HIGHLANDS INSTITUTE SERIES 2

New Essays in Religious Naturalism

edited by
W. Creighton Peden
and
Larry E. Axel

PEETERS

MERCER

ISBN 0-86554-426-3 MUP/H346

New Essays in Religious Naturalism

Mercer University Press, Macon, Georgia 31207

Printed in the United States of America

The paper used in this publication meets
the minimum requirements of American National Standard
for Information Sciences—Permanence of Paper
for Printed Library Materials, ANSI Z39.48-1984.

Library of Congress Cataloging-in-Publication Data

New essays in religious naturalism /
edited by W. Creighton Peden and Larry E. Axel.
viii+250 pp. 6x9" (15x23cm.)—(Highlands Institute series : 2)
Papers presented at the Conference on American Religious Thought, held June 1990 in Highlands NC and sponsored by Highlands Institute for American Religious Thought.
Includes bibliographical references.
ISBN 0-86554-426-3 (alk. paper)
1. Religious thought—United States—20th century. 2. Philosophical theology—congresses. 3. Naturalism—congresses. 4. Empirical theology—congresses. 5. Liberalism (Religion)—Congresses. 6. Chicago school of theology—congresses. I. Peden, W. Creighton, 1935– . II. Axel, Larry E., 1946–1991. III. Highlands Institute for American Religious Thought. IV. Conference on American Religious Thought (1990: Highlands NC). V. Series.
BL2525.N486 1994
200'.973—dc20 93-37812
CIP

Contents

Preface

The essays in this volume were selected from those presented at the Conference on American Religious Thought sponsored by the Highlands Institute for American Religious Thought. The conference was held in Highlands, North Carolina, in June 1990.

The Highlands Institute is a community of productive scholars with diverse theological and philosophical perspectives. The Institute contributes to the academic study of religion through interpretive, critical, and constructive reflections whose principal focus is on distinctively American religious thought. It fosters broad discussion of relevant options through its sponsorship of conferences, seminars, workshops, and publications.

The work of the Institute emphasizes

(1) the interface between theology and philosophy, especially where theological efforts have utilized the American philosophical tradition;
(2) the history and development of liberal religious thought in America;
(3) themes pertinent to the "Chicago School" of theology, and
(4) naturalism in American theology and philosophy.

—*W. Creighton Peden*
Highlands, North Carolina
June 1990

In Memoriam

LAWRENCE EUGENE AXEL
1946–1991

BERNARD EUGENE MELAND
1899–1993

Meland and Loomer: Forging an Alternative to Patriarchal Secularism

Rebecca C. Axel

Recent years have brought about the rise of highstyle fashions for children—from fur coats to sequined tennis shoes. The prices of the clothes are appalling; but interviews with parents are even more so. One mother complains, "It's all Forenza, Generra, and Esprit. If you don't have the real things, they don't like it. It's pretty ridiculous, but what do you do if they won't wear anything else?"[1] (Offhand, I can think of a few things "to do!") Unfortunately, if this kind of "parental paralysis" is very widespread, we may very well produce a generation of soullessness unprecedented even in American society.

Such materialism has been around for a long time, constantly steering our culture into what I can only describe as a shallow secularism. I hesitate to use the word "secularism," because it is so overworked as to be almost meaningless. But, if we listen to Bernard Meland, we may understand anew the dreadful legacy secularism leaves to a culture. He defines secularism as:

> an attitude and a procedure within society which ignores the primal depths and takes events on face value as simply human events with no understanding of the formulative elements of great depth and antiquity [that] continue to cradle and nurture the human spirit. . . .[2]

I would define our particular brand of secularism as *patriarchal,* because it is an attitude and procedure forged and preserved by a male hierarchy, "a social system in which men are perceived as inherently superior and more powerful than women."[3]

Further, this patriarchal secularism patterns its society on the model of a pyramid. Analyzing our society's structure as pyramidal is not the result of traditional research, nor is it the product of quantifiable data or analysis. It is a description fashioned largely through inference and intuition; for, although there is evidence of this dehumanizing pyramid all around us, we rarely discuss it explicitly.

---

[1]*Newsweek* (22 December 1986) 59.

[2]*Faith and Culture* (Carbondale: Southern Illinois University Press, 1972) 131.

[3]Nelle Morton, *The Journey Is Home* (Boston: Beacon Press, 1985) 36.

But if we listen to our conversation, if we heed our writings, our organizations, and our personal relationships, I believe we will find the pyramid underneath it all.

The patterns of coercive power and control and the pursuit of money within the pyramid define our relationships as competitive. The most "successful" of us have moved up through the lower levels to occupy increasingly exclusive strata, enjoying more and more privilege. That this pyramid is patriarchal is clear, for the structure generally makes it easier for men (especially *white* men) to "rise through the ranks." Indeed, both the "ranks" and the methods for rising are defined by men.

In addition, a whole ontology has grown up to support this pyramidal model. Patriarchal secularism presents us with a "God the Father" who sits at the top of this pyramid, condoning and reinforcing the hierarchical nature of human relationships as patriarchal secularism defines them. The closer we "climb" to God in the pyramid, the "better" we are than our brothers and sisters. In using the metaphor "God the Father" to justify its definitions and structures, patriarchal secularism fosters a blatant, double idolatry. First, our society's real object of worship is power (and money, through which more power can be attained) rather than God. Second, this system of patriarchal secularism actively perpetuates an image of God as a manipulable object that can be used to justify its practices and its pursuit of coercive power.

Patriarchal secularism, then, gives rise to a model of society that may be called a "patriarchal power pyramid." I use the term "model" here to indicate that mental structure of reality which functions to organize human relationships, both between individuals and among groups. Now, this model is less visible (and, therefore, less open to examination) than is its attendant metaphor, "God the Father." Its invisibility notwithstanding, the model of the patriarchal power pyramid defines and organizes a great deal of our thinking about "reality." This patriarchal power pyramid:

- Defines as "good" the climb to an ever higher level in the pyramid;
- Defines the goal of human existence as the acquisition of coercive power (the more power, the better);
- Defines the structure of human relationships in terms of verticality—subordination to higher authorities and control over underlings;
- Defines the nature of human relationships as basically competitive and individuated;
- Defines "proper" behavior as submission to the pyramid's "powers that be" and rewards with money and power those who "play by the rules";
- Offers "God the Father" as the ultimate authority figure who sanctions the exercise of coercive power within the pyramid to keep order;
- Organizes reality in terms of coercive power, competition, alienation, privilege, elitism, hierarchy, and stratification;
- Utilizes various kinds of exclusionary practices (such as sexism, racism, ageism, and militarism) to insure that those with power keep it.

Bernard Loomer eloquently describes this understanding of power as "unilateral."[4] Unilateral power is generally one-sided, involving a change in the one upon whom the power is exercised. Of course, the one wielding the power may be influenced by the very exercising of power or by the response of the one being acted upon. But the primary aim of this kind of power is to create the greatest effect on the other and to minimize the influence of the one who is assigned a subordinate role. In fact, the less-powerful other is often seen as a threat to the one who occupies the dominant place in the pyramid, for to be susceptible to influence is understood as weakness. As one struggles to obtain even more coercive power, it becomes essential that the other's freedom and influence be minimized and thus be brought under control.[5]

Unilateral power tends to corrupt because the exercise of it brings estrangement and alienation. If our egoism goes unchecked, the power we acquire adds to our sense of worth; so we do not voluntarily give it up. Thus the inequalities between individuals and among groups are deepened.[6] I would add that the exercise of linear power corrupts because it furthers and enlarges the alienation that already belongs to an ego-centered self which understands itself primarily as independent. Unilateral power is based on a noncommunal and nonrelational understanding of the self. We aim for as much self-sufficiency as possible, and we see others merely as helpers or obstacles to our attempts to "actualize" our purposes.[7] It seems to me that Loomer's analysis goes to the heart of the individualism which is so indigenous to the American character.

Finally, this unilateral power and its attendant sense of alienation deny us the ability to understand the concrete situations of others, to practice true "presence" with them. Aiming to influence and control others, we cannot allow them to be themselves in their "concrete freedom."[8] Instead of dealing with the concrete lives of individuals, unilateral power deals in abstraction. Dedicated only to the furtherance of our own ends, we relate to others:

> in terms of abstract classes, or stereotypes, or groups looked at in a cross-sectional manner, without reference to their peculiar histories. In this fashion we fail to deal with the inexhaustible and variegated complexity, the confusing complexity, and the omnipresent and intertwined ambiguities present in the concreteness of individual and group life.[9]

---

[4]This discussion is based on Loomer's article "Two Kinds of Power," *Process Studies* 6 (1976): 5-32.

[5]Ibid., see 8-11.

[6]Ibid., 11 and 14.

[7]Ibid., 12.

[8]Ibid., 14.

[9]Ibid., 24-25.

Further, this understanding of power has its birth in, and perpetuates the dualism so characteristic of the patriarchy. Adrienne Rich puts it this way. "The language of patriarchal power insists on a dichotomy: for one person to have power, others—or another—must be powerless."[10] This reflects the patriarchal definition of human relationality: human beings are essentially isolated individuals who exist in I-it relationships to other essentially isolated individuals. Obviously, the exercise of coercive power thrives in such an environment.

Our paralysis in the face of this patriarchal secularism poses two grave dangers. First, it teaches our children that there is really not very much to them—not much, at least, beyond a shallow wish to have certain egotistical desires satisfied. Reared in such a system, they cannot hope to learn compassion or empathic understanding for anyone outside their own small group. They cannot find the deep fulfillment to be found from living beyond their own physical, personal selves. Left to our culture's reigning values, they cannot develop the depth necessary to appreciate and participate in the texture, subtlety, and variety of human experience.

Second, our children may internalize an enslaving herd mentality. Those mothers mentioned at the beginning of this paper apparently do not see the bankruptcy of their daughters' relational lives. When we cave into such peer pressure we teach our children that such superficiality is not only acceptable, but it is desireable. Worse, they learn that such superficiality and herd conformity should never be questioned. So, we often send our children mixed signals. We want our children "fit in," so we help them to conform to peer standards in clothes and cars. Yet, we expect them to "just say no" to that same peer pressure when it attempts to coerce them into drugs or into casual and demeaning sexual relationships. We must choose between teaching our children independence or capitulation. We cannot have it both ways.

It is incumbent upon us adults (whether we are parents or not) to offer the children of our culture a finer vision of relationality than they can find in the pyramid of patriarchal secularism. I prefer the more horizontal model of "web." This particular model was concretized for me one day when my daughter Jenny and I were walking in the woods. We chanced upon two saplings which anchored a large and impressive spider web. Its lovely pattern sparkled in the early morning sunlight, which caught the dew drops that still clung to its webbed strands. We were awestruck. We humans, endowed with higher-order brains and sophisticated neurological structures, were humbled by the wonderful work of our tiny, talented sister.

The picture of that wonderful creation comes to me as I struggle to understand, and speak about, this rich and perplexing experience of being human. I like to imagine that web multiplied many times over, each duplication in a different plane, all the planes intersecting and all faces of the web connected. The complexity of

---

[10]*Of Woman Born* (New York: Norton, 1976) 67.

that multidimensional web extends in all directions in my mind's eye, far beyond my capacity to follow all its paths. Further, I like to envision us humans living in such a web, exploring our connectedness to other aspects of the web but forever falling short of comprehending the whole.

This alternative model of web is rooted in creaturalism, in the belief that we find our best living as creatures, here and now, in what Meland describes as "the vivid arena of decision and act" where we must find ultimate meaning.[11] This alternative is also rooted in feminism, in a fierce belief that patriarchal understandings of relationality are hollow and bankrupt, shallow and superficial. The possibilities within our human experience far surpass the limited definitions promulgated by a Western corporate mentality; there is depth and richness available to us if we are open to it. Our human structure is limited, to be sure, but not so limited as we normally believe, not so limited as our patriarchal and secular society wants to teach us.

As adults, we bear responsibility for the society we shall bequeath to America's children. That very serious sense of obligation should leave us deeply distressed about the patriarchal secularism that defines our present culture. We adults must reclaim our roles as teachers and counselors for our young people and help them to explore the possibilities beyond the shallow secularism that our society offers them. And we begin that reclamation with Meland, who teaches *us adults* that there are resources of richness and depth within our creaturehood. We have only to be responsive to the texture of the immediacies of experience.[12]

For Meland, the most important human experiences, feelings, and issues are to be found in the common immediacies of our lives, in the "living, immediate context of the human situation."[13] If we have any hope of finding release from the competition and alienation that patriarchal secularism offers us, that release must be found within this "texture of existence,' within this web we call home. However, that release will come only if we develop the appropriate attitude, what Meland terms a "creatural stance."

Unfortunately, too many of us refuse to recognize our creaturehood, refuse to acknowledge that we are fragile and that our lives—physical, emotional, spiritual, relational—always hang by a thread. No amount of sandbagging can alter our

---

[11]*The Realities of Faith* (New York: Oxford University Press, 1962) 115.

[12]"Myth as a Mode of Awareness and Intelligibility," *American Journal of Theology & Philosophy* 8 (1987): 115.

[13]*Faith and Culture,* 102. See also *The Realities of Faith,* 116ff. The model of "web" may be humble, but Adrienne Rich reminds us that behind its imagery lies the ancient and honored tradition of web-spinners, who (the ancients believed) held the power over life and death. "The spider who spins thread out of her own body, Adiadne providing the clue to the labyrinth, the figures of the Gates or Norns or old spinning-women who cut the thread of life or spit it further" are all associated with this process. See *Of Woman Born,* 101.

temporariness, but we sandbag with a vengeance anyway. We pile up vast amounts of "things" around us, building walls to keep the fear and insecurity at bay. It is all a quite vain attempt to feel worthy and secure; for it cannot work. We cannot purchase security with any kind of coin: not with great wealth or physical prowess, not with fine reputations or hordes of friends, not with grand philanthropic work or multinational corporations. We cannot purchase security, but we can achieve a very real peace when we give up trying to be what we are not. Adopting a creatural stance and accepting our impermanence can infuse our experiences with poignancy and power. And the possibilities for depth and richness within those experiences multiply when we practice what Meland calls "appreciative consciousness."

This "appreciative awareness" (as he also calls it) is "an orientation of the mind which makes for a maximum degree of receptivity to the datum under consideration," recognizing that "what is given may be more than what is immediately perceived, or more than one can think."[14] A description of facts or a recording of the observations of the senses(however poignant they may be) does not exhaust the possibilities of a particular event or object. Meland says we must come to understand observable data in organic, not mechanistic, terms. Thus, our attention must be twofold: (1) to the sense of fact and description; and, (2) to the meaning which transcends the fact and enlarges our scope beyond the bare description of fact.[15]

Precision, analysis, and related mental activities are one aspect of appreciative consciousness; but their data are tentative and subject to revision "before the great ongoing mystery in which our lives are cast—a drama of existence in which wonder, inquiry, and the appreciative mind play creative roles."[16] Appreciative awareness is an orientation which will open us to the depths of experience.

A number of years ago, my grandmother gave me her ruby ring. Recently, I needed to have the stones rest, because the original setting broke. The new band has caused me to see the stones with new eyes and with renewed understanding of what that ring means to me. Anyone with even a small amount of aesthetic sensibility can look at the ring and appreciate the depth of its color and the way it winks and sparkles in the light. When I look at it, however, my appreciation transcends such lovely, but (to me) rather superficial, aspects. My eyes see beyond its shape and color to the woman who so largely influenced my life. I see her, tiny and unsinkable, self-educated and tough, circumscribed by her times but a sweet survivor. And captured in her frame, I see the whole history of my mother's people. Knowing the depth of experience that is represented in my grandmother's ring, I must understand that other ordinary objects function profoundly in *other* peoples' live, as well.

---

[14]*Higher Education and the Human Spirit* (Chicago: University of Chicago Press, 1953) 63 and 175. Please see all of chap. 5 for a full discussion of appreciative consciousness.

[15]Ibid., 71-72.

[16]Ibid., 77.

Wonder and awareness must infuse the concrete immediacy of our existence if we are to live fully and well. The character of this immediacy is relational, both to past and present events—as the interconnected strands of the web model suggest. Mutuality means just what it implies: an abandonment of the hierarchy upon which patriarchal secularism thrives. Each human being, as event, is born into a situation of relating to other events. All structures and creatures (human, nonhuman, plant, inanimate) are coinhabitants of the web. Meland says, "It is literally true that human nature, like creature life at every level, is defined by this interdependence and mutuality."[17] We must unlearn the egocentric individualism that defines patriarchal secularism. We must recognize that the human creature, bearing the intent of creation, participates in the immediacy and concretion in two ways: as an individuated event (self) and in interdependence (community).[18] The web cradles us in a complex pattern of selfhood and relationship, each bearing the mark of creaturehood. Mother Earth herself may be spoken of as one "structure" within the web of the universe. The linkages between ourselves and our cocreatures reveal to us constant resources for renewal.

In the course of my growing up, I have learned a great deal from my mother. That process continues to this day, even though she now suffers from Alzheimer's Disease. She taught me to see lacy leaves in spring and bright cardinals against the dreary winter landscape. She taught me to hear wind in the cottonwood trees and to love the smell of freshly cut grass. I know that she gave me presents for birthdays and Christmas, but I don't remember very many of them. The gifts that stay in my heart came wrapped in her love for Mother Earth. I watch my own children respond to their grandmother now with love, respect, and constant good humor—not because she showered them with toys at Christmas, but because she taught them to stand very still to watch a robin in the bird bath, because she helped them search for the first yellow crocuses peeping through the March snow. I am not sure why it is that flowers contribute more to a nourished life than do toys. I only know that it is true and that my mother was wise enough to teach us so.

This emphasis on relationality can be found in Loomer as well. He states unequivocally that the actualities (including the complexity of actual occasions we know as "human being") which constitute our immediate experience are made up primarily of their relations. Loomer himself uses the metaphor of web to describe this interrelatedness. Within this web, our own possibility emerges; our own opportunities for becoming exist only in our relationality. "As interrelated individuals we create the web and the web creates us. Within this relational web we are also self-creative and thereby transform the web—for better or worse."[19]

---

[17]"Myth as a Mode," 136.

[18]Ibid., 143.

[19]"The Size of God," in *The Size of God: The Theology of Bernard Loomer in Context*, ed. William Dean and Larry E. Axel (Macon GA: Mercer University Press, 1987) see 24-25.

How, then, do we transform the web, and ourselves, for the better? The answer for Loomer lies in his concept of *size,* or *stature,* and *relational power.* Those who live by the pyramidal model define power in terms of coercion and control. However, Loomer contends that the ability to *absorb* an influence is as much a mark of power as is the ability to *produce* an influence.

> The world of the individual who can be influenced by another without losing his or her identity or freedom is larger than the world of the individual who fears being influenced. The former can include ranges and depths of complexity and contrast to a degree that is not possible for the latter. The stature of the individual who can let another exist in his or her own creative freedom is larger that the size of the individual who insists that others conform to his own purposes and understandings.[20]

In this rendering of power, the focus is always on the relationship; and that relationship functions *internally.* In the pyramidal model, by contrast, power relationships are external. I may be able to coerce another into doing my bidding; but I have effected no internal change in the other, because we have no internal relationship. We function as sealed individuals, pushing each other around but never entering into each other's internal worlds. In the web, however, power is understood as the ability "to sustain a mutually internal relationship."[21] Those who participate in such a relationship often

> seem to be almost indistinguishable and their roles appear to be interchangeable. Often the greatest influence that one can exercise on another consists in being influenced by the other, in enabling the other to make the largest impact on one's self.[22]

Thus, both participants in the relationship develop their own relational power.

Just as the concept of power in the web is relational, so, too, is the concept of the self. The self's very life springs from the relationality of communal life. Indeed, we live in our web and our web lives in us. Possibilities are not inherent in the individual; they emerge out of the relationality which the self experiences in community. This emerging relationality creates possibilities. Freedom, then, becomes an occasion not for the exercise of self-interest and unilateral power, but relational growth. Loomer puts it well: "We are most free in all the dimensions of our

---

[20]"Two Kinds of Power," 18.

[21]Ibid., 22.

[22]Ibid. I wonder about Loomer's term "indistinguishable" here. It is difficult to believe that he believes two people in such a relationship will, in an unhealthy manner, lose their identities. I think describing their roles as "interchangeable" is more helpful.

freedom when we enter more deeply into those relationships which are creative of ourselves as people of larger size."[23]

Relational power must deal with the concrete life of the other, in the richness of its many dimensions. Those who practice unilateral power have an easier task, of course. For them, others exist as stereotypes, fitted into neat categories that mask the very real disorderliness of human life. Those who practice relational power, on the other hand, dive into the disorder; for they know that therein lies the only possibility for authentic relationships. "Power, to be creative and not destructive, must be inextricably related to the ambiguous, contradictory, and baffling character of concrete existence."[24] The person of greater size will be able to recognize that the forces which produce tragedy and evil are inseparable from the forces which can produce good. Such a person will be able to take within himself or herself "greater evil and greater good without losing personal integrity."[25] That ability will empower the person to stand against the forces of evil. We achieve our fulfillment in the finer relationships we work to create and which, in turn, sustain us. When we engage in such creative work, we sustain our web of relationality and nourish all of life.

Our creatural stance of awareness draws us out of our egocentrism and into the relational life of community. As it does so, it draws us into a *new* kind of centeredness: an awareness of self and place and a confidence in relationality. This centeredness, no longer organized around the ego, gives one the courage to take on the risks of relationality—risks of being known, being hurt, being rejected, being loved, being wrong, being fulfilled.

It seems clear to me that we adults have much to learn from Loomer and Meland. They offer us a compelling alternative to patriarchal secularism and its pyramid. *Our* responsibility lies in teaching our children such an alternative vision. Much of what they learn from us comes, of course, through the subtle medium of example. Our understanding of relationality manifests itself in the way we live our lives—in a creatural stance, in appreciative awareness, in the practice of relational power. But we need also to accept our responsibility for overt teaching as well. We must talk to our children, *name* for them the character of good human relationality, teach them that the web:

- Defines the care of our co-creatures in the web as "good";
- Defines the goal of human existence as the deepening of our connections to our co-creatures;
- Defines the structure of creatural relationality as horizontal;
- Defines the nature of creatural relationality as cooperative and connected;
- Fosters equality among all co-creatures;

[23]Ibid., 21.

[24]Ibid., 25.

[25]William Dean, "Introduction: From Integrity to Size," *The Size of God,* 16.

•Organizes reality in terms of relational power, cooperation, connectedness, equality, and horizontality.

Let us abandon our sad "parental paralysis." Let us assume our responsibility for our children's future and pledge to teach them this vision of webbed relationality. If we do, they may be able to offer *their* children not only a better *vision* but a better *world.*

Pragmatism, Process, and Courage

J. Edward Barrett

This paper is an attempt—in two parts—to discuss two related issues: (1) the courage to do theology, and (2) a theology of courage. The two are not the same, though they are related. *How* they are related will also be discussed. After writing and refining it (with all the appropriate scholarly qualifications), it occurred to me that a more appropriate title would be "A Walk through a Garden of Parentheses."

I

Without being rigidly committed to any methodological tradition, I nevertheless approach theology from the perspective of American "pragmatism." By this I mean that: (1) I try to stay close to evidence (or what can be confirmed by experience); (2) I am satisfied with tentative answers; and (3) I assume that truth itself is "in process"—developmental, dialectical, and (as I will later explain) helpfully informed by the familiar model of archaeological method. The problem that emerges from this epistemological position is: where do we find the courage to live without absolutes? (I suspect this bears some ironic semblance to the question as to how we can have government without tyranny.)

(1) I try to stay close to evidence, even while recognizing that in order to say anything important one must venture beyond the obvious. As Bertrand Russell said (He said so many incompatible things): "The practical man may be pardoned if he comes to the conclusion that truth is unattainable except when it is unimportant."[1]

In seeking to know what *is* important, I try to limit speculation considerably, and exclude dogma totally. I usually avoid "high-rise" rationalistic structures, preferring to stay close to ground level. I make no appeal to supernatural revelation and, while intuition plays some role in all investigation, I seek to appeal only to evidence that is available to everyone. Staying close to experience need not, I think, mean avoiding attempts to gain perspective on life, and to "get it all together." (This has always been the real function of metaphysics, and it is a perfectly valid and impor-

---

[1]Bertrand Russell, "Philosophy In The Twentieth Century," *Twentieth Century Philosophy*, ed. D. Runes (New York: Philosophical Library, 1947) 227.

tant function for human beings. We are the animal who asks BIG questions, and develops as answers "imaginative constructions.")

(2) I am satisfied with tentative answers, which are "practical" descriptions of experience (or working ideas), and which surely fall short of being comprehensive, logically necessary, or final descriptions of ultimate reality. For me, the word "ultimate," unless used with great care, is likely to be an idolatrous, nonreferential, and fatiguing idea. (I do not intend this remark as a slur against or an indictment of Tillich, who uses the word with considerable care, which I appreciate and endorse.) The possibility of doing theology includes the certainty that it is finite, and that it can and will be faulted by colleagues.

(3) I assume that truth itself is in process. Truths about human existence (and the deep things of life) are not usually discovered by (1) logical syllogisms, in the tradition of Descartes and perhaps also of Hartshorne (Emerson said that "a foolish consistency is the hobgoblin of little minds"[2]), or by (2) publicly provable fact, but instead by (3) *excavation*. The model of an archaeological dig is quite instructive, and important for understanding this paper. As the director of a dig assembles a team of experts, so too the theologian must become familiar with the conclusions of many different disciplines. The team is expected to discuss, debate differences (for differences there always are), revise judgments, and suggest possibilities. At some point, however, the director must evaluate the evidence, make decisions, and draw conclusions, producing a report that is always subject to review (and review there will be).

So it is with the theologian. The hard work of others in exploring human existence must not be ignored and should always be appreciated. One cannot dig deeply into the stuff of human life without the sweat and toil of others. And, such digging is seldom tidy—meaning it is sometimes difficult to give a perfectly clean account of "how I got there."

Most important, the director achieves credibility not by ignoring but by taking into consideration evidence to the contrary. In a similar way, theological proposals gain credibility not just by marshalling evidence in their support, but by honestly wrestling with contrary evidence and conclusions. Digging that uncovers deep truth often requires approaches from many different sides. So too the theologian only gets into the depths of life by an excavation that requires dialectic and dialogue, a discussion that amounts to a digging back and forth for the unknown. Philosophical discussion that is worthy of the name is punctuated with "yes, buts." It is never quite resolved, though it does get deeper. Also, while digging conspicuously involves depth, the issue for the archaeologist is exploring a distance created by time (the past). Conversely, while the theologian's digging occasionally involves the

---

[2]Ralph Waldo Emerson, "Self-Reliance," *The Writings of Ralph Waldo Emerson* (New York: Modern Library, 1950) 152.

past, the issue is exploring a distance created by the fathomless breadth and depth of the ecosystem, of which human life is a part.

Henry Nelson Wieman spoke of the need for two levels of commitment. On the first level, we should commit ourselves to the best we know (empirically, scientifically, experientially) about the source of human good, that which transforms human life by expanding the range of what we know, control, and appreciate or value; but on the second and deeper level, we must be finally (ultimately) committed to whatever it is that *in fact* transforms human life in the direction of the good, no matter how different that operating reality may be from our ideas about it. I confess that Wieman's position on this point makes more sense to me than any other prolegomena I know of in the libraries of theological literature.

Theology can be considered a blessing to the human community when its undertakings sufficiently display two characteristics (in a reasonable and aesthetic balance). They are *humility* and *courage*. Paul of Tarsus made the point when he wrote to the Philippians: "Work out your own salvation with fear and trembling; for God is at work in you, both to will and to work for divine good pleasure" (Philippians 2:12,13). Humility requires that the theologian proceed with fear and trembling, knowing the human capacity for error. Courage is grounded in the possibility that the theologian is in touch with resources beyond failure, and may therefore be right, or at least partially and perhaps substantially so. Theology is always an act of *courage*—in which the cowardly do not know the joy of tasting truth, and the foolhardy imagine that because they have tasted it, they have digested it.

I have so far spoken of the courage to do theology. But, can I propose a pragmatically persuasive theology of courage? That is to say, do I have the theological courage to propose a theology of courage? The pragmatic method allows one to be light and debonair (both its weakness and its glory); the challenge is now to explore beneath the surface, to excavate the deep and difficult human reality we call *courage*.

The rest of this paper will examine and evaluate selected theories and manifestations of courage (part II), and then seek to identify the source and ground that nourishes courage (part III).

II

A theologian who is a methodological pragmatist must still deal with the issue of definition. What is meant by courage? For a "working" definition, Tillich's magisterial study, *The Courage To Be*, helps more than a dictionary. He writes:

> The courage to be is the ethical act in which human beings affirm their own being in spite of those elements of their existence which conflict with their essential self-affirmation[3].

---

[3]Paul Tillich, *The Courage to Be* (New Haven CT: Yale University Press, 1952) 3.

Or again:

Courage is self-affirmation "in-spite-of." . . .[4]

Once this general description is accepted as a "working" (pragmatic) definition, the *real* issue for theology becomes developing a theory about courage and identifying the source and ground of courage.

In the following survey, I will be the archaeological director, evaluating the evidence and suggesting conclusions.

1. *Courage explained by or arising from absolutes. The* chief illustration of this approach to courage is Islam. More so than historic Christianity, Moslem faith proceeds from a theory of absolute truth (Allah's revelation to Muhammad), combined with promises of reward and punishment for those who do or do not honor and obey. Courage arises from knowing you are absolutely right. The courage of absolutes has little to contribute to the analysis of a theological pragmatist, but it is an empirical fact that absolutes have been important in history (including our own Western history), and continue to be for many people around the globe. Still, it is precisely what can *not* provide a ground for the courage of modern thinkers, among whom claims to absolute truth seem naive, manipulative, phony, just plain wrong. So, enough of that.

2. *Courage explained by or arising from detachment.* The chief illustration of this approach to courage is BUDDHISM. Recognizing the passing (process) character of reality, Buddhist courage is (paradoxically) grounded in the possibility of abandoning all attempts to find a ground, since all supposed grounds (like wealth, power, and knowledge) are judged to be illusory. *Satori* is the recognition of this paradox, and the courage of the buddha-life flows from it. The courage of *detachment*, in either its philosophical Buddhist or cynical secular forms (Nothing matters, I don't give a damn), has the great danger of intentionally avoiding *relational responsibility.* I consider that defiance of the established conclusions of modern psychology, sociology, history, and ecology enough to disqualify it as a serious option for a pragmatist.

3. *Courage explained by or arising from metaphysics.* The chief illustration of this approach to courage is HINDUISM. Proceeding from a large and complex metaphysic, Hindu courage is nourished in the serenity of acceptance of one's *karma.* The world is said to be uncontestably just, and those who accept their fate are promised the possibility of better luck next time. Courage arises from the confidence that the vicissitudes of life are understood, and will ultimately prove to be good.

For a more modern example, there is a highly metaphysical painting by the nineteenth-century artist Casper David Friedrich, titled "The Wanderer above the Mists." In it we see a nineteenth-century "gentleman," his feet planted firmly on a mountain peak, surveying below him the clouds and haze (and by implication the

---

[4]Ibid., 32.

ignorance) of former generations, which had been fated to the fog of the unenlightened. In this instance, courage is born of confidence that (at last) the world is understood (in this case in scientific and technological categories, which present us with a comprehensive *Weltanschauung*).

The courage of metaphysics, like the courage of absolutes, suffers from the weakness that (no matter how rational and unanswered its arguments) it's proposals can be doubted—and doubt drains courage of its strength. Still, I would argue that metaphysics is on the boundary (more precisely, the intellectual boundary) of the ground for courage, that one may hold a metaphysic within a pragmatic epistemology, that every life implies some world-view (*Weltanschauung*) or other, and that the attempt to develop an empirically informed and rationally consistent metaphysic *is* an aspect of human courage. Metaphysics is daring to think it through, even if doing so leaves us in the grips of what William James called "ontological wonder-sickness."[5]

4. *Courage explained by or arising from defiance.* The chief illustration of this approach to courage is STOICISM, in its pessimistic form. Optimistic stoicism found a *logos* in nature and history with which human life could live in tune, by using the discipline of reason (Cicero, Seneca, Aurelius). Lost with the decline of Rome it reappeared in Western history during the Enlightenment. But pessimistic stoicism finds no *logos* or reason operative in nature and history. Courage arises in defiance of circumstances, and seeks to live a reasonable life without any help from a larger reason, a rational life in an irrational world. William Ernest Henley's popular poem *Invictus* illustrates the point:

> Out of the night that covers me,
> Black as the Pit from pole to pole,
> I thank whatever gods may be
> For my unconquerable soul.
>
> In the fell clutch of circumstance
> I have not winced nor cried aloud;
> Under the bludgeonings of chance
> My head is bloody, but unbowed.
>
> Beyond this place of wrath and tears
> Looms but the Horror of the shade,
> And yet the menace of the years
> Finds and shall find me unafraid.
>
> It matters not how strait the gate,
> How charged with punishment the scroll,

---

[5]William James, "The Sentiment of Rationality," in *Essays in Pragmatism* ed. Albert Castell (New York: Hafner Publishing Company, 1949) 9.

I am the master of my fate;
I am the captain of my soul.[6]

There is a lot of hokum in Henley's poem, as there is when Sinatra sings, "I Did It My Way." I am *not* the master of my fate or the captain of my soul, and can be excused for suspecting that Henley was not either. I am just a finite individual with a limited allotment of time and talents. These talents have been nurtured by a world that is not "dark as a pit from pole to pole," (*that* is an inadequate metaphysic). I am not the master of my fate *or* the captain of my soul (that is inadequate self-assessment, if not a pretentious boast). But the courage of defiance does recognize that there is always an in-spite-of quality to courage, and that in human beings courage can reach unpredictable and fascinating degrees of nobility. Bertrand Russell illustrated the courage of defiance in its more noble form (still pessimistic stoicism) when he wrote:

> Brief and powerless is man's life; on him . . . the slow, sure doom falls pitiless and dark. Blind to good and evil, . . . omnipotent matter rolls on its relentless way; for man, . . . it remains only to cherish . . . the lofty thoughts that ennoble his little day, . . . despite the trampling march of unconscious power.[7]

The courage of defiance is also an element in the American psyche, though it is probably more akin than is Russell to optimistic stoicism. About this Tillich wrote:

> There is something astonishing in the American courage for an observer who comes from Europe: . . . A person may have experienced a tragedy, a destructive fate, the breakdown of convictions, even guilt and momentary despair: he feels neither destroyed nor meaningless nor condemned nor without hope. When the Roman Stoic experienced the same catastrophes he took them with the courage of resignation. The typical American, after he has lost the foundations of his existence, works for new foundations."[8]

That is self-affirmation in-spite-of, and what is meant by the courage of defiance.

5. *Courage explained by or arising from history.* The chief illustration of this approach to courage is the modern day idea of PROGRESS. Rooted in the Judaeo-Christian ideas of providence and eschatology, given philosophical dignity by optimistic stoicism (*logos* philosophy), and seemingly confirmed by biological

---

[6]William Ernest Henley, "Invictus," *The Best Loved Poems of the American People* (New York: Doubleday, 1936) 73.

[7]Bertrand Russell, "A Free Man's Worship," *Why I Am Not a Christian* (New York: Simon & Schuster, 1957) 115-16.

[8]*The Courage to Be*, 107-108.

evolution and developing technology, it has in the past two hundred years become thoroughly secularized for many people in Western Civilization (who usually do not know the quite distinctive historic roots of their secular faith). The courage of progress is, I believe, the uniquely *Western* form of courage, particularly as it unites both Jewish eschatology with Graeco-Roman universalism, formulated as a vision of what God is doing with the world.

Courage arises from participation in the big event, what is believed to be "really" happening in human history, or (theologically considered) working with God toward a divine goal. The fall of the Roman Empire seriously sapped the strength of this courage for a thousand years, and it was not rediscovered until the Renaissance. Today, however, it is the courage of progress which fires hope around the world. Born in the Middle East, first flowering in Western Civilization, the courage of progress is today a globally embraced ground and shaper of courage. And, however much we may experience it as an embarrassment or burden, America is its chief exemplar. Tillich writes that this courage (arising from progress in history):

> is what makes of present-day American courage one of the great types of the courage to be as a part. Its self-affirmation is the affirmation of oneself as a participant in the creative development of mankind.[9]

My own understanding of courage (as an American, no doubt) is considerably shaped by this courage of progress, or what Tillich called the "affirmation of oneself as a participant in the creative development of mankind."

6. *Courage explained by or arising from biology (or nature).* The chief illustration of this approach to courage is Vitalism, attributing courage to the biochemical constitution of the organism. Courage is understood to be the volitional quality of life. This interpretation does justice to the undoubtedly real continuity of human courage with animal courage: the drive to affirm one's self, to fight, to flee (Even fleeing is a kind of courage, for it affirms that it is better to be than not to be). The courage of biology, or *vitalism*, is as deep as a strictly scientific method permits one to go. That is plenty deep, and points to depths of mystery beyond the limitations imposed by its own methodology.

A pragmatic and persuasive analysis of courage should begin with vitalism. It is the best point of entry into the subject. Occasionally we encounter a statement whose simplicity and clarity in expressing the "neglected-obvious" is such that it can be considered wisdom. In this case I am thinking of Albert Schweitzer's empirically demonstrable and experientially confirmable dictum that: "I am life that wills to live, in the midst of life that wills to live."[10] Any thoughtful person recognizes, both personally and universally, the primordial, central, and vital truth expressed in those words. I recommend them as the starting point for any serious theology.

---

[9]Ibid., 107.

[10]Albert Schweitzer, *The Teaching of Reverence for Life* (London: Peter Owen, 1965) 25.

That struggle or willing is what could be called "generic courage," and it is universal—across the entire biological realm, and perhaps in some primitive way operative in the inorganic as well. To make this observation is not to trivialize courage—it is to recognize its ontological dignity. Courage is a *quality* of existence, much as wetness is a quality of water. Courage is the volitional quality of existence, and self-affirmation is a universal, ontological phenomenon. From protozoa to porpoises, from gypsy moths to giant redwoods, from babies crying to Beethoven composing, from soaring gulls to soaring human intellects—all evidence a process of self-affirmation in spite of difficulties.[11]

In human beings, however, this struggle to live takes richly diverse forms which, like the colors of the spectrum, are often highly individualistic—distinguishing human courage, or what could be called "personal courage" from generic courage. The ballet dancer for whom the struggle to live means exceptional aesthetic discipline, the cancer patient who struggles with suffering and mortality, the poverty fated mother who struggles just to feed her children, the politician who struggles for new levels of justice, the business executive who struggles to keep a faltering company solvent, the theologian who struggles to discover and express the meaning of it all—these are assorted forms of courage, in the manifold richness which appears only on the human level, but which nevertheless have in common that they are a process of individual self-affirmation in-spite-of.

Tillich defined human courage as an "ethical" act. He meant by "ethical" not that human courage is always righteous, but that humans are *accountable* for the form their self-affirmation takes. Nevertheless, the relationship of courage to ethical consequences is interesting.

On the one hand, there are forerunners of ethical courage on pre-human levels—as when animals fight to defend their young. In these instances self-affirmation is sometimes transmuted into self-sacrifice. On the other hand, not every human act of self-affirmation is ethically commendable.

If we think of "heroes" as exemplary instances of human courage, we may have to rule out sulking Achilles and wily Odysseus as failing in ethics, and demonstrating only a pre-human or inferior form of courage. Sports heroes, by comparison, may either fascinate or bore us, but they are usually ethically neutral, and therefore an improvement over gore and death. Ethical heroes, however—Socrates and Jesus, St. Francis and Luther, Jefferson and Schweitzer, Lincoln and King—are clearly qualitatively richer expressions of courage.

This means that heroes (and by contrast cowards) have a function other than to sell Wheaties. They remind us of something restless but ignored, dimly seen but

---

[11]If courage is the volitional quality of existence, we should not try to explain it in terms of something else, but rather we should begin with courage, and explain much if not everything else in terms of it. Instead of asking how we can explain courage, given the nature of reality—we should then seek to explain the nature of reality using courage as a clue.

deeply loved, inside all of us, summoning us to new possibilities of self-affirmation. When we delight in hero stories (as all cultures do and have done), perhaps it is because these exemplary instances of courage tell us who we are, who we are not, and what we are called to be. It was Thomas Carlyle who urged that the central question every person must ask is: "Wilt thou be a hero or a coward?"[12]

III

But, is there a "ground" of courage, or, more accurately, a ground which supports and nourishes courage? When we speak of a "ground," the image suggests "something to stand on," in a word, *sub-stance*—not a very honored image among process thinkers, but one that is suggestive.

So far as I can determine, however, a pragmatist must meet with devout agnosticism all proposals concerning a supranatural ground for courage, something outside of natural existence that nourishes and summons us. We do not enjoy the luxury of either arrogant atheists or arrogant theists. We simply do not know, and suspect no one else does either. The ground of courage which a pragmatist seeks is a "working" reality *within* existence, as we are within existence.

Is there such a working ground? Most assuredly, if by that we mean something about existence itself, something constitutive of natural-historical life as we personally experience and can publicly verify it, that provides for and nourishes us (Dare we say *en-courages* courage?). This is the (not always consciously acknowledged, considered, or even known) web of life, the network of relationships, the connections of consequence, that create us, support us, and make demands upon us. *It is an empirical fact that we are nourished by nature and history,* by that great network of connections that support and sustain us on our transient pilgrimage through life. And we are therefore the ground of one another's existence, and of one another's courage.

> For men and women are not only themselves; they are also the region in which they were born, the city apartment or the farm in which they learnt to walk, the games they played as children, the old wives' tales they overheard, the food they ate, the schools they attended, the sports they followed, the poets they read, and the God they believed in.[13]

These but illustrate the seemingly endless expanse of nourishing connections of consequence—family and friends, schools and sports, language and literature, financial and artistic, vocational and recreational, personal and institutional. We *are* surrounded by "so great a cloud of witnesses" (Hebrews 12:1) that cheer us on.

---

[12]L. P. Jacks, *Religious Perplexities* (New York: Doran, 1923) 11. See Thomas Carlyle, *Heroes and Hero Worship.* See also Joseph Campbell, *The Hero With a Thousand Faces.*

[13]W. Somereset Maugham, *The Razor's Edge,* as quoted in *Journal of the American Academy of Religion* 66/3 (Fall 1988): 397.

Even when overt support is absent, the thrust of this fathomless ocean's waves wash on, and (as with a skillful surfer) can be ridden.

This is why courage that is concerned about ethical consequences is the highest form of courage. A consumate courage does not just draw upon the rich relationships that nourish us, *but also contributes to them*. A courage which draws from but does not itself enrich the ecosystem is in danger of being parasitic. Of course, we often do not know the consequences of our choices, or the value of even our best achievements. The artist, who was unappreciated in his own time but treasured by later generations (Vincent Van Gogh), would present an obvious example. Pragmatists have no absolute criterion for making ethical-aesthetic judgments. Perhaps it is enough to keep the concern ever before us.

I am proposing that the ecological system in which we surely "live and move and have our being" (Acts 17:28)—or call it nature and history, with all the appropriate sub-departments that academics study—is the ground that nourishes courage. We are en-couraged by supportive connections of consequence—from solar energy to the toil of farmers, from mother's love to constructive theologies. Perhaps when we stand before oceans and deserts, the beauty of mountains and of valleys, the night sky and the glory of sunrise, the awe we experience is not because we are biologically afflicted by acrophobia (though that may be present). Rather, it is that nature awakens us to heights and depths of reality which we have neglected—namely, the magnitude and complexity of relationships that both support and summon us. These nourishing and challenging relationships, as described in the halls of academia (but experienced everywhere), are the receding horizon beyond which knowledge fades into mystery, and experience expands into a felt quality of holiness. There *is* a "more" beyond the horizon, but it is beyond the horizon, and therefore not available for scholarly discussion.

So, I would suggest, remote to but continuous with this empirically approachable ground for courage there lies a rich ocean of mystery, a depth of complexity and quality, which the pragmatic theologian can gladly acknowledge and sometimes symbolize, but cannot reduce to definitions, except in the form of personal and idiosyncratic, but not therefore condemnable, "overbeliefs" (James).[14]

---

[14]William James, *Varieties of Religious Experience* (New York: Modern Library, 1902) 503 and passim.

Marginalizing the Life of Language: Radical Empiricism as a Critique of Gadamer

Delwin Brown

What originally constituted the basis of the life of language and its . . . productivity . . . is now marginalized and instrumentalized into a rhetorical figure. —Gadamer, *Truth and Method* (1989)

Introduction

Theological inquiry today is tied closely to hermeneutics. Some say theology *is* hermeneutics. This association, however close it may be, exists not merely in the sense that theology has to do with understanding the religious past and/or the contemporary situation. The association of theology and hermeneutics exists also, and more importantly, in the sense that theology has to do with understanding what it means to understand at all. To some extent the current affiliation of theology and hermeneutics is only the latest step in theology's fascination since Schleiermacher with methodology. As such it reflects the now dominant emphasis of the modern methodological discussions—away from traditional considerations of faith and reason, for instance, and toward the analysis of human subjectivity that started with Kant.

This essay, like the larger project on the nature of tradition of which it is a part, reflects the view that the recent turn toward the subject in theology must move still further.[1] Specifically, in order to be more adequate to our own experience of selfhood in Western culture and also in order to be more consistent internally, the turn toward the subject must not only issue into a kind of historicism, as presently it is doing; it must also move toward a form of naturalism. It must place the human in a historical context and history in the context of nature. Even more specifically, theology must move from hermeneutics to tradition or, better, to tradition analysis.

To propose tradition as a desirable analytical framework for theology might seem odd, perhaps even dangerous. It might be thought dangerous because "tradi-

---

[1]*Boundaries of Our Habitations: Tradition and Theological Construction* (Albany: SUNY Press, 1994). Portions of this essay appear in chap. 2 of that volume.

tion" is a favored category of conservative ideologies. How can the elevation of this category do other than encourage the most retrograde forces in our society? And the attention I propose to give to tradition might seem odd simply because it is accompanied by the claim that hermeneutics must become historicism and historicism must be grounded in nature. How can this claim demand or even tolerate tradition analysis? What hath nature to do with tradition, or vice versa?

This paper will address these questions implicitly, but its explicit focus will be the work of Hans-Georg Gadamer who has done as much as any contemporary thinker to reopen the topic of tradition. The paper will assess elements of Gadamer's work on the nature of tradition from the standpoint of one who believes that radical empiricism has something important to add to his position. The assessment will proceed as follows. First, there will be a summary of the structure of Gadamer's analysis of tradition. Then Gadamer's reflection on the nature of play, which is central to my interpretation of his concept of tradition, will be considered. The final section will discuss what I take to be missing from Gadamer's analysis that should lead to the thesis of radical empiricism.

The Structure of Gadamer's Argument

Gadamer's chief work is *Truth and Method,* and though he has written much since its publication in 1960, *Truth and Method* still represents the framework of his point of view.[2] Gadamer's aim is to develop and defend a view of the truth of humanistic studies, in contrast to the truth of the natural sciences. His strategy is to juxtapose hermeneutics, which he says is the procedure of the humanities, with the methodical procedures of the hard sciences. For him, however, hermeneutics is not simply or primarily the science of text interpretation. For Gadamer as for Heidegger before him, "the real question is not in what way being can be understood but in what way understanding *is* being."[3] And since both hold that "understanding is the way in which the historicity of human being [Dasein] is itself carried out,"[4] Gadamer and Heidegger see an account of understanding to be at the same time an account of what is distinctive about human being. Thus, what is the nature of humanistic understanding? and what is the character of its truth? are the dominating questions of *Truth and Method.*

Truth and Method begins with a consideration of the way that the question of truth emerges in the experience of art (part I). Crucial to this discussion is an extended argument to the effect that the appreciative self comes into being through a

---

[2]*Wahrheit und Methode* (Tübingen: J. C. B. Mohr, 1960). References in this paper will be to *Truth and Method,* 2nd rev. ed. (New York: Crossroad, 1989).

[3]Hans Georg Gadamer, *Philosophical Hermeneutics,* ed. David E. Linge (Berkeley: University of California Press, 1976) 49.

[4]Ibid.

social process of "formation, education, or cultivation (Bildung)."[5] An essential part of this formation is an openness to the other, the alien. The process of openness entails the self's movement from itself into the alien, but also the self's return to itself which, however, is always changed by this process.[6] The vocation of the human spirit is this perpetual alienation, return, and therefore perpetual transformation.

In a discussion of tact, common sense, taste, and judgment Gadamer argues that this process is communally formed and *re*formed. Far from issuing into a kind of subjectivistic aestheticism, the aesthetic process is a mode of knowing and a source of truth—or more precisely, it is a socially formed mode of knowledge that yields claims to truth. Art is experienced as an assertion of meaning, Gadamer says.[7] Art is an interpretation of our existence, which by presenting its interpretive challenge calls us to the interpretive task.[8]

But how can aesthetic interpretation be so construed? How can it escape the specter of "hermeneutical nihilism,"[9] which holds that the work of art in itself means nothing at all and thus that it offers no interpretation of its own? How can we make credible the claim of an objective element in the experience of art, and, especially, how can we understand the relationship of the object's alleged claim to truth and our interpretation of it? Gadamer's way of responding to this kind of question—which is really the question about going beyond objectivism and relativism—is to recall that interpretation is historical, traditioned. For a clarification of the difference this makes Gadamer turns to a discussion of play. I shall consider Gadamer's discussion of play at some length in a moment, but first, as background, I shall to summarize two or three other aspects of the argument in *Truth and Method.*

Gadamer contends for what we might call the constitutive necessity of tradition. His is more than the claim that we are all historical creatures and therefore that the past is the inescapable ground *upon which* our future will be made. He argues also that the past is the material *with which* the future is made. Tradition is not simply formative, it is *in*formative or constitutive of the creation of the future. This claim leads to Gadamer's famous critique of the Enlightenment's "prejudice against prejudice":

> The historicity of our existence entails that prejudices, in the literal sense of the word, constitute the initial directedness of our whole ability to experience the world. They are simply the conditions whereby we experience some-

---

[5]*Truth and Method*, 9.
[6]Ibid., 14.
[7]Ibid, 92.
[8]Ibid., 100.
[9]Ibid., 95.

> thing.[10]

Or again, in a most revealing statement, Gadamer says:

> In fact history does not belong to us; we belong to it. Long before we understand ourselves through the process of self-examination, we understand ourselves in a self-evident way in the family, society, and state in which we live. . . . The self-awareness of the individual is only a flickering in the closed circuits of historical life. *That is why the prejudices of the individual, far more than his judgments, constitute the historical reality of his being.*[11]

The overtone of "determination" in the above statement, the sense that the past is an inescapable prison, is resisted by Gadamer in several important ways. For one thing, he argues that prejudices, the *fore*-understandings given by tradition, are the conditions of understanding[12]; thus in the sense that understanding is creative it follows that prejudice is a condition of creativity. Moreover, against both the Enlightenment and Romanticism, Gadamer contends that tradition does not in fact constrain freedom, creativity.[13] This is so in part because tradition is a conflictual variety of voices and it exists "only in the multifariousness of such voices."[14]

But the freedom of tradition is also accounted for by the fact that traditions are never insulated, hermetically sealed from encounters with and transformations by other traditions.[15] What Gadamer says about the perpetual journey of the human spirit—the movement into the alien and the return home of a changed self—applies no less to the movements of traditions. Both individually and collectively the flow of life is never a confrontation of self-contained subject and fixed object; understanding is always a mutual interaction in which two subjects are each transformed by the other. This is what Gadamer refers to as the "fusion of horizons"[16] that characterizes the hermeneutic experience.

Still, as much as Gadamer wishes to accent the vehicles of creativity in his view, most readers find in his work a persistent conservatism. As much as he attempts in *Truth and Method* and in subsequent responses to his critics to affirm the creativity that belongs to life in tradition, the mood that lingers throughout his work is nicely captured in the words: "history does not belong to us; we belong to it."

My own view is that Gadamer does not dispel this mood because his systematic analysis will not allow him to do so. The primary impediment is his point of departure—the "question of truth as it emerges *in the experience of art*" (emphasis

---

[10]*Philosophical Hermeneutics,* 9; cf. Truth and Method, 269ff.

[11]*Truth and Method,* 276-77 (emphasis original).

[12]Ibid., 277.

[13]Ibid., 276.

[14]Ibid., 284.

[15]Ibid., 304.

[16]Ibid., 306.

added). The point to be noticed is that "experience" here refers fundamentally to the experience of the observer of art, not the creator. This emphasis on the observer's orientation can fairly easily be missed because Gadamer's discussion of play—which is actor oriented, for the most part, not spectator oriented—is a prominent part of his larger investigation of the experience of art, and Gadamer even tells us that play is "the mode of being of the work of art."[17]

The important thing, however, is what is not said. We are not told that play is the mode of being of the *creation* of art; it is a clue to the appreciation of art. And, in fact, the play that turns out to be a clue to the being of art is play that has acquired, and is thus transformed by, the appearance of an audience—play, as Gadamer says, that has been "transformed into structure." In point of fact, the topic of play appears rather abruptly in Gadamer's analysis and after 30 pages or so it disappears almost completely from the discussion. What Gadamer says thereafter about the nature of understanding (aesthetic understanding and understanding in general) is determined by Gadamer's opening account of the *observer's* experience of art. In sum, play clarifies but does not alter a discussion whose parameters have already been set by Gadamer's initial interpretation of the observation of art.

How might Gadamer's analysis of tradition have been different if he had begun with an analysis of play? To speculate on that we need to examine what Gadamer says about play.

Gadamer's Analysis of Play

Gadamer looks to the phenomenon of play for "an alternative to the Cartesian model that rivets our attention on `subjective attitudes' [Vorsellung] toward what is presumably `objective'."[18] In this regard he notes that those who enter the game are taken up into and become one with its activity. The game "absorbs the player into itself."[19] We cannot think of the playing of the player as a subjective activity that is distinct from and stands over against the game as an object. The game cannot be reduced to the activity of the player or players, of course, but the game's reality is not instantiated except as it is instantiated in the activity of the player. In play, the specter of subjectivism disappears; subject and object presuppose one another.

Gadamer views play as a natural phenomenon whose "to-and-fro" activity is self-extending and self-renewing.[20] It is also freeing. Indeed, the "peculiar freedom and buoyancy" of play, Gadamer says, "determines the consciousness of the

---

[17]Ibid., 101.

[18]Richard J. Bernstein, *Beyond Objectivism and Relativism* (Philadelphia: University of Pennsylvania Press, 1983), 21.

[19]*Truth and Method*, 105.

[20]Ibid.

player."[21] So much so that "the players are not the subjects of [the] play."[22] The play plays the players. "All playing is being-played."[23]

The game has its own distinctive space or place, denoted not only by boundaries or a playing field, but also by the boundaries of appropriate activities usually called rules. Indeed, the rules or patterns of propriety are the most prominent features of the reality of the game apart from its instantiation in the play itself. The rules constitute the canon of the game.

What Gadamer fails to explore adequately, in my view, is the creativity of the player. That is understandable if, as I claim, Gadamer's effective model of analysis is not play or artistic creation but the observer's experience of art. In any case, while Gadamer does talk about the player's creativity, it is primarily his or her creativity in instantiating the game, which for Gadamer is already about as "fixed" as a sculpture or a painting. My contention is that if we focus on playing, i.e., if we escape the confines of Gadamer's restrictive starting point, we will see that all playing is indeed being-played, as he says, but, equally, all being-played is playing, creating, constructing.

There is, first, the obvious point that rules or canons for play are simply the outer limits which, precisely as limits, also direct the player's attention to the task of multiplying the possibilities within. The stipulation of what is not permitted is also an invitation to explore and expand from within what is permitted. Limitation, as Jonathan Z. Smith has said in his discussion of canon, calls forth ingenuity.[24] Hence as much as it is true to say that the game plays the players, the players also develop and alter the game by exploring and expanding the game from within, both with respect to what is possible (strategy) and how it is possible (technique). Players play the game, change the game from within.

The changes that occur in play do not simply succeed what went before, they inherit what went before. Prior play is constitutive of succeeding play even when what follows moves far beyond it. In games, the past is not necessarily inhibitory, but it is obligatory at least in the sense that what follows must somehow take it into account. If it does not, it is another game. The past is taken up into what follows and makes a difference to what follows. The change within games displays constitutive, not merely successive, continuity.

But rules also change. Especially in free play—for example, children playing house, adults engrossed in conversation, couples making love—the canons of play are fluid. Their fluidity varies, of course. There is more than a little evidence that in modern Western culture this variation relates partly to gender roles. According

---

[21] *Philosophical Hermeneutics*, 53.

[22] *Truth and Method*, 103.

[23] *Philosophical Hermeneutics*, xxiii.

[24] Jonathan Z. Smith, "Sacred Persistence: Towards a Redescription of Canon," in *Approaches to Ancient Judaism,* ed. Jacob Neusner (Atlanta: Scholars Press, 1978) 27.

to the research of Janet Lever as reported by Carol Gilligan,[25] boys tend to view the rules of games as inviolable and thus they make rules applicable to new situations by the addition of rules of arbitration. (In religions this is called commentary.) For girls the rules of games per se are usually subservient to the more important rules of relationships, so that a conflict within a game may simply end the game in order to continue the relationship. Variations in the fluidity of rules also relates to cultural differences. But the basic point is this: In play, there is a changing of the rules as well as a changing within the rules.

Gadamer's acknowledgement of the creativity of the player is therefore much too timid. The game plays the players, *and* the players play (play with) the game. Still, the most important thing, as Gadamer rightly observes, is that "playing with" and "being played" are not experienced as the interaction of separable subjects and objects. Gadamer has indeed found a model for relationships that avoids the Cartesian cul de sac. And when this analysis of games is applied to the relationship of individuals and their traditions, including their religious traditions, the results are interesting:[26]

(1) Traditions are not simply reducible to the activity of individuals and groups within them, but neither do they have a reality except as they are instantiated in their quite varied activities.
(2) Traditions are natural phenomena whose very "to-and-fro" movements are the ground, so to speak, of their being extended and renewed. They live precisely in the dialectic of continuity *and* change.
(3) Traditions have their own distinctive spaces and places, which we usually call canons. They are the principle of identity as well as the font of ingenuity or imaginative construction within a tradition.
(4) The vocation of creativity within a tradition applies not only to an expansion of the alternatives *within* a canon but also to an expansion of the alternatives *for* a canon. The "freedom and buoyancy" of traditions is greater than Gadamer allows.
(5) The past of a tradition is constitutive of the changes that follow, both within the canon and to the canon. The past is taken up into the present as an agent of its *re*formation.

The Ground of Play

My view is that enlarging the role of creativity in Gadamer's theory of tradition is helpful, but it is not yet enough. What we still lack is an adequate account of *how*

---

[25]Carol Gilligan, *In a Different Voice: Psychological Theory and Women's Development* (Cambridge: Harvard University Press) 9-10.

[26]The significance of the model of games, and play in particular, for understanding the dynamics of religious traditions was first suggested to me in conversation by Sam D. Gill, whose important work on the topic is forthcoming.

it is that tradition is efficacious in the present. Gadamer's analysis of the power of the past is limited almost exclusively to an examination of language, canonical language or "classics" in particular. In this respect Gadamer continues the modernist preoccupation with the human, limited not to the dictates of reason or the structures of the mind but to the patterns and functionings of human linguisticality. Yet Gadamer's own discussion occasionally betrays the insufficiency of this "linguicentrism." What I shall do in this final section is examine the telling "slips" in Gadamer's discussion and say why and how I think they should be taken seriously.

Gadamer persuasively argues that all understanding is interpretive, and that all conscious interpretation is linguistic. But this leaves open a question: Is there a prelinguistic, largely nonconscious mode of apprehending whatever is given, out of which emerges our conscious, interpretive, linguistic understandings?

Gadamer's own account of the power of language in the final pages of *Truth and Method* suggests, and perhaps even presupposes, the hypothesis of a preconceptual mode of awareness or "prehension" (Whitehead). At one point, for example, Gadamer writes:

> Language often seems ill suited to express what we feel. In the face of the overwhelming presence of works of art, the task of expressing in words what they say to us seems like an infinite and hopeless undertaking. The fact that our desire and capacity to understand always go beyond any statement that we can make seems like a critique of language.[27]

Two pages later Gadamer is reflecting on the process of conceptual interpretation:

> We have seen that conceptual interpretation is the realization of the hermeneutical experience itself. That is why our problem is so difficult. The interpreter does not know that he is bringing himself and his own concepts into the interpretation. The verbal formulation is so much part of the interpreter's mind that he never becomes aware of it as an object.[28]

As we have noted, Gadamer says that all understanding is interpretation and that interpretation is linguistic. But here, interestingly, he has to postulate an element of the process of understanding and interpretation that is not conscious. What he seems to mean is that we are conscious of the outcome of the process of thinking and speaking, but not of the process itself. At the very least what follows is the reality of a preconceptual element that is powerfully efficacious in the understanding process. If Gadamer wants still to insist that this preconceptual process—"bringing one's own concepts into the interpretation"—is linguistic, he must now conclude that all linguisticality is not conscious.

---

[27]*Truth and Method*, 401.

[28]Ibid., 403.

In fact, much earlier in the book Gadamer had already toyed with the idea that, as we might put it, knowing exceeds being conscious. He says:

> We do not understand what recognition is in its profoundest nature if we only regard it as knowing something again that we know already. . . . The joy of recognition is rather the joy of knowing *more* than is already familiar [or, in Warnke's translation, "The joy of recognition is rather that more is known than only the known"].[29]

A passage in *Philosophical Hermeneutics* contains the same suggestion:

> Reflection on a given preunderstanding brings before me something that otherwise happens *behind my back*. . . . For what I have called *wirkungsgeschichtliches* [effective historical consciousness] is inescapably more *being* than consciousness, and being is never fully manifest.[30]

One can dismiss such statements as slips that a more careful writer should and would avoid. I prefer, for reasons to be mentioned later, to explore the possibility that these references to a level of nonconceptual experience, where subject and object are presumably intertwined, are insightful. Their insight can be expressed in a paraphrase of Gadamer:

> Even as we understand through the process of conscious examination, we apprehend at the prelinguistic and largely nonconscious level where we most fundamentally live. The focus on language and thus consciousness, taken alone, is a distorting mirror. The consciousness of the individual is only a flickering in the closed circuits of our bodily and historical life.[31]

This, of course, is the claim of radical empiricism. I would summarize the radical empiricist hypothesis about the human relationship with the rest of the world in four points.

The first is the proposal that our primary connectedness with things is at the level of largely nonconscious feeling. Whitehead, for example, acknowledges the central importance of sensory experience which is vivid and precise. But he insists that there is another, more fundamental, dimension of experience "vague, unmanageable . . . , heavy with the contact of things gone by."[32] This is our bodily commerce with the world—intuitive, felt, tacit. On Whitehead's view, we do not first experience the world through one or more of the five senses; sense experience and intel-

---

[29]Ibid., 114; cf. Georgia Warnke, *Gadamer: Hermeneutics, Tradition and Reason* (Stanford: Stanford University Press, 1987) 60.

[30]*Philosophical Hermeneutics*, 38.

[31]Cf. *Truth and Method*, 276, quoted above.

[32]Alfred North Whitehead, *Symbolism: Its Meaning and Effect* (New York: Macmillan, 1959) 43-44.

lection are fashioned out of a more basic sense of the world that is given in dim, imprecise feeling.[33] Experience at the primitive level is probably best described as an activity of the body, or at least of the self as an embodied organism, rooted in, and interacting with, the rest of nature.

A second element of radical empiricism is the judgment that feelings at the preconceptual and largely preconscious level are always weighted or patterned. They are not innocent, indifferent buzzes. They are forces, values. They incline us, influence us, move us. Like strong winds they bend us in particular directions. They are "meanings." I say this with some hesitation because we are predisposed to associate "meaning" with language, and thus to ask about such feelings, "what do they mean?" The most adequate answer is that they mean themselves. They are powers, and their meaning is what they do to us, including what they enable us to do, to see, to think, to imagine, to create.

A third supposition is that the relationship of the human subject and her or his given environment is, in either case, neither simply "causing" (creating, imagining, constructing) nor "being caused" (receiving, picturing, corresponding). Each is to some degree creative subject and to some degree created object, plastic or malleable coparticipants in an interconnected process. Hence the relationship of "self" and "world" (both social and natural) is best described as interactive, codeterminant, or reciprocal.

This brings up a fourth aspect of the radical empiricist hypothesis, concerning the interactivity within the self. In human experience, the more primitive level of feeling is intertwined with sensation and reflection. Our conscious sensory awareness of the world, and then our imaginative reflection on this conscious awareness, are abstractions constructed out of the raw material of inchoate, largely preconscious feeling. Feeling, in other words, permeates sensation and thought. But the opposite is true, too. The worlds of sensation and ideas also impact the more basic level of feeling. So formed feelings at the level of our most primitive awareness of the world both influence and are influenced by what we experience in the five senses and what we think about.[34]

Radical empiricism, in sum, is the hypothesis that we are bodies more than we are minds, even though minds are absolutely essential, and that the dimension of largely preconscious feeling, which our bodies receive and enact, should be, no less

[33]Radical empiricism, if it is to be taken seriously, must offer a plausible hypothesis as to how the kind of experience it posits might give rise to sensation and reflection. Whitehead's theory of concrescence is one way to give an account of such an emergence.

[34]This interaction at the human level (as well as the fact that such feelings, even if considered in isolation from sensation and reflection, are always affected by the "bias" of particular spaces and times) means that there is no such thing as "pure experience" if that term suggests that a subject can take account of a datum "as it is." All experience is perspectival. "Interpretation" refers to perspectival appropriation insofar as it is cognitive.

than language, a part of any theory about how it is that we relate to our environments, "know" our world, and inherit and transform our particular traditions.

There are, it seems to me, a number of reasons for taking this hypothesis seriously, most of which, because of limited space, I can only mention.

First, the hypothesis of a preconceptual and largely preconscious mode of awareness provides a plausible interpretation of the way "lower" forms of life take account of their environments, and since humans evolved from and remain rooted in nature it would be odd if through evolution humans had managed to abandon this mode of awareness entirely. Indeed, some such way of taking account of the world appears to be an appropriate description of the relatedness of the newborn humans and their environments. Again, it would be odd if this kind of awareness were simply to cease as human beings mature.

Secondly, this hypothesis, implying as it does a continuity between humans and nonhumans, is one way of overcoming the deleterious dualisms of mind and body, and humanity and the rest of the natural order. Thirdly, the notion of bodily inheritance can account for memory and for the experience of causality. Fourth, there is some reason for supposing that such a mode of awareness manifests itself at the edges of our consciousness, in so-called "personal knowledge" and in more intuitive senses of our connectedness to things.

In this context, however, I should like to emphasize a fifth consideration.[35] The radical empiricist hypothesis—which holds that the fundamental connectedness of humans and their worlds, including their pasts, occurs at a level of preconceptual awareness and inheritance—helps us to understand the power of the affective or noncognitive dimensions of traditions. It indicates that our cultural and religious traditions are transmitted fundamentally at the level of bodily feeling where our immersion in nature is most intense. This judgment finds support in recent ritual studies which, however much they may differ in other respects, suggest I think that rituals do things and convey meanings that are not communicated by language, certainly not by language alone.[36] Studies of oral traditions and varying forms of

---

[35]It should be noted that I eschew entirely two arguments rather commonly marshalled in defence of radical empiricism.

The hypothesis of radical empiricism has no special relevance to the accrediting of religion or religious sensibilities. If there is a preconceptual mode of awareness, it does not follow that this awareness necessarily includes a "sense of the whole," or, if it does, that this sense of the whole has anything to do with religion.

The claims of radical empiricism are useless, too, with respect to the task of adjudication. Radical empiricism does lead us to suppose that there is a "givenness" that constrains us and our knowledge claims to some degree. But in the assessment of competing knowledge claims the radical empiricist is no more able than anyone else to appeal to an experiential given undefiled by an interpretive framework that includes in particular the grid imposed by linguistic convention.

[36]Here one thinks in particular of the analyses of ritual by Sam D. Gill, Ronald Grimes,

literate traditions indicate, too, that the power of the past cannot be reduced to the conscious and conceptual.[37] The efficacy of traditions is located very significantly—perhaps largely—in rites of bodily enactment, in the felt dimensions of community, and in the largely precritical play of symbol and myth. Radical empiricism makes sense of this.

Conclusion

I do not argue that Gadamer gives inadequate attention to the creative play within religious traditions because he pays insufficient attention to the preconceptual dimensions of experience, or vice versa. I do observe, however, that the two emendations of Gadamer proposed in this essay are mutually supportive. The preconceptual dimensions of traditions are fonts of creativity as well as continuity. If, as Gadamer and Ricoeur have claimed, the inherited past is multifarious or plurivocal, then the tensive richness of the past communicated at the level of bodily feeling would in fact serve to undermine repetition. The valuing of sameness, the elevation of conformity over creativity, is not an inherent characteristic of tradition; it is likely the product of conceptual strategies—theologies—intentionally cultivated to protect the status quo. When grounded in the richness of feeling, conserving traditions are also creating. A vital tradition is a tradition at play.

With Nicholas of Cusa, Gadamer speaks of creativity as the life of language.[38] But Gadamer himself neglects the effusive, precognitive ground from which creativity springs. In his theory of tradition, to quote Gadamer speaking about another matter, "what originally constituted the basis of the life of language . . . is . . . marginalized."[39] Fortunately, Gadamer's intuition is more adequate than his theory. Taking seriously the insights that language is often "ill suited to express what we feel," that the role of the past is "inescapably more being than consciousness," and that in human experience "more is known than only the known"—adhering to these insights allows us to ground in nature the human creativity that Gadamer's analysis of play, further developed and consistently focused, shows to be central to the life of traditions.[40]

---

and Jonathan Z. Smith, historians of religions, and anthropological studies by Clifford Geertz, Sally Moore and Barbara Myerhoff, and Victor Turner.

[37]The varied works that come to mind here are those by Jack Goody, Walter Ong, Paul Ricoeur, and William Graham.

[38]*Truth and Method*, 434.

[39]Ibid., 432.

[40]The work of two graduate students, Harold Anderson and John Minear, was helpful to me in the preparation of this paper. I also benefitted from the probing questions and suggestions of William Dean and, especially, Sheila Davaney.

A Functional-Empirical Approach to the "Whitehead without God" Debate

David E. Conner

> My own method is to distinguish each thing according to its nature, and to specify how it behaves.
>
> —Heraclitus of Ephesus, *On the Universe,* frag. 1

> The ultimate test is always to widespread, recurrent experience; and the more general the rationalistic scheme the more important is this final appeal.
>
> —Alfred North Whitehead, *Process and Reality* (1929) 25

A noteworthy event in the relatively brief history of process theology was the appearance in 1965 of John B. Cobb's *A Christian Natural Theology*. Among the responses to the ideas in this book one of the most memorable is a chapter entitled "Whitehead without God" by Donald Sherburne in Brown, James, and Reeves's *Process Philosophy and Christian Thought* (1971). This chapter led in turn to a series of articles by Professors Cobb and Sherburne that appeared in the then-new journal *Process Studies* under the title "The Whitehead-without-God Debate."

The focus of the debate (Cobb taking pro and Sherburne con) is whether any idea of God is really needed in Whitehead's metaphysics, especially in light of the changes in that metaphysics undertaken by Cobb in chapter 5 of *A Christian Natural Theology*. After almost two decades this debate still makes for stimulating reading, if for no other reasons than the intellectual fluency and stature of the two disputants, the spirited character of their exchanges, and the extraordinary moment of the topic itself.

The purpose of this paper is not to engage Cobb and Sherburne on their own ground so as to add to or even resolve their discussion. My aims instead are briefly to call attention to the rationalistic character of the methods embraced within their debate and to offer, in contrast to that rationalism, a more functional-empirical approach both to Whitehead's concept of God and to the larger question of God's very existence. The point is not to prove Cobb and Sherburne mistaken either in their reasoning or in their interpretation of Whitehead, but to provide an example of how a functional-empirical reading of Whitehead offers a feasible and, indeed, appealing alternative in process theology.

A Review of the Debate

In *A Christian Natural Theology* John Cobb advocates that Whitehead's theory of God as the only nontemporal actual entity be jettisoned in favor of the belief that God is a personally ordered society of actual occasions.[1] Cobb's reasoning is too complex to be restated here, but the essential point for present purposes is that Cobb's primary methodological consideration in reaching this conclusion is the criterion of *coherence.*

> My conclusion, then, is that the chief reasons for insisting that God is *an* actual entity can be satisfied by the view that he is a living person, that this view makes the doctrine of God more coherent, and that no serious new difficulties are raised.[2]

Cobb argues that Whitehead's God-concept is additionally improved by the assertion that God is omnispatial. This position, also, is supported by the criterion of coherence. "If the nonspatiality and omnispatiality of god are both equally allowed by Whitehead's metaphysics, we can chose between them only on the basis of coherence."[3] The idea that God is an omnispatial, personal being proves to be central to the disagreement with Sherburne.

In his chapter, "Whitehead without God," Sherburne begins not by referring directly to Cobb's revision of Whitehead's god-concept, but by proposing to "naturalize" Whitehead's metaphysics. By "naturalized" metaphysics Sherburne means metaphysics in which all ideas of God have been eliminated. While philosophical naturalism may legitimately be defined so as to entail atheism, it should be noted that many theologians would not choose to equate naturalization or naturalism with godlessness, and one may wonder whether Sherburne has simply overlooked the theological possibility that Whitehead's God can be understood naturalistically, namely, as an intrinsic aspect of the world. Be that as it may, after listing the roles god plays in Whitehead's philosophy, Sherburne writes:

> A naturalistic reinterpretation of Whitehead's scheme has to show (1) that in some one, at least, of these roles the concept "God" violates the fundamental metaphysical principles of the system and thereby introduces incoherence into the scheme, and (2) that the system can be so interpreted and modified that each of these roles is superfluous. . . . My first concern . . . will be to show that on either the orthodox interpretation of Whitehead . . . or on the interpretation offered by Charles Hartshorne and John Cobb,

---

[1]John B. Cobb, Jr., *A Christian Natural Theology* (Philadelphia: Westminster Press, 1965) 188-92. Chap. 5 of this book is reprinted in *Process Philosophy and Christian Thought*, 213-43 (see n. 4 below).

[2]Ibid., 192.

[3]Ibid., 195.

there is incoherence.[4]

Sherburne's first section centers on the question of how Whitehead's God can influence or relate to actual occasions and on the interdependent question of how God can preserve the past or the values achieved in the past. Two relevant issues are (1) whether God is required to prehend contemporary occasions (Whitehead had said that contemporaries can not prehend one another) and (2) how God can prehend occasions which are included with God's own region. This second problem, termed "the problem of regional inclusion,"[5] is a complicated one which, however, our present purposes do not require us to address at length. The essence of the question is how God, assuming Cobb's affirmation of omnispatiality, can prehend concrescing occasions when they must be included within the region in which God also is concrescing. Sherburne contends that it is impossible to defend regional inclusion without either making God an exception to systematic principles or else introducing a *reductio ad absurdum* in which it becomes necessary for single prehensions to belong to two subjects.[6] In all of this it is obvious that Sherburne has in mind the alterations which Cobb, seeking greater coherence, has made in Whitehead's idea of God, and that Sherburne is actually criticizing not Whitehead's idea of God but Cobb's revision of Whitehead's idea of God.[7]

In a second, shorter section Sherburne seeks to explain how the incoherence attributed to Whitehead and Cobb can best be addressed. The answer proffered is, not surprisingly, to excise any idea of God from the scheme. It then remains in a third and final section for Sherburne to demonstrate that any functions of Whitehead's God which have not already been discussed can likewise be explained by referring to Whiteheadian principles which do not implicate God. The divine functions which Sherburne mentions at this juncture are (1) the function of providing an ontological ground for the eternal objects and (2) the function of providing subjective aims for actual occasions. The first role, Sherburne says, does not require God because "if there is at least one actual entity in the world characterized by at least one eternal object . . . then this actual entity provides all the ontological ground required for the realm of eternal objects—an appeal to God is not necessary."[8] As for the source of subjective aims, Sherburne holds that these can as well be furnished by the past as by God.[9] Again, God is not needed.

---

[4]Donald Sherburne, "Whitehead without God," in *Process Philosophy and Christian Thought,* ed. Delwin Brown, Ralph James, and Gene Reeves (Indianapolis: Bobbs-Merrill, 1971) 306-307. This article was first published in *The Christian Scholar* 50/3 (Fall 1967).

[5]Ibid., 310-20.

[6]Ibid., 309, 312-13.

[7]Sherburne is actually very sparing in his citations of Whitehead, while Cobb is cited repeatedly at each point in the polemic.

[8]Sherburne, "Whitehead without God,"326.

[9]Ibid., 328.

It is unfortunate that in a twenty-four-page article Sherburne takes only three pages for this concluding section. These final two points, and especially the last, might well be considered the most critical issues that have been raised. In Whitehead's metaphysics the divine provision of initial[10] aims is integral to the explanation of how novelty comes into being and of how wholes emerge and evolve in the world. At least at first it is difficult to see how genuine originality can occur if, as Sherburne claims, subjective aims are restricted to the past for their derivations.

In his critique of Sherburne's position Cobb indicates his agreement with Sherburne that in Whitehead's system God is not needed as the ground of the givenness of the past—but this, Cobb notes, was never asserted by Whitehead in the first place.[11] Furthermore the issue of regional inclusion is not as decisive to the coherence or incoherence of process theism as Sherburne thinks; nevertheless this matter "has important consequences for how God is to be conceived in his relation to the world," and therefore it is worthy of continued discussion.[12]

Thus Cobb devotes most or his answer to Sherburne to the problem or regional inclusion, taking only two final pages to respond to Sherburne's comments on the ontological ground of the eternal objects and the source of each actual entity's subjective aim. Then, stating his disappointment that Sherburne has given a misleading impression of Whitehead's doctrine, Cobb adds:

> Further, eternal objects cannot be the reason for their own ordering, at least in so far as this has relevance to ingression. Here again an actual entity is required as agent. Apparently Sherburne attributes these functions to past occasions, but I see no sign that he has wrestled with the immense difficul-

---

[10]Though Professors Cobb and Sherburne refer to the "subjective" aim as being derived from God, I am using the term "initial aim" because (1) I wish to emphasize the initiating function of the divine lure, and (2) I believe it may be more correct in Whitehead's own terms to think of the *initial* aspect of the subjective aim as the aspect stemming from God. Whitehead writes that "the subjective aim limits the ontological principle by its own autonomy. But the *initial stage* of its aim is an endowment which the subject inherits from the inevitable ordering of things, conceptually realized in the nature of God. . . . Thus the *initial stage* of the aim is rooted in the nature of God, and its completion depends on the self-causation of the subject-supersubject. This function of God is analogous to the remorseless working of things in Greek and Buddhist thought. The initial aim is the best for that impasse. . . . What is inexorable in God is valuation as an aim towards 'order'; and 'order' means 'society permissive of actualities with patterned intensity of feeling arising from adjusted contrasts.' In this sense God is the principle of concretion; namely, he is that actual entity from which each temporal concrescence receives that *initial* aim from which its self causation starts." (*Process and Reality,* 373-74, or 244 in the Griffin-Sherburne edition; emphasis added.)

[11]John B. Cobb, Jr., "'The Whitehead without God' Debate: The Critique," in *Process Studies* 1/2 (Summer 1971): 92.

[12]Ibid., 93.

> ties that prevented Whitehead from doing so. The ordering of the entire realm of possibility seems a truly amazing feat for even the highest grade occasions, but Sherburne must attribute it to the simplest as well. One must also ask whether all individual occasions order the whole realm of pure possibility identically. If so, is not some explanation required for this truly amazing identity?[13]

Here Cobb hits the nail on the head; essentially he is asking how Sherburne can explain the world's manifest structure, order, and emergent novelty without referring to God. To reiterate, this in my view is the most momentous question which has so far been broached, one that might have been given a preemiment position in the ensuing discussion. However Cobb does not press this point—and his words, "an actual entity is *required*," suggest once more the belief that logic makes demands on actual things. At any rate Sherburne in his rejoinder makes no explicit reply to this question but returns instead to the problem of regional inclusion, again basing his fundamental divergence from Cobb and Whitehead on the purported incoherence of their opinions.

> I stick to the claim . . . that "without this explanation of the givenness of the past Whitehead's system is incomplete." In this context the question of whether or not past entities are actual becomes very important, for if they are, the explanation about the givenness of the past via God is superfluous, but if the are not, as I have argued, then it seems that God is required to do this job in the system. But given that God is required to do this job, it was the burden of my "Whitehead without God" article to show that God could not perform the role without violating the categories of the system. This state of affairs . . . is one reason for looking with some interest toward a naturalistic reformulation of Whitehead's system.[14]

For Sherburne, also, concerns for rational inference and integrity of system continue to predominate.

The final segment of the debate, "Regional Inclusion and the Extensive Continuum"[15] is comprised of two statements by each author in alternation. As indicated by the title, the arguments remain focused on the problem of regional inclusion and on related matters such as what Whitehead meant by the term "region." Questions about propriety in the exposition of Whitehead and about

---

[13]Ibid., 99.

[14]Donald Sherburne, "The 'Whitehead without God' Debate: The Rejoinder," *Process Studies* 1/2 (Summer 1971): 108. In the first sentence of the indented paragraph Sherburne is quoting William Christian, *An Interpretation of Whitehead's Metaphysics* (New Haven CT: Yale University Press, 1959).

[15]John B. Cobb, Jr. and Donald W. Sherburne, "Regional Inclusion and the Extensive Continuum," *Process Studies* 2/4 (Winter 1972): 277-95.

systemic coherence remain as the focus of attention, and the debate ends with no major concessions made by either author.

This has been the briefest of reviews of "the Whitehead without God Debate," and it is worth repeating that the primary goal has not been to summarize the content of the debate itself but to give some indication of the rationalistic nature of its methods and goals. I will now suggest how the subject of the "Whitehead without God" debate can be approached from a functional-empirical standpoint.

Some Rationalistic Elements to Relinquish

I now emphasize that the objective in what follows is not to denigrate the achievement of Professors Cobb or Sherburne but to show how the debate over the existence of Whitehead's God is altered and simplified by the emphasis of differing methodological criteria. Whitehead is quoted not in order to prove that an empirical reading is the only correct reading (perhaps an impossible task, anyway) but to indicate that it is a plausible reading. This entails a somewhat critical approach to the existing debate, but the aim is to reformulate prior themes—not reject them altogether. I am in sympathy both with Sherburne's desire to 'naturalize' Whitehead's thought (if we may redefine 'naturalize'!) and, especially, with Cobb's wish to retain the idea of God in process cosmology.

(1) The most significant point of agreement between Cobb and Sherburne in the "Whitehead without God debate" is that *coherence* is the foremost methodological consideration. However, in order to develop a functional-empirical approach to the matters over which they have wrestled, it is desirable to *demote the criterion of coherence* from its paramount position and *elevate instead criteria such as adequacy* (to observed facts) *and exemplification* (or applicability).

Exponents of the rationalistic rendition of process philosophy may object that to make such a methodological shift is to flirt with inconsistency, indefensibility, and outright confusion. Why not simply strike a balance between coherence on the one hand and criteria such as adequacy and exemplification on the other? Surely, the rationalist says, one can pursue adequacy and exemplification without neglecting coherence.

But this in a sense is exactly what the empiricist denies. It is not that the empiricist is antirational, seeking wisdom as some theologians have in paradox, enigma, or some other form of the deliberate subjugation of reason. The point is rather that, however much consistency and coherence we may achieve, there is still at the heart of life a mystery which is, if not contradictory to reason, still not entirely amenable to it, either. In Bernard Meland's well-known words, "We live more deeply than we can think."[16]

---

[16]Bernard E. Meland elaborates on this apothegm in many places, e.g., in "The Empirical Tradition in Theology at Chicago," in *The Future of Empirical Theology*, ed. Meland (Chicago: University of Chicago Press, 1969) 13, 48. On Meland's view of mystery, see his "Myth

Chemists freely admit that many reactions cannot be explained theoretically. For example, twenty years ago when I was taking chemistry courses no one knew why the addition of tetraethyl lead to gasoline would reduce engine knocking and raise the octane rating. Just the same it worked, and it was added to the gasoline. There are times when, in like fashion, theology is entitled to speak of divine workings even when systematic explanations are difficult or impossible. This kind of mystery is the result of plain ignorance.

Another kind of mystery is associated with phenomena which prompt astonishment, wonder, and appreciative depth, despite the fact that we can explain them rather well. Anyone who has taken part in or even merely witnessed the birth of a child knows this feeling. The mastery of subjects such as physiology and obstetrics may enhance but is not essential to the richness of the experience, and indeed a preoccupation with theories and facts often detracts from a profounder appreciation.

A third kind of mystery, noted eloquently by Meland and Whitehead, has to do with those elements of experience which, though vague and often only partly conscious, are yet pervasive and powerful. For example, feelings about food and eating, sexual feelings, and feelings related to our self-image and to our bodily presence all massively qualify our lives in spite of the obvious fact that they defy rational analysis and the Cartesian criteria of clarity and distinctness.

A functional-empirical theology is attentive to what 'works' in life, and to these senses of mystery. The achievement of coherence and the construction of systems are seen as supportive tools in the clarification of experience rather than as ends-in-themselves. Whitehead made statements which reveal his sympathy with this orientation: "The elucidation of immediate experience is the sole justification for any thought." "The success of the imaginative experiment is always to be tested by the applicability of its results beyond the restricted locus from which it originated."[17]

> But the universe stretches beyond our finite powers of understanding. The great thinkers from whom we derive inspiration enjoyed insights beyond their own systems. They made statements hard to reconcile with the neat little ways of thought which we pin to their names. . . .
>
> Plato and Hume illustrate that system is essential for rational thought. But they also illustrate that the closed system is the death of living understanding. In their explanations they wander beyond all system. Thus they illustrate in their own procedures that our primary insight is a mixture of clarity and vagueness.[18]

---

as a Mode of Awareness and Intelligibility," *American Journal of Theology & Philosophy* 8/3 (September 1987): 109-19. I thank Charles Milligan for drawing my attention to this article.

[17]Alfred North Whitehead, *Process and Reality* (New York: Macmillan, 1933) 4 and 8.

[18]Alfred North Whitehead, *Modes of Thought* (New York: The Free Press, 1968) 82-83.

Regarding theology itself Whitehead wrote:

> I am suggesting that Protestant theology should develop as its foundation an interpretation of the Universe which grasps its unity amid its many diversities. The interpretation to be achieved is a reconciliation of seeming incompatibilities. But these incompatibilities are not hypothetical. They are there on the stage of history, undoubted and claiming interpretation. There stand in the public view the persuasiveness of the eternal ideals . . . and the compulsoriness of physical nature. . . . Nature changes and yet remains. . . . It is the business of philosophical theology to provide a rational understanding of the rise of civilization, and of the tendernesses of mere life itself, in a world which superficially is founded upon the clashing of senseless compulsion.[19]

Phrases such as "they are there on the stage of history," "there stand in public view," and "theology should develop as its foundation an interpretation of the Universe," provide more than a hint that a theology which begins and ends with observation and experience is wholly compatible with Whitehead's philosophy.

(2) Concomitant to the relinquishment of coherence as the primary methodological criterion is the relinquishment of the belief that *the existence of actual realities can be established or disestablished on the basis of abstract reasoning.* Most rationalists believe, and a good many empiricists do not believe, that if a proposition affirming the existence of something is *logically* necessary then the existence of that something has been established in actual fact.[20] Possibly the underlying differences between rationalists and empiricists on this issue are ontological rather than methodological, having to do with how terms such as "existence," "actual," "reality," and "fact" are defined. Concerning rationalism in the Middle Ages Whitehead comments:

> By this rationalism I mean the belief that the avenue to truth was predominantly through a metaphysical analysis of the nature of things, which would thereby determine how things acted and functioned. The historical revolt was the definite abandonment of this method in favour of the study of the empirical facts of antecedents and consequences.[21]

---

[19]Alfred North Whitehead, *Adventures of Ideas* (New York: Macmillan, 1933) 216-18.

[20]This means of differentiating between rationalistic and empiricistic process theologies was noted during the "Conference on Methodological Alternatives in Process Theology" at the Iliff School of Theology, February 23-25, 1989, although I am aware that this point has been discussed at least informally for many years previously.

[21]Alfred North Whitehead, *Science and the Modern World* (New York: Macmillan, 1925) 57. Whitehead is commenting here on medieval rationalism, but his observation is germane for the present discussion as well. Consider also this: "No logical argument can demonstrate this gap. Such arguments are merely subsidiary helps for the conscious realiztion of

In other words, for rationalists the requirements of the system were actually believed to "determine how things" did function or could function in the world. Though sometimes Whitehead's ideas are indeed based more upon reason than upon experience, he more typically distances himself from the rationalistic temper, as in the pithy remark: "The thesis that I am developing conceives proof, in the strict sense of that term, as a feeble second-rate procedure. When the word *proof* has been uttered, the next notion to enter the mind is halfheartedness."[22] The justification of his own metaphysical concepts relies

> mainly upon their direct elucidation of firsthand experience. They are not, and should not be, the result of an argument. For all argument must rest upon premises more fundamental than the conclusions. . . .
>
> The above set of metaphysical notions rests itself upon the ordinary average experience of mankind, properly interpreted.[23]

The conviction that tenable notions of God ultimately call for the formulation of doctrines of God which are integral to coherent schemes of thought leads to the attitude that the chief function of apologetic theology is to defend philosophical-theological systems *qua* systems. Thus we see Sherburne denying and Cobb defending points of systematic coherence. Though these antagonists have nominally limited themselves to rather narrow issues, there is a clear impression that the coherence or incoherence of the system will be a telling factor for each thinker's own theism or nontheism. In contrast, a more functional-empirical orientation sees apologetics as the *description* of existence in such a way as *persuasively to reveal the functioning of the divine* within the world and within human experience. As Nancy Frankenberry puts it,

> Evident in both the older ontological approach and in the newer linguistic approach is a tendency to treat the problem of God primarily as a conceptual rather than as a perceptual problem. Whether it is approached ontologically or linguistically, the problem of God has been consistently viewed as a *conceptual* problem, having empirical and existential implications, rather than as an empirical and existential problem, having conceptual and logical implications. What has been forfeited, as philosophy or religion has steadily assumed more and more the status of logical and semantic explication, is any concerted or sustained attempt to describe empirically the structures

---

metaphysical intuitions. —*Non in dialectica complaciut Deo salvum facere populum suum.* This saying, quoted by Cardinal Newman, should be the motto of every metaphysician." (*Adventures of Ideas,* 380.) My attempt at the Latin yields, "To save his own people is pleasing to God not according to (or subject to) logic," or, less literally, that God's pleasure is saving his/her people cannot be the discovery or the result of dialectic or argument.

[22]Whitehead, *Modes of Thought,* 48.

[23]Whitehead, *Adventures of Ideas,* 379.

pertaining to the actual operation of deity in human and natural existence.[24]

A similar tone is discernible in Whitehead's familiar statement that

> God is the ultimate limitation, and His existence is the ultimate irrationality. For no reasons can be given for just that limitation which is stands in His nature to impose. . . . The general principle of empiricism depends upon the doctrine that there is a principle of concretion which is not discoverable by abstract reasoning.[25]

Whitehead refers to God as "the ultimate irrationality" not because the principle of concretion is an affront to reason but because no functioning principle of limitation could have been predicted or inferred on the basis of previously articulated metaphysical principles. The divine functioning is not a matter of deduction but of observation. Accordingly one may conclude that "the Whitehead without God Debate," as well as other ways of questioning God's existence, will prove more fruitful when God-concepts are associated more closely with observable functions and less closely with inferential reasoning.

(3) A third rationalistic element of the Cobb-Sherburne debate which can be relinquished in a functional-empirical theology is *the conception that God is a serially ordered society of entities*, that is, a personally ordered being who endures through time. Cobb evinces little support for this thesis other than the consideration of coherence, and it is therefore not inappropriate to lay it aside when the primacy of coherence has already been abandoned, especially if there are other good reasons for doing so. Though Whitehead's God-concept allows us to think of God as functioning in several ways, I will propose below that the most observable of the functions of Whitehead's God is the function of providing initial aims or, in less technical language, the function of luring reality into originality and emergent wholeness. I will also argue that it is not necessary to think of God as a personal-temporal Being in order to envision God as fulfilling this function.

In the meantime it is relevant to note that within the Whitehead-without-God debate Cobb's assertion that God is a personally ordered society actually becomes an item of contention in its own right, for the idea of God as a living person connotes, if it does not actually avow, the existence of a distinct cotemporal Being

---

[24]Nancy Frankenberry, *Religion and Radical Empiricism* Albany: State University of New York Press, 1987) 25. See also p. 26, where Frankenberry associates a type of rationalism with "the way in which traditional theists typically proceed by first stating without question what a thing must be prior to inquiry, and then trying to demonstrate that God must conform to this prescription. One may wonder whether anything at all can be known on the basis of such a priori procedure. An empirical approach would insist, to the contrary, that knowledge should come as a consequence of inquiry, not be prescribing before inquiry begins what it must discover." This statement is relevant to my suggestions below.

[25]Whitehead, *Science and the Modern World,* 257.

whose particular ontological status is then such as to invite scrutiny and possible denial. It is remarkable that, as zealous as Sherburne is to "naturalize" Whitehead's metaphysics, he in no instance denies the *functions* of Whitehead's God. *What he in effect does deny is the need for an ontologically distinguishable divine Being to perform these functions.*

Surrendering the idea of God as a living person contributes substantively to the functional-empirical perspective now to be outlined.

A Functional-Empirical Overture to Process Theology

In our finer moments, when we are not preoccupied or self-absorbed, life spontaneously provokes within us a sense of esthetic appreciation and, indeed, of astonished marveling. From primordial cosmic blasts of light there have arisen not merely innumerable life forms but the arts and sciences, friendship and love and self-sacrifical behavior—not to mention the numberless lesser delights of daily existence. To be sure, life entails considerable pain and tragedy which are unwanted and, in many instances, unnecessary; and yet in the main the world is eminently suited for something much better than bare redundance or stark, physical survival.

Proponents of evolutionary, naturalistic worldviews speak of the source or sources of this "something much better" in various ways. Wieman writes of "creative interchange." Teilhard refers to "complexification." Potthoff develops the theme of "the dynamic reality making for wholeness" or "the character of reality in its wholeness." Whitehead says we must ask "whether nature does not contain within itself a tendency to be in tune, an Eros urging towards perfection."[26] The functioning realities which lie behind these concepts are so conspicuous in our experience and so apparent in their truth that it is not always easy to sympathize with the enthusiasm of much postmodern philosophy for topics such as fallibilism, anti-foundationalism, deconstruction and, in short, with what William Dean aptly and critically calls "methodologism."[27] On the other hand, in a more circumspect frame of mind we recognize that we are still struggling to remedy the defects of the Cartesian and Newtonian worldviews whose presumed realities we regarded until relatively recently as being, indeed, so conspicuous in our experience, and so apparent in their truth.

No details of epistemology can be presented here, but it is arguable that in a functionally oriented metaphysics (which identifies reality not with substances but with processes), problems related to perspective, verification, and imaginative construction are lessened or minimized. Most likely Kant presupposed not functions but some sort of substance when he spoke of the unknowable *Ding an sich*. The conviction that functions or behavior or "energy events" are more real than sub-

---

[26] *Adventures of Ideas,* 323. The phrase of Harvey Potthoff's is from *God and the Celebration of Life* (Chicago: Rand-McNally, 1969) 190ff.

[27] William Dean, *History Making History* (Albany: State University of New York Press, 1988) 22, and esp. chap. 6.

stances or neutral stuff or things-in-themselves meliorates the problems of construction and deconstruction. Admittedly, regardless of whether we believe we are observing substances on the one hand or activity on the other, our observations will still be *theory related* or even *theory dependent*—but, I would say, not *theory determined*. Beyond variations in perspective there are parameters which lead to significant agreement, especially when our metaphysical stance looks for reality not in internal constitutions but in outward activities, that is, in what William Henry Bernhardt called "checkable consequences." Whether we are speaking of electrons or fruit trees or athletic teams we find analysis a great deal easier if we forsake the search for some presumed internal essence and turn instead to observed structure and behavior.

Holding in abeyance the many questions prompted by this line of reasoning, my wish is simply to draw attention to the vindicable character of a functionalistic rendering of Whitehead's God concept. Whitehead's own vision is that the cosmos is filled with many things, and yet they are one in their potential for interrelation, causation, and organization. In this welter of togetherness we observe not a mere chaos, like neutral particles colliding haphazardly; we observe instead degrees of purpose and intelligence. We observe final causes interacting with efficient causes. We observe "civilization" and "the tendernesses of mere life itself" amidst the "clashing of senseless compulsion." In the groping, often forceful, and sometimes violent interaction of individuals with individuals and with environmental structures there persists evidence that wholeness and complexity are bolstered, that esthetic contrast and intensity of feeling are favored, and that errors are sometimes naturally and gracefully converted into occasions for growth. This higher influence is not such as to suggest an absolute heavenly goal but rather a variety of informed divine responses or 'lures.' These lures exemplify relevance for each occasion, but they do not, as a rule, crop up in such a way as to suggest an anthropomorphic deity who variously intervenes and withdraws or who exercises some kind of absolute sway.

In seeking to explain the evident interplay between efficient and final causes and the pattern and originality which are the apparent results of this interplay, Whitehead describes reality as constituted of discrete, atomic occasions which are internally made up of nontemporal phases. He develops an idea of God not for religious reasons but because, as unlikely as it may seem to Sherburne and others that there is any divine agency coordinating the ingression of lures or ideals for actualization, it is, upon reflection, *even more unlikely that the world as we experience it has come into being without any coordinated application of lures or ideals whatsoever*. I submit that *a functional-empirical process theology may more appropriately envision God not as a personal being who provides these lures or ideals but as the very provision itself of those lures and ideals*. In other words God is not a being (at this stage of the discussion, anyway), but a metaphysically general activity or a structure of concrescence.

As opposed to those who see so much of Plato in Whitehead, I believe that we should affirm as Whitehead's most important contribution to theology the point at which Whitehead says Plato "only achieves the feeblest of solutions," for

> Plato grounded these derivations from God upon his *will*, whereas metaphysics requires that the relationships of God and the World should lie beyond the accidents of will, and that they be founded upon the necessities of the nature of the God and the nature of the world. . . . The point is the recourse to a doctrine of mutual immanence.[28]

In agreement with Whitehead I suggest that process theology should consider God and the World as each being physically (not logically) necessary to the other, as if they were the two sides of the same coin.

In summary, I am proposing

(1) that we regard all of reality as populated not by beings but by functions,
(2) that we therefore identify God, also, not as a being but as a function, and
(3) that we recognize the agreement of both of these proposals with Whitehead's own philosophy.

Let us take Whitehead seriously when he says, "The process is itself the actuality, and requires no antecedent static cabinet"[29]—and let us apply this assertion equally to the world, and to God. Instead of identifying God as a distinguishable divine, personal Being whose existence may then be questioned, let us identify certain observable functions of evident metaphysical generality—that is, patterns or structures which appear pertinent to every occasion—so that only *after* identifying these functions do we investigate their religious availability and the appropriateness of their designation as "God."[30]

Using Whitehead's terms, we may say that God is not a living person but a function or a process which somehow takes place in the initial phase of every concrescence. *This in effect 'naturalizes' the situation, but without endorsing Sherburne's suggestion of atheism.*

As noted already, Sherburne and Cobb agree concerning the existence of *this function*. What sort of ontological unity might pertain to such a God is a much more complex matter. On one side of the issue it is, as John Cobb indicates (see above),

---

[28]*Adventures of Ideas,* 215-16.

[29]*Adventures of Ideas,* 356 (276 in Free Press edition). "The process is itself the actuality, and requires no antecedent static cabinet. Also the precesses of the past, in their perishing, are themselves energizing as the complex origin of each novel occasion. The past is the reality at the base of each new actuality. *The process* is its absorption into a new unity with ideas and with anticipation, *by the operation of the creative Eros*." (Emphasis added.)

[30]On this subject of the religious availability of Whitehead's God, see Charles S. Milligan, "Religious Values of Whitehead's God Concept," *The Iliff Review* 9/3 (Fall 1952): 117-28. Over the years I have found myself referring to this article repeatedly.

difficult to imagine that "all individual occasions order the whole realm of pure possibility identically," that is, that the world's order has resulted from the uncoordinated, particularized valuations of each entity. The unlikelihood of this scenario leads to the idea that there is indeed an interconnectedness or unity of coordination and gradation. But the other side of the matter is that any conclusions regarding the nature of God's ontological unity must depend upon inference and speculation, if not in fact upon some degree of arbitrary conjecture. Harvey Potthoff has written,

> To speak of wholes raises the question as to whether there is some final, all-inclusive whole with definable characteristics. The only answer at this time is: We do not know. . . . There are some persons who believe that back of all this there is a single power which originates and in some measure orders this scheme of things. The truth of such a belief can neither be verified nor falsified.[31]

Specifically concerning Whitehead's doctrine of God, Bernard Loomer states his impression that

> Whitehead's concept of the consequent nature of God can be established only by rationalistic methods. Hartshorne's ontological argument is an attempt to prove by rational means that Whitehead's concrete God necessarily exists, that the universe is one organic unity and that it necessarily exists. . . . But this option is not available to an empirical theology.[32]

Process theologians who are more rationalistically oriented will protest that a coherent explanation is needed to support my statement that there is a divine function or process which somehow takes place in the initial phase. They will also protest that Whitehead's ontological principle requires that all functions be attributed to one or more actual entities, and that adherence to this principle is surely one major reason why Whitehead departed from the "principle of concretion" of *SMW* in order to propound in *Process and Reality* the belief that God is an actual entity. My response is twofold: (1) that these protests lose a good deal of their force when we relinquish the primacy of coherence and the other elements of rationalism noted in Section II, above; and (2) that in any case the goal of this paper has not been to present a fully developed doctrine of God but to show how a functional-empirical stance within process theology transforms or even obviates the questioning of God's existence in the manner of the "Whitehead without God" debate. Supporting the idea of God's existence by equating the divine with observable functions frees the theologian to explore themes based on reason or speculation to the degree that this

---

[31]Harvey H. Potthoff, *God and the Celebration of Life,* 189-90.

[32]Bernhard M. Loomer, "Empirical Theology within Process Thought," *The Future of Empirical Theology,* 167-68.

is deemed feasible. I might add my own feeling that Whitehead's theory of God as the only nontemporal actual entity merits further analysis and development—and possibly on empirical grounds.

For functional-empirical theologies the issue is not so much whether God exists but which, if any, existing patterns or functions may appropriately be identified with the Divine. God is envisaged as a functioning reality, intrinsic to every natural process. A functional-empirical process theology thus alters controversies such as the Whitehead without God debate so as to offer significant avenues for rapprochement and perhaps even reconciliation.

Directions in Historicism: Language, Experience, and Pragmatic Adjudication

Sheila Greeve Davaney

In his recent book *History Making History*, William Dean contends that an outlook and set of assumptions are emerging within contemporary American thought which he labels an American historicism.[1] According to Dean, this historicist orientation characterizes a wide range of thinkers and intellectual perspectives, including philosophical neopragmatism, forms of literary criticism, neopragmatic philosophies of religion, postmodern and constructivist theology, radical empiricism, and historicized naturalism. While the thinkers who are forging these perspectives represent various disciplinary commitments and work out of disparate intellectual and political agendas, increasingly they share a set of presuppositions that suggest a common ground for conversation and debate, if not the basis for a readily agreed-upon and widely affirmed consensus. Among the fundamental premises these thinkers espouse, Dean states, are acceptance of "only historical references," the affirmation of "pragmatism, pluralism and the constructive power of the imagination," and "rejection of foundationalism, the transcendentalized subject and a correspondence-theory-of-truth realism." In sum, Dean argues, "they acknowledge that historical reality is created through interpretation of the historical subject—that it is history that makes history."[2]

It is my present task to focus on two representatives of this orientation who are working out its implications for the disciplines of philosophy of religion and theology. By examining the constructivist theology of Gordon Kaufman and the radical empiricism of William Dean, we may clarify what these positions hold in common and elucidate divergences, whether of emphases or more fundamental premises.

A central lament of Dean's book is that while he discerns a historicist orientation typifying much American thought today, it is characterized by an ironic amnesia, a forgetting of the very history that has provided, at least in part, the context for the renewed historicism of today. With this in mind, it is perhaps appropriate to begin this paper by historically locating the thinkers upon whom I will be focusing

---

[1]William Dean, *History Making History: The New Historicism in American Religious Thought* (Albany: SUNY Press, 1988) 12.

[2]Ibid.

my analyses, for they come to *this* conversation from other, different conversations and it is important to note these, if only briefly and in passing.

Gordon Kaufman and Constructivist Theology

Gordon Kaufman's constructivist view of theology has been forged in relation to a set of influences that include a Mennonite religious background, with its insistence that the quality of life is more important than claims to truth; an intellectual heritage shaped by Kant and Hegel and the Continental rendering of the modern project; the neo-orthodox visions of Barth and H. R. Niebuhr, with their emphases upon the problem of idolatry and the critical function of God-talk; and the American strand of theology and philosophy associated with James and Dewey and the Chicago School, with their naturalistic and sociohistorical orientation and their articulation of an American pragmatism. Moreover, certain contemporary insights and issues have also shaped Kaufman's theological agenda. In particular, recognition of religious pluralism, realization that we live under a self-imposed nuclear threat and the possibility of the annihilation of all life, and acknowledgment that not only is experience shaped by language and culture, but that such shaping has to do in the most profound way with power and its unequal distribution—all of these have given particular direction to Kaufman's thinking.

In conversation and critical struggle with these influences and issues, Kaufman has developed a view of theology as imaginative construction that stands in contrast to a number of other theological options on the current scene. In particular, this understanding of theology is in opposition to authoritarian models of theology (whether they discover some final truth in the past or in ahistorical reason, or in experience, or in revelation) *and* to more recent deconstructionist efforts that, while they historicize everything, appear to give up all interest in or hope of normative visions in terms of which persons might live fruitful and humane lives. In contrast, Kaufman has steadfastly argued for an interpretation of theology that is thoroughly historicist, in character, eschewing all claims to absoluteness or certitude but insisting upon the possibility, indeed the necessity, of normative visions in relation to which we might live our lives.

William Dean comes to this discussion from a different dialogical location than Kaufman, for Dean has developed his position in primary conversation with the line of American thought that stretches from James and Dewey to contemporary American pragmatists, though he rejects the repudiation of religion and the radical empiricism that has marked so much of neopragmatism today. On the other hand, he has attempted to engage more rationalist and speculative process thinkers in conversation concerning the repercussions of an empirical rendering of process thought, and to move away from the metaphysical and rationalistic emphases still prominent in much process thinking. By so doing, he hopes to bring process thought more fully into the current theological and philosophical debates upon whose fringes it has so long lingered. Finally, Dean has forthrightly sought to converse with other historicists, such as Kaufman, and deconstructionists such as Mark C. Taylor, to see what these positions might contribute to one another.

In light of the fact that both Kaufman and Dean eschew any spectator view of knowledge, it is perhaps important to note that I, no mere spectator, have been influenced by both these perspectives. I was a graduate student of Kaufman and John Cobb, and through the vagaries of history have found myself teaching at Iliff School of Theology, long a bastion of naturalism and radical empiricism, and presently have as my colleague in theology Del Brown, with whom conversations more often than not turn to the issues I will be exploring here. Hence, it has increasingly seemed appropriate that I look at these perspectives in light of one another, and to that task I now turn.

Gordon Kaufman has been arguing for years for a view of theology that he terms imaginative construction.[3] Such a constructivist approach is grounded in an interpretation of human life as emergent from and shaped within both a long natural process of biological evolution and a historically formed social and cultural matrix. Through these natural and historical processes, human consciousness, and with it distinctively human life, appeared and developed. From early on, human life was characterized not only by blind physiological adaptations to the natural environment but also by the development of culture and language. In this view, culture was not added to a finished animal but was integral to the evolution, survival, and development of the human form of life. Hence cultural resources have been both created by and creative of distinctively human life; indeed, without them, human life would not have been possible.

For Kaufman then, culture and language are ingredient in all human forms of being and modes of activity. The possible ways humans enact their humanity, the roles they can take, the forms of activities open to them, *and* their interaction with the natural world are all made possible through and are dependent upon the linguistic and symbolic visions that human communities create. This dependence upon culture and language is manifested on all levels of human life, but it finds fundamental expression in our need for overarching frameworks of interpretation by which reality is organized and the human place within the scheme of things is given definition. According to Kaufman, the absence of such a broad and inclusive vision of reality and of humanity's place within the cosmos would render human life impossible: "We cannot gain orientation in life and cannot act without some conception or vision of the context within which we are living and moving, and without some understanding of our own place and role within that context."[4] Moreover, these frames of orientation are not merely broad interpretive schemes without much defi-

---

[3]Gordon D. Kaufman, *An Essay on Theological Method* (Missoula MT: Scholars Press, 1975); *Theological Imagination: Constructing the Concept of God* (Philadelphia: Westminster, 1981); *Theology for a Nuclear Age* (Philadelphia: Westminster, 1985).

[4]Kaufman, *Theological Imagination*, 27.

nition, but are focused and given specification through central symbols that embody their fundamental convictions about reality and the values that are embedded in such convictions.

If Kaufman argues for an anthropological theory in which overarching schemes play a central role, he also insists that these interpretive grids within and through which humans gain orientation are not the result of a direct reading of the nature of reality, or of some direct access to the nature of things. They are, rather, imaginative pictures, built up through history and culture of what we take existence to be about and of our human place within the cosmic context. That is to say, these networks of meaning, these worldviews, are quite thoroughly cultural and social creations that are developed through historical processes. And the symbols that focus them are equally the product of human imaginative activity.[5]

Furthermore, such inclusive visions grow out of, reflect, and often reinforce the societal contexts in which they take shape, including the values and power arrangements of those contexts. Hence human visions of the nature and meaning of reality as a whole and of humanity's place within the cosmos are not disinterested accounts of a readily accessible and objectively knowable reality, but value- and interest-laden interpretations of life and its purposes.

Kaufman extends his theory of worldviews and their human constitution to what we have come to call religious understandings of reality and the symbols that center them. That is, the comprehensive frameworks we label religions and their symbols are also cultural artifacts. This is so no less for Christianity than for Buddhism, Islam, or Marxist humanism; no less for the theistic idea of God than for such symbols as emptiness, humanity, and nature. Such religious visions and symbols are also imaginative renderings, not names for directly or even indirectly experienced realities. They are human constructs, fabricated out of the bits and pieces of human life, embodying the basic convictions, values, and hopes of the traditions within which they emerged, and in turn shaping, undergirding, and giving direction to life within these historical strands.[6]

Out of such presuppositions Kaufman has fashioned an interpretation of theology as imaginative construction whose primary task is not the articulation of apodictic truth claims about reality or God but the "analysis, criticism and reconstruction" of comprehensive frameworks and, in particular, their symbols so that these might better serve their function of ordering and giving direction to human life.[7] Theology is thus, for Kaufman, carried out for the highly pragmatic purpose of providing orientation in life. Comprehensive interpretive systems and their symbols are human products, arising from the fundamental human need for order, meaning, and a sense of purpose for life. Hence our theological thinking is not an

---

[5]Ibid., 28.

[6]Ibid., 100-101.

[7]Kaufman, *Theology for a Nuclear Age*, 22.

end in itself, but seeks to contribute to the evaluation and restructuring of such systems so they may further enhance human life in the contemporary period. Therefore, in Kaufman's view, both theology, as a form of reflection, and the worldviews and symbols to which it attends are, in the final analysis, to be judged by the modes of human life they make possible. Kaufman focuses such pragmatic criteria by stating that the ultimate norm for theology and for worldviews and their symbols is humanization, or the creation of more humane forms of human existence.[8] In *The Theological Imagination*, Kaufman states his case bluntly when he says, "The central problem facing the present generation is the construction of a genuinely humane order—lest we destroy ourselves completely. If theological reflection is to be justified in this crisis, it must contribute to this work. A theology that makes an essential contribution to our humanization is the *only* sort we can afford today."[9]

If Kaufman has found himself opposing those who seek or think they have found certain truth, of whatever origin, he has also differentiated himself from those who would argue that recognition of our radical historicity leads ineluctably to a chaotic relativism or a nonoffensive but vapid tolerance in which no judgments, relative or absolute, can be proffered. Humanization, in Kaufman's view, gives us a norm for adjudication; it provides us the means by which critically to engage our past, and to evaluate our present visions of reality as well as those of others.[10] Such a norm is neither infallible nor absolute. Its content is utterly historical, forged in conversation with our history and our contemporaries, tested for validity in terms of the repercussions it generates, both for our sociocultural life and for our relation to the broader context of the natural world in which we live. The content of humaneness is certainly open to debate, but claiming it as the central theological norm allows us to acknowledge our responsibility for theological construction and to place our critical attention on the only issue that finally matters—what kind of lives are made possible by living our various interpretations of reality.

As I stated at the beginning, Gordon Kaufman has been proposing this view of theology for quite a while. But in his most recent book, *Theology for a Nuclear Age*, he presented it with greater urgency, for he suggests that we face an unprecedented crisis which demands, if we are to survive, much greater self-consciousness of our role in the construction of our interpretations of reality and a more critical analysis of the repercussions of living out of (in particular) our Western theistic heritage. According to Kaufman, we face the possibility, which no other generation of humanity has ever faced, of total annihilation—not partial destruction, but the complete and final end of life, and not only human reality but also the web of life within which humanity resides. In light of this situation, Kaufman asserts that the responsibility to reexamine our traditions in terms of their adequacy for today is

---

[8]Kaufman, *Theological Imagination*, 168, 199.

[9]Ibid., 168.

[10]Ibid., 168.

imperative if humanity is to survive, and if it survives, to create more humane and just forms of community. Thus Kaufman in this work undertakes the constructive theological project he argued for in his methodological discussions, and he does so, in part, through reexamination of the Christian symbol of God. This critical analysis elucidates Kaufman's theological program as well as indicates the direction of his current thought.

According to Kaufman, the symbol *God*, as it developed in Western theistic history, has been envisioned as the ultimate point of reference, the most central reality, in relation to which all life is to be lived and in terms of which the meaning of human life is to be understood. As such, Kaufman argues, this symbol has come to fulfill two central functions: relativizing all human life and effort, and grounding all forms of humaneness.[11]

As relativizer, the symbol God has functioned to remind humans of their finitude and that they are not ultimate, the center of all life and meaning. Again as relativizer, the idea of God has undercut the seemingly all-pervasive human tendency toward self-idolatry. As humanizer, the symbol God has embodied the conviction that humanity is of value, and that that from which human life originated and is sustained is supportive of human possibility and meaning.

Now while Kaufman contends that the symbol God has had these two functions (though not always in the same proportion) the images, metaphors, and concepts that embodied these functions have differed over the ages and in different historical communities. Yet Kaufman suggests that one strand has had, if not continual expression, a fairly consistent presence in Western theistic schemes, and that is the interpretation of God as omnipotent creator and controller of all reality. In concrete images, such omnipotent power has been embodied in the metaphors of God as Creator, Lord, King, Father, and the like.

A major contention of Kaufman's book is that, though he affirms the need for the symbol of God that continues to function as relativizer and humanizer, humans can no longer afford this understanding of God as omnipotent controller of reality. Such a view in a nuclear age is dangerous, for it contributes to the evasion of human responsibility for our situation. It leads humans to assume that either God will save us from such destruction or that the annihilation of life is part of the divine providential plan. In either case, such an idea engenders passivity and irresponsibility in the face of an enormous threat.[12]

In light of this, Kaufman suggests that we reconstruct the idea of God, forgoing the notion of omnipotence and the ancient images and metaphors that expressed this power. Instead, we should reconceive God as the symbol of those biological and historical forces that have brought forth life, both human and nonhuman, and have

---

[11]Kaufman, *Theology for a Nuclear Age*, 32-34.

[12]Ibid., 7-8.

been the foundations out of which consciousness and history have emerged. "God should today be conceived in terms of the complex of physical, biological and historico-cultural conditions which have made human existence possible, which continue to sustain it and which may draw it out to fuller humanity and humaneness."[13] As such, the symbol God would not be mistaken for the name of a personlike reality, but would be identified as that which "holds together in a unity that complex reality which grounds and sustains our human existence."[14]

In this reconstructed view, God would no longer be interpreted as the omnipotent controller of reality who could save us from our madness by divine fiat, but the symbol for those life-engendering aspects of reality that we, in this age unlike all others, can destroy. God, in this vision, is a source of ongoing support for life and humane possibilities, but can provide no guarantee that we will not put an end to not only present life but the prospect of all future life. Such a view, Kaufman thinks, is more adequate to our situation and more productive of creative and responsible action on our part.[15]

Before leaving the thought of Gordon Kaufman, I want to highlight several points that I think may focus the comparison with Dean's proposals. First, language is central to Kaufman's understanding of experience and reflection upon experience. Experience is a fairly specified term for him, indicating those dimensions of human existence that can be identified and delineated linguistically. This is not to say that we humans do not interact with our environments on nonlinguistic levels, nor that humans are not receptive of influences from those environments. It *is* to say that we can only know and attend to such interaction through linguistic means.

Second, theology is a complex and high-level form of reflection whose primary focus is on complex linguistic and conceptual constructions. Its attention is not to the "non-linguistic depths of experience," nor does it purport to refer to "reality" in any direct descriptive manner. Instead, theology entails linguistic constructions dealing with other linguistic and symbolic constructions.

Third, this view does not mean that theology has, so to speak, nothing to do with "reality"—an accusation often leveled at Kaufman. Our comprehensive frameworks and their symbols are built out of our local and episodic experience—all, of course, linguistically mediated—and our reflection on them should be carried out to enhance our experience—that is, to enable us to function better in the world. As such, these frameworks and their symbols "intend the real"; that is, they embody our most fundamental convictions about the nature of reality, and it is our at least implicit, if not uncritical, confidence in their adequacy that allows us to function more or less effectively.

---

[13]Ibid., 42.
[14]Ibid., 43.
[15]Ibid., 45.

Fourth, despite our intentions, we never are in a position to verify which of our worldviews and symbols refer most adequately to reality. Reality has, in a sense, the final word, in that if we utterly destroy ourselves, we can assume that the principle of falsification is at work. Short of that, however, we are confronted with multiple interpretive schemes and symbol systems, each offering illuminating and plausible pictures of reality and of human life and purposes. The only way to evaluate these internally and to adjudicate their competing claims is therefore by reference *not* to a self-attesting reality, but only to the pragmatic consequences of living in each.

This last point is important, for Kaufman's recent move to speak of God in naturalistic terms has been read by many, friends and critics alike, as a major shift toward more directly referential language in relation to God.[16] Depending on the perspective, Kaufman's conception of the God symbol in terms of biological and historico-social forces is interpreted either as inconsistency or the dawning of truth. Either reading is, I think, mistaken. Rather, I believe the idea of God articulated in *Theology for a Nuclear Age* and other recent writings is precisely the embodiment of Kaufman's constructivist project, not its repudiation. For this idea, no less than its theological and religious predecessors, is a symbolic construction built up through our imaginative activity, just as were earlier notions of God as transcendent and omnipotent creator. Hence the tests of its validity continue to be the insight and guidance it gives us, not suddenly its adequate correspondence to the "way things really are."

This interpretation of Kaufman is reinforced by his increasing use of the term *mystery*. In his 1972 book, *God the Problem*, Kaufman distinguished between the "available" and the "real" God, depicting the former as our humanly created notion of the ultimate point of reference and the latter as that limiting idea which undermines all our tendencies to think we have it right.[17] Kaufman has replaced the notion of a real God, with its unintended but powerful theistic prejudices, with the vaguer notion of mystery. This idea confesses, Kaufman says, to our "unknowing." It is "an acknowledgement . . . that we do not know how the images and metaphors in terms of which we conceive God apply; since they are always our own metaphors and images, infected by our limitations, interests, and biases."[18] Again, he states: "Today we are forced to take with greater seriousness the fact that we do not know, and we can see no way in which we will ever be able to plumb the true meaning

---

[16]See Ronald Cole-Turner, review of *Theology for a Nuclear Age* in *Cumberland Seminarian* 24/1 (1986): 31; and David Pailin, review of *Theology for a Nuclear Age* in *Perkins Journal* 39/3 (1986): 5-36.

[17]Gordon D. Kaufman, *God the Problem* (Cambridge: Harvard University Press, 1972) chap. 5.

[18]Gordon D. Kaufman, "'Evidentialism': A Theologian's Response," *Faith and Philosophy* 6/1 (1989): 43-44.

of human life—or whether there even is such a thing."[19] Thus the Kaufman of today is more of an agnostic than ever and just as committed to his constructivist project.[20]

With these thoughts in mind, we now turn to the proposals set forth by William Dean.

William Dean's Historicism, Radical Empiricism, and Pragmatism

I am considering the work of William Dean because I think that, of all the people working on the revival of radical empiricism, his sympathies and vision most closely approximate Gordon Kaufman's. In his two recent books, *American Religious Empiricism*, and *History Making History*, as well as in some current articles, Dean carries on a dialogue not only with his naturalist and radical empiricist forebears in the figures of James and Dewey and Meland and Loomer and the like, but also with more contemporary historicist thinkers such as Richard Rorty, Mark C. Taylor, and Gordon Kaufman. Out of his exploration of what some might term disparate positions, Dean has begun to fashion an intriguing (if not always clear) position that intertwines historicism, radical empiricism, and pragmatism. The combination of these three dimensions represents, according to Dean, a third way beyond the impasse of a foundationalism that seeks sure ground for our ideas and claims to truth outside the vagaries of the historical process and a subjectivism that forgoes all interest in broader appeals for justification, being content with seemingly arbitrary statements of preference. In developing his view, Dean does not claim to be offering a definitive metaphysics, cosmology, or epistemology. Instead, we offer something of an imaginative world-picture and a theory of experience that, from the outset, admits its tentativeness and speculative character while suggesting good reasons for proceeding in this manner.

The first leg, so to speak, of Dean's position is his historicism. For Dean, there is no reality that we can know, have experience of, or have access to or relationship with outside historical time and space, nor are there extrahistorical principles to which we might have recourse as the basis for our understandings of reality. There are instead only the contingent realities of history and our time- and place-conditioned understandings of them. Stated even more strongly, the history we have is composed not of facts or things or events that we can know with some kind of pure objectivity, but rather is an endless chain of interpretation whereby the past is appropriated in ever-changing and new ways.[21] Hence Dean's historicism sets itself in opposition to foundationalist approaches that seek certainty in extrahistorical sources, realisms that assume the capacity for unbiased and objective access to reality, and to views of the human subject that, in their emphasis on universal common

[19]Ibid., 44.

[20]Ibid., 44.

[21]William Dean, "Naturalism and Methodologism," *American Journal of Theology & Philosophy* 10/2 (1989): 108.

characteristics, dislocate individuals from their concrete, particular locations in history.

On these points, Dean is in clear agreement with many forms of historicist thinking that are so prevalent today. However, he is convinced that the historicism of many of these thinkers does not go far enough, in that it confines itself to human social and cultural history. The natural sphere is either completely ignored or rendered in nonhistorical categories. The "new historicists," as he labels them, "limit history to language and culture, thus omitting natural events." Contrary to this humanistic historicism, Dean proposes a historicized naturalism in which nature too is seen as a process of interpretation upon interpretation whereby the natural world constitutes itself. This move permits Dean to overcome the bifurcation of human cultural history and the processes of nature; although language deeply shapes the interpretive process within human history and makes it distinct from the natural sphere, nonetheless, Dean contends, there is a parallel interpretive process by which nature constitutes itself—a kind of nonlinguistic hermeneutics, if you will. Moreover, this historicized view of nature is important not only because it rejects the dualistic opposition of nature and history, but because it will be seen to complement Dean's radical empiricism (which includes a theory of how such natural events can be ingredient in human experience) and his pragmatism (which argues that we must test our ideas and beliefs, not only in terms of human culture and history but also in terms of the sphere of nature).

The second "leg" of Dean's position is radical empiricism. If Dean's historicized naturalism sets him apart from most of the other historicists today, his theory of experience, centered on the claims of radical empiricism, represents an even greater departure from these thinkers and constitutes his most distinctive contribution to these conversations. Dean insists that the linking of historicism, radical empiricism, and pragmatism has a long history in the thought of James and Dewey and the Chicago School. This history, Dean suggests, has been unfortunately forgotten not only because amnesia distorts these persons' positions but because the severing of historicism, radical empiricism and pragmatism weakens the viability of these approaches (today in particular) by moving historicism and pragmatism toward a form of subjectivism.

Many recent-day historicists and pragmatists, including Gordon Kaufman, have focused upon the linguistic character of human experience and have claimed that there is no such thing as unmediated, nonlinguistically structured experience and that the only world we have, so to speak, is constituted through the power of language. As Kaufman stated in his paper for this [1990] conference, "there is no such thing as 'raw experience'; experience completely free of all symbolic and linguistic coloring and interpretation and, thus, the real focus of 'realities' to which our words and symbols can only lamely and abstractly "'point'."[22]

---

[22]Gordon D. Kaufman, "Empirical Realism in Theology: An Examination of Some

For Dean, the insights into the role of language and culture articulated by these thinkers are an all important part of a theory of experience. They are, however, partial, leaving out much and truncating the explanatory power of their interpretations of human experience. In particular, they leave out of their accounts all nonlinguistic forms of human awareness and nonlinguistic elements in human knowledge; they remain essentially dualistic, shutting the body off from the human imaginative spirit, the human off from the natural world. Again, for Dean, radical empiricism can give a fuller account of these dimensions of human experience, while not denying that in many (though not all) ways, language plays a constitutive role in the determination of experience.

In the radical empiricist version of experience, linguistically shaped and interpreted experience is not the only way human beings relate to our world. Instead, in this view, we are also aware of and connected to our world in a largely pre- or nonlinguistic and mostly unconscious manner. Human beings not only perceive their world through the five senses, and conceptualize and shape such perception linguistically, but have another, fundamental mode of relationship with their environment, both social and natural, by which we literally feel the world, physically and causally, impinging upon us.

There are a number of elements in this claim that experience has to do with more than that which can be identified and expressed linguistically. First, what is experienced in this mode are not only things, separate facts, but primarily relations that are felt as *given* in experience. Second, experience in this mode of primal feeling is valuational. On one hand, the experience itself is not neutral but is laden with value and significance; on the other hand, that which is experienced is also encountered as valuable and quality filled. Value is thus not something that is only imposed upon the world, but is ingredient in the world as well. Third, this way of being aware of and connected to the world is often not separable from our linguistically defined knowledge and experience, but a dimension of them, and hence clear-cut distinctions between these modes are difficult. Moreover, even those moments of experience that are not primarily constituted by language are nonetheless always particular, concrete, and local.[23] That is, experience is always from a particular perspective and that perspective shapes it, albeit not always linguistically. Hence it is always contingent and relative to its context; that is, in Dean's terms, it is always historical. And fourth, experience in this mode of feeling is always, in Dean's words, "dim, confusing, vague, unknowable, unabstracted, inchoate, at the margins, akin to the edges of sleep," and therefore not readily available for conscious consideration. Thus whatever we may say about it will not only be tentative and lack certitude but will also involve speculation and imaginative reconstruction.

Themes in Meland and Loomers," in this volume, below.

[23]William Dean, "Empirical Theology: A Revisable Tradition," in *Process Studies* 19/2 (Summer 1990): 87.

When Dean speaks of religious sensibilities and God, it is to this dim, vaguely perceived sense of value and direction that he refers. For he argues: What appreciative awareness senses, albeit unclearly, is the movement toward greater historical value understood as aesthetic complexification or the increase of diversity within unity. Such a "tropism toward complexity" is, as we have seen, always experienced locally and in a transitory fashion, but when such local experience of value is extended by a kind of leap of faith, to assume a general movement in history, then, Dean suggests, we can speak of religious sensibilities. Dean states, therefore, that "the religious person would be distinguished from the non-religious person by his or her faith "that the tropism toward greater historical value is real and that it can be sustained through greater reinterpretation."[24] Moreover, it is this movement toward greater complexity and, hence, increased aesthetic value that, according to Dean, "provides much of that vitality that makes life, including human life, possible and valuable."[25] As such, it elicits wonder, mystery, and commitment and suggests an understanding of morality as loyalty to this directionality and pursuit of its increase through moral action.[26] For these reasons, Dean asserts it is legitimate to refer to this tropism toward increased value as "God."[27]

Thus Dean can be seen to contend that there is a world, as he states it, "beyond the linguistically-posited world," that is apprehended through feeling, through a kind of affectional sensibility. The world, so encountered, is heavy with significance and direction, but we are only aware of it from our particular locations in history, and we only sense it in a nebulous fashion. This version of radical empiricism keeps faith with Dean's historicism for it asserts unequivocally that nothing that is experienced in this manner is outside history and that this mode of awareness represents, on a nonlinguistic level, a form of interpretive process that is replicated on conscious and linguistically shaped levels of experience. Also for Dean, it represents a way of enriching historicism, by first insisting that the historical world is not only given value through our linguistic construals of it, but that it is already rich in value to be appropriated. Moreover, Dean's radical empiricism is suggestive of ways we not only exist within human history, creating meaning and receiving value from our social worlds, but also how we live in interaction with the natural world and how we are aware, albeit dimly, of values that inhere there. Finally, Dean's radical empiricism delineates a naturalist and historicist interpretation of religious experience and God that does not appeal to any kind of immediate or pure experience, that rejects any extrahistorical referent for the divine, and that takes seriously the constructive character of our idea of God—for the *general* movement

---

[24]William Dean, *American Religious Empiricism* (Albany: SUNY Press, 1986) 60.

[25]Ibid., 62.

[26]Dean, "Naturalism and Methodologism," 108.

[27]Dean, *American Religious Empiricism*, 62.

toward complexification is, for Dean, never experienced, but, through the imaginative extension of more local experience of value, comes to be affirmed.

If Dean argues that a fuller account of experience must include felt values and relations, it is also clear that, for him, this form of awareness does not yield clear or certain norms and criteria against which we can easily test our linguistic construals of reality and of humanity's place in the cosmos. Dean contends, therefore, that the norms for evaluating the viability of our ideas and beliefs must finally be pragmatic ones; that is, we must test our visions of reality against the effects and consequences they engender within history. But just as Dean develops his broader view of historicism, he offers a distinctive version of pragmatism that sets him off from other pragmatists on the scene today.

First, Dean concurs with many pragmatists that we assess our ideas and conceptual systems, including our religious and theological notions, in the arena of human culture and history through conversation in historical contexts and with historical traditions. Thus he can assert, with other pragmatists, that "history is both gatekeeper and judge, both stages of new variations and slaughterhouse of old ones."[28] But, in a manner parallel to his analysis of historicism, he contends that this stage is too small, it is too confined to human history. Against this narrowing of consequences, Dean argues that we must also test our linguistic interpretations in terms of nature and natural events. Although we certainly construct our ideas of nature, nature exists, for Dean, in real independence from how we may conceive of it and, hence, as that against which we can, at least broadly speaking, check our versions of it. This does not reintroduce a new foundationalism or correspondence theory of truth, for Dean contends such tests are never exact, nor do they issue forth in any final confidence that our ideas have reality exactly right. Such tests do, however, indicate to us the limits of our ideas in a broader realm than the solely human ones of history and culture.

Dean's pragmatism can therefore be seen to embrace both human history and the natural sphere as arenas of consequence within which to evaluate our human conceptual efforts, as well as the various modes of human activity in the world. But the distinctiveness of Dean's version of pragmatism does not stop with this inclusion of nature, for he is not only interested in the fact that finally we test our ideas and constructions pragmatically, he is also concerned with how we decide what counts as an acceptable or satisfactory consequence. "On what grounds," Dean asks, "is something declared valuable or not?"[29] Many pragmatists would simply answer that such decisions are made historically through the contingent conversation of historical persons, and that there are no grounds or sources beyond such human deliberations. Dean sees in such an answer the dangers of subjectivism, of mere preference. While he agrees that what counts as valuable is indeed delineated in historical con-

---

[28]Dean, *History Making History*, 105.

[29]Ibid., 82.

texts, he again proposes that this is not a full enough account of how our conceptions of value arise. Instead, he turns to his radical empiricism and suggests that history, both human and natural, is the bearer of both conscious and unconscious value. While we are, at best, only dimly and occasionally aware of this value, attention to this deeper context of value provides a fuller way to understand how history yields criteria, and perhaps a way to develop, or at least argue for, notions of what is satisfactory and valuable in a less arbitrary manner. That is to say, we know not only our own local interests, but also, though vaguely, we are aware of the interests of broader segments of the world in which we exist.

This claim links Dean's pragmatism with his radical empiricism and may be the most interesting part of his whole project, yet it is also the most problematic. For on one hand, Dean has acknowledged so thoroughly the constructive human role in the creation of norms; on the other, he has testified to the utter vagueness of our awareness of nonlinguistically transmitted value, that it is difficult to see how appeal to this level of experience yields anything very concrete or how, in fact, it substantially avoids the subjectivism that he finds so dangerous elsewhere. Dean himself acknowledges this when, in *History Making History*, he proposes that what is needed in a historicist epistemology that would clarify how "history yields criteria" and how the dim, vaguely felt values referred to by radical empiricists become ingredient in our conscious forms of knowledge.[30] Until such an epistemology is more fully developed, the linking of radical empiricism and pragmatism will be an interesting but tension-filled proposal whose pragmatic repercussions are not all that clear.

In sum, William Dean is in the midst of developing a distinctive proposal that couples his versions of historicism, radical empiricism, and pragmatism and that purports to give a more adequate account of human experience in the context of nature and history and of the generation of the values in relation to which we assess our ideas of and actions within this world. I believe Dean's proposals share a good deal in common with Gordon Kaufman's, though their positions contrast with one another as well. It is to these similarities and to their critical differences that I want to turn in closing.

Conclusion

A number of similarities and shared assumptions characterize the positions of Kaufman and Dean. First, they both work in a historicist perspective that affirms that humans exist within an interdependent social and natural context that is dynamic and processive and is literally constituted by the chain of human and nonhuman appropriations of the past, which they call history. For both, moreover, there is no reality outside of this contingent human and natural web of existence to

---

[30]Ibid., 83.

which we have access, and there is nothing within this historical matrix that will provide us absolute or unchanging foundations. Second, both men promote pragmatic norms for assessing the validity of our claims, and each includes the natural sphere as somehow a part of the conversation that will determine what is beneficial for humanity. Third, Kaufman and Dean are developing substantive ideas of God, along naturalistic lines, and these ideas have at least a family resemblance. Increasingly, Dean seems to be distinguishing his position from some fellow radical empiricists by emphasizing the speculative and constructive character of our idea of God, and distancing himself from any claim that we *experience* the whole of reality or even a *general* direction within history. Thus Kaufman and Dean seem to be converging on a more constructivist position vis-à-vis God. Fourth, because of their shared historicism and Dean's understanding of experience, these two thinkers eschew any idea that their formulations represent any claims to final or absolute truth. They are positing, instead, explanatory models that each thinks offers an account of human experience that is illuminating and points in a viable direction for the development of a normative vision of the human.

Although these similarities represent a "genuine convergence of interest," differences remain between these two positions, and highlighting several of them may help us to avoid too hasty an assumption of agreement while indicating problem areas in each position. One way to focus this final part of this exploration is to return to the beginning, to the conversations from which Dean and Kaufman come. In the end, the position of each is deeply influenced by strands of thought that, though they show certain convergences, take quite distinct directions.

First, Kaufman's proposal is deeply indebted to his Kantian and Hegelian roots, and especially to Kantian assumptions concerning the constructivist and agential character of all human knowing. Although Kaufman has wanted to continue to affirm these Kantian epistemological insights, he has increasingly repudiated the dualistic ontology that historically accompanied them. Thus, with greater purposiveness, he has turned to nature and the body and to the question of their impact on human linguistic construction. Yet, despite this turn, Kaufman's central (indeed, almost exclusive) focus has remained upon conscious and linguistically structured experience and upon the productive power of the imagination. While he acknowledges reality external to the human self and nonlinguistically determined elements of human existence, he nonetheless continues to insist that, ultimately, the nature of such modes of reality remains a mystery whose depths we will never be able to fathom and whose influence upon us we may assume but cannot clearly discern. Thus, even within his system, where both self and world are constructs of the imagination, he develops a picture of the relationship between the two that is unidirectional, in which the constructive agency is almost exclusively on the part of the human knower. And though Kaufman grants that if our imaginative construals of the world are to function, they cannot contradict reality, his proposal does not give an account of how such reality shapes, contributes to, constrains, or impacts our linguistic versions of it. This is especially the case in relation to what the radical empiricists have called the affectional mode of feeling by which we interact with our environment. Thus while Kaufman concedes this level of experience and acknowledges that we receive physical input from our world, his position continues to have difficulty explaining how such input influences our eventual linguistic constructions or, in the end, judges them. Hence Kaufman's human self, while located in a biosocial world, often appears oddly disembodied, the possessor of a productive imagination whereby it creates a world but not clearly a co-participant with a world, which has agency of its own, in the reciprocal creation of the natural and historical process. This lingering dualism stands in tension with and undermines much of the direction of Kaufman's current thought, and how it is resolved will determine how consistently and persuasively he can develop his present line of argument.

On the surface, William Dean does not have the same problems. His position is not grounded in such dualist assumptions, but in a vision that presupposes the mutual interaction and reciprocal influence of the human self and the human and nonhuman world it inhabits. Dean's analysis of affectional sensibility is precisely an attempt to show how such interaction takes place on the nonlinguistic, preconscious level of feeling. Thus Dean proposes a theory of human experience that does not leave the human self-enclosed in lonely agential isolation, but in real, mutual, and codetermining relation with the world. On the level of an explanatory theory, this proposal seems to avoid the problems of Kaufman's lingering dualism, for it overcomes (at least theoretically) the bifurcation of self and body and humanity and the rest of the world. Yet it runs into similar problems, as Kaufman's proposal does, for Dean has yet to tell us how, in fact, such primal and fundamental levels of experience shape, if at all, our linguistic constructions. Although Dean has acknowledged the need for a historicist epistemology that can provide the link, so to speak, between the nonlinguistic and linguistic levels of human experience, without such a theory, Dean finally leaves us in much the same position as Kaufman, acknowledging that on a conscious level, experience and knowledge are primarily shaped by language; and while asserting other levels of experience, he has no clear way to speak of their creative role in our linguistic constructions.

Another issue in terms of which intellectual roots point to current differences is the idea of God. On one level, Dean and Kaufman appear to be headed in a similar direction. Each has rejected supernaturalistic renderings of God, and substantively each has utilized naturalistic metaphors that forgo notions of omnipotence. On a more subtle level, however, I think Kaufman's God remains the moral God of his Kantian intellectual heritage and Mennonite religious background, and Dean's deity bears all the marks of the process aesthetic God. For Kaufman, God is a construct whose purpose is to provide orientation in life and to guide human beings in the creation of a *humane* order—that is, the primary function of the idea of God is a *moral* one. Hence Kaufman, though using naturalistic metaphors, does so because he believes they are more able to nurture a just, equitable, and sustainable human way of life today. Dean's process God is rather the symbol for the movement toward increased aesthetic value in reality. Commitment to this movement, as I noted above, involves a form of morality that is understood as loyalty to and service in the increase of beauty, and hence is not irrelevant to practical and moral concerns. However, when this idea of God is developed along the lines of Bernard Loomer's notion of a concrete God embracing good and evil, it becomes less clear whether the aesthetic idea of God developed by Dean can be allied with the moral aims so central to Kaufman's position. The pursuit of goodness—interpreted here as humaneness—and the quest for aesthetic value may not be totally divorced, but neither can they be reduced to one another, and their relation to each other in these two proposals merits further clarification.

In closing, I want to point to one further issue among the many that might be raised. Both William Dean and Gordon Kaufman have done admirable jobs in focusing our attention on the fact that humans exist not only in human culture and history but also within the web of natural events, and they have rightly pointed out that our conceptions of human life and the symbols that focus it must be framed, if they are to be adequate for today, in biosocial terms and images. However, it must be remembered that the webs of reality within which we exist are, especially on the social level, networks of power and that our construals of both human life and the natural sphere are not benign or innocent but are expressions of fundamental relations of power. As such, the processes by which we name these interconnected matrices, human and natural alike, are profoundly conflictual and bear enormous political and social repercussions. And while both Dean and Kaufman occasionally acknowledge this, their analyses rarely focus upon this dimension, and until they do, Kaufman's appeal to the "humane" and Dean's articulation of the empirical will fail to develop a fundamental insight of contemporary historicist consciousness, that is, the nature of power and its conscious and unconscious transmission in our world.[31]

---

[31]This paper was published in *Zygon: Journal of Religion and Science* 26/2 (June 1991): 201-20.

The Persistence of Experience: A Commentary on Gordon Kaufman's Theology

William Dean

Gordon Kaufman works very promisingly and almost alone at the juncture of postmodern religious constructivism and American religious naturalism. His writings after 1974 will constitute one day, if they do not constitute already, a major option in American theology.

However, even after reading Kaufman's powerful argument that experience is not a theological resource, I am unconvinced. Rather, experience is persistingly important as a theological resource.

Kaufman refuses to trace theological ideas to empirical sources or to ask how religious experiences might provide at least weak indicators to guide the formation of theological ideas. For Kaufman theological ideas are cobbled without experience in the workshop of the imagination as it communicates only with a tradition that itself was cobbled in the workshop of the imagination. The effect is to make the imaginative construction itself a surd, and its truth a matter of chance.

Paradoxically, Kaufman's ostensible elevation of imagination diminishes rather than exaggerates its importance. When the imagination itself is treated as an unexaminable *terminous a quo*, emphasis is taken away from its creativity (how it moves beyond the ground level of experience) and turns to imagination's function (how it affects the future). While this pragmatism is valuable, taken alone it neglects the extent to which the religious imagination creates out of experience not only the concept but the reality of God.

Both concerns—that of making imaginative construction a matter of chance and that of underrating its creativity—can be resolved through a greater, but different, emphasis on experience.

I. Kaufman's Unique Position in Recent American Theology

Among current American theological options Kaufman's is distinctive. That distinctiveness can be approached through examining the gap separating his 1960 *Relativism, Knowledge, and Faith* and his 1985 *Theology for a Nuclear Age*. Kaufman very believably acknowledges that the 1960 book was guided "to a far greater extent than footnotes suggest"[1] by Wilhelm Dilthey, R. G. Collingwood, and Paul Tillich—two neoKantians and a Schellingian. His 1985 book was closer to the classical American tradition represented by John Dewey and Henry Nelson Wieman than to Kant and Schelling. And yet, Kaufman not only retains elements from the earlier tradition but integrates implications from each tradition into a new theological whole that is not only unique but singularly effective in the current American historical situation.

As Kaufman has acknowledged,[2] the amalgam has required shifts from divine revelation to human imagination, from God's transcendence to God's immanence, from a neoorthodox historicism to a version of postmodern historicism. And in these moves Kaufman has influenced a remarkable crop of students—George Rupp, Mark C. Taylor, Wayne Proudfoot, Karl Raschke, and Sheila Davaney, to name a few.

Finally, in ways first really evident in his *Essay on Theological Method* (1979), Kaufman has laid out a distinct alternative both to what would come to be postmodern theologies and philosophies of religion and to American empirical and process theologies. First, Kaufman shares much with postmodern deconstructive, neopragmatic, and narrativist theologies. He locates theology in one among a plurality of histories rather than in a transcendental ego, in an ontological foundation, or in a core religious experience; he tests theology pragmatically rather than epistemologically (or, by reference to how it came to be). But while postmodernists tend to limit history to the personal and communal, Kaufman conceives of history as political and natural as well as personal and communal. While, for example, Mark C. Taylor will see theological expression as a form of playful erring and George Lindbeck will see theological expression as a from of linguistic expression specific to a community of faith, Kaufman urges a historicism attentive also to nature[3] and to politics,[4] particularly to issues of ecology and nuclear war.

Second, Kaufman's new emphasis on naturalistic and political issues allies him with the American pragmatic philosophy and with the "Chicago School," the empirical, and the process theologies that grew out of that philosophy. Kaufman's

---

[1]Gordon D. Kaufman, *Relativism, Knowledge, and Faith* (Chicago: University of Chicago Press, 1960) xii.

[2]Gordon D. Kaufman, *God the Problem* (Cambridge MA: Harvard University Press, 1972) xii; "Apologia pro Vita Sua," in *Why I am a Mennonite*, ed. by Harry Loewen (Scottdale PA: Herald Press, 1988) esp. 134-35.

[3]However, see Carol P. Christ's complaint that Kaufman still has an anthropocentric world in "Rethinking Theology and Nature," in *Weaving the Visions: New Patterns in Feminist Spirituality*, ed. Judith Plaskow and Carol P. Christ (San Francisco: Harper & Row, 1989) 314-25.

[4]However, see Sheila Davaney's complaint that Kaufman is inattentive to "the political analysis" of his position, particularly to how "the fusion of power and knowledge" contributes to theology, in "Options in Post-Modern Theology," *Dialog* 26 (1987): 200.

1985 *Theology for a Nuclear Age* emphasizes evolutionary biology, the environmental and political consequences of theories, and the social construction of truth.[5] But, unlike those classically American theologies, Kaufman's work retains from the Continental tradition an appreciation of the imaginative or speculative base of all knowledge. Ironically, this has made his pragmatism, pluralism, and historicism more crucial than they were for the American theologians who first advanced them.[6] While many of the Chicago, empirical, or process theologians foster hopes for a rationalistic grasp of deep structures or an empirical induction from the facts of nature or history, Kaufman, working without these safety nets, must rely almost entirely on a combination of a situational imagination and historical pragmatics. Consequently, in many respects Kaufman can better answer the current sociologists of knowledge, philosophers of science, deconstructivists, and neopragmatists who refuse to use "how we know" as a test for the truth of what we know.

Kaufman's emerging theological position is significant, then, as a corrective and a positive alternative not only to the postmodernists but also to the classical American theologians. It is this that makes Kaufman's notion of God so crucial today.

II. From Epistemology to Imaginative Construction: The Overt change

As early as his 1960 *Relativism, Knowledge, and Faith*, Kaufman cites Kant and Hume[7] and argues that all we know is based on our own forms of knowing, so that what we know of the external world is, in fact, a kind of "imaginative construction." In the 1968 *Systematic Theology* Kaufman treats experiential epistemologies as insufficient and rejects natural theology.[8] Nevertheless, of overriding importance in his earlier work was Kaufman's claim that revelation, unlike other knowledge, includes an element beyond imaginative construction; for revelation is the process whereby the self receives a positive self-disclosure from a personal God who is beyond human history.[9]

---

[5]Kaufman argues, "The theological imagination devotes itself to the continuing critical reconstruction of the symbol 'God,' so that it can with greater effectiveness orient contemporary and future human life" (*The Theological Imagination: Constructing the Concept of God* [Philadelphia: Westminster Press, 1981] 12). Compare this to John Dewey's "faith in the continuing disclosing of truth through direct cooperative human endeavor" (*A Common Faith* [New Haven: Yale University Press, 1952] 26).

[6]From the list of these theologians I would exclude George Burman Foster, who took pragmatism and pluralism seriously in *The Finality of the Christian Religion* (Chicago: University of Chicago Press, 1909; orig. 1906) and *The Function of Religion in Man's Struggle for Existence* (Chicago: University of Chicago Press, 1909).

[7]Kaufman, *Relativism*, 35.

[8]Gordon D. Kaufman, *Systematic Theology: A Historicist Perspective* (New York: Scribner's, 1968) esp. 109-12.

[9]Ibid., chaps. 2, 3, and 7.

Kaufman first broke the grip of this neoorthodox revelational epistemology, I believe, in the transitional essay "God as Symbol" in his 1972 *God the Problem.*[10] In that essay the notion of positive revelation is missing and Kaufman unhesitatingly claims that the concept of God is itself an imaginative construct. Nevertheless, in this book as a whole Kaufman has taken what he calls then and later a "tentative" stance.[11] This book and his *Essay on Theological Method* are earmarked with the ambivalence typical of a writer in transition. On one hand *An Essay on Theological Method* begins with the claim that religious knowledge is socially based in language, so that the only God we can know "is the God that we, with the help of a long tradition developing before us, construct in our imagination as the ultimate point of reference for all life and thought and reality."[12] Kaufman argues with increasing seriousness that in the order of knowing the concept of God arises from imaginative construction. But at the same time he insists that this does not deny that in the order of being God may be present in both revelation and in experience. On one hand Kaufman acknowledges that notions of revelation beg all the important epistemological questions and he maintains that the experience of God is never direct—that, in fact, religious experience always already has been interpreted by culture. On the other hand he allows that theological construction may be based, in fact, on divine self-disclosure; and the epistemological effort to validate a truth by tracing it to its source still has status in *God the Problem* and in *An Essay on Theological Method.*

By the 1980s Kaufman's apparently Kantian reluctance to claim to know the objective world had grown, for by then he contends that neither revelation nor experience can be trusted to translate the objective world itself into theological truths. Kaufman abandoned what Kant had seen as the pretense that experience can be founded on noumena, or things-in-themselves; and with this he abandoned language of divine self-disclosure (and, accordingly, of God as a person who discloses). Kaufman appears to accept the kind of admonition Kant offers when he says "we must not seek universal laws of nature in nature by means of experience, but conversely must seek nature, as to its universal conformity to law, in the conditions of the possibility of experience which lie in our sensibility and in our understanding."[13] Accordingly, for Kaufman theological knowledge now is based entirely on imagination and tests of imagined images. Theological knowledge is a function of the pres-

---

[10]See Kaufman's comment on this essay in "Apologia pro Vita Sua," 134, and in *Theological Imagination*, 12.

[11]Kaufman, *God the Problem*, xi; *Theological Imagination*, 11.

[12]Gordon D. Kaufman, *An Essay on Theological Method* (Missoula MT: Scholar's Press, 1975, 1979) 27.

[13]Immanuel Kant, *Prolegomena to any Future Metaphysics*, ed. Lewis White Beck (New York: Liberal Arts Press, 1950) 66.

ent imaginative construction in interaction with the heritage of imaginative constructions and pragmatic tests of those constructions.

If epistemology is the effort to make sense of appearance already within one's mind, then Kaufman is very much still an epistemologist. At the very least, he remains an epistemologist in what Jeffrey Stout calls the "innocuous sense," as "reflection of any sort about knowledge."[14] Kaufman remains an epistemologist in the sense that he will both propose those general notions of imaginative construction that can organize perceptions and he will test those notions by a kind of Kantian pragmatics, examining what Kant called "the use of representations in the understanding, and not their origin."[15]

Nevertheless, Kaufman has made a significant epistemological move. He has abandoned what I will call "strong epistemology," or "epistemology" as the neopragmatists invidiously use the term. He has abandoned the epistemological claim that how we came to know (from what source) says something about the truth of what we know.

Accordingly, in the 1981 *The Theological Imagination* Kaufman describes theology as "essentially a constructive work of the human imagination"; in fact, Kaufman says, "our awareness and understanding here [with regard to the reality of God] is gained entirely in and through the images and concepts themselves, constructed into and focused by the mind into a center for the self's devotion and service."[16] And in *Theology for a Nuclear Age* it is possible to talk simply of "Christian theology as imaginative construction."[17] Here revelation not only begs the question, but illicitly imposes the conclusions of an earlier age on a later age (much as John Dewey thought "religion"—as opposed to the "religious"—was the imposition of an earlier people's adjustment to its environment on a later people's task of adjustment). Experiential resources for a concept of God now hardly warrant comment.

Nevertheless, this development is surprising. Just as Kaufman introduced this strong notion of theological construction, he made a counterbalancing move. As early as "God as Symbol" Kaufman said that the God in imaginative construction is only an "available referent" and not the "real referent"—as though there were a "real" referent. Just as he began to move away from neoorthodoxy's interpersonal realism and began propounding an almost-Feuerbachian subjectivism, he introduced a new realism into his talk. Attempting to allay the suspicion that God was "merely imaginary," Kaufman insists that God is "himself 'objective' and 'real.' "[18] Kaufman moved from a revelational window to the Transcendent into a sociology of

---

[14]Jeffrey Stout, *Ethics after Babel: The Language of Morals and their Discontents* (Boston: Beacon Press, 1988) 295.

[15]Kant, *Prolegomena*, 39.

[16]Kaufman, *Theological Imagination*, 11, 21.

[17]Kaufman, *Theology for a Nuclear Age*, (Philadelphia: Westminster Press, 1985) 22.

[18]See *God the Problem*, 88, 92, 114.

knowledge, only to counterbalance that move to the left with a countervailing move—the claim that God is literally a reality in cultural and physical history. This deliberate tension prevails in Kaufman's discussion of God in his two books of the 1980s. At the same time that he treats God as a construct of the imagination, he claims that God lives outside the imagination in nature and history or not at all. In *The Theological Imagination* God really is a "a cosmic movement";[19] in *Theology for a Nuclear Age* God really is a "hidden creativity."[20]

III. From Epistemology to Chance: The Covert change

The foregoing account appears to leave open a question: If revelational and experiential ways of knowing the God external to the self are dead, how can imaginative constructions within the self ever reach a God beyond the self? Once the theological imagination is asserted so strongly, why is not a theological realism simply dead?

Let me elaborate. The marriage of imaginative construction and historical realism gives a notion of God that is both strong and accident prone. Making God a reality in nonhuman nature as well as public history not only moves Kaufman beyond postmodern subjectivism but connects Kaufman with American classical theologians. Making God an imaginative construct not only carries Kaufman beyond the classical American theologians but puts Kaufman in touch with the postmodernists. Further, Kaufman's new theological naturalism enables him to address problems of nuclear war, environmental destruction, and the implications of physical science with a facility simply absent in most historicist theologies today. But the obvious question is, How can Kaufman hold all these desirable qualities together? If he accepts postmodern relativity and imaginative construction, must he not simply abandon realism? Conversely, if he embraces a naturalistic and public realism, must he not also simply abandon postmodernism? Is it not simply inconsistent first to discover God in the subjective imagination of the individual and of the historical community alone and then to discover God in nature and public history as well?

There is one immediate answer to this question. It is that I have created an artificial problem by mixing modes, confusing questions of order of knowing and order of being, questions of genesis and outcome, questions of how we know and of what knowledge works pragmatically, questions of subjective origination and of the realism of the conclusion. The origination of knowledge of God in the human imagination has nothing to do with the validity of the claim that God is real in nature and public history. In Kaufman's own words, "It is the content of the notion of God, not the manner in which that notion is created and shaped in human consciousness, that determines whether God is a proper object of worship and devotion."[21] His point is

---

[19]*Theological Imagination,* 50-51.

[20]Kaufman, *Theology for a Nuclear Age*, 41.

[21]Kaufman, *God the Problem*, 113.

to separate the question of how ideas are reached from the question of their validity. And Kaufman's answer in *God the Problem* and in every book thereafter is that the validity of imagined theological truths must be tested pragmatically. Thus, a theological truth should be judged not in terms of how we came to it, but "in terms of the adequacy with which it is fulfilling the objectives we humans set for it."[22]

With these distinctions, it could be said that there is no incongruity between the imaginative origin of ideas about God and realistic claims those ideas might make. They simply have nothing to do with each other. It is just this distinction that leads neopragmatists such as Richard Rorty and Jeffrey Stout to argue that epistemology is dead; by this they mean not only that you can 't prove the truth of an idea by tracing its origins, but that the pragmatic meaning of the idea has nothing to do with origins anyway—so that even if you were given the magic to discover epistemological foundations, they would be irrelevant.

However, it is worth remembering that the founders of pragmatism, particularly James and Dewey, concluded that it simply was not pragmatic to rely on pragmatics to the exclusion of epistemology. They knew that the effectiveness of what you know has something to do with how you know. Today it seems clear—fashions of thought to the contrary notwithstanding—that, for example, how politicians know the world suggests what they will do. Why else would we ask for the politician's life story? Why else would we assume that female and minority leaders are probably most capable of helping women and minorities? Equally, affirmative action policy acknowledges that an employer's knowledge of a wide applicant pool is likely to influence the employer's hiring decision. Equally, which rap you get for murder depends on whether you premeditated. Equally, while we do not ignore lucky guesses, we rightly take educated guesses more seriously.

The point is that some epistemological effort to trace the source of a claim to its origin has something to do with the success of the claim. Using epistemology in this sense, it might be said that while pragmatism may point to the proof that is in the pudding, epistemology has something to do with the recipe. When any consideration of the source of a claim is made irrelevant to the truth of a claim, then you've got the same kind of problems a cook has without recipes. Equally, the imaginative construction one places on God had better have something to do with at least minimal knowledge of God or at least of the world, or the construction is simply a wild guess and is no more likely to work out pragmatically than any other wild guess.

My concern is not that Kaufman and others have no right to be skeptical of strong epistemologies or of foundationalism—for, surely, they do. Nor do I find their skepticism, itself, unhealthy, for it is not—even when it is directed to the empiricist pretensions of American classical theology. Rather, my concern is that this

---

[22]Kaufman, *Theology for a Nuclear Age*, 19; see also Kaufman, *Theological Imagination*, 46-51 and 255-60.

skepticism can turn into a simple rejection of any epistemology except innocuous epistemology, and then another problem arises, the fallacy of dichotomous thinking.

The dichotomy lies in one basic alternative: either (1) simple correspondence to facts or to noumena or (2) no epistemology at all. The problem arises this way. Practically speaking, the epistemology of the correspondence theory of truth can be used when we approach discrete objects; here truth is found in a correspondence between the object out there and my knowledge within myself. But when we deal with what Kaufman calls the "world-itself," "there is nothing outside our conception against which we can place it to see whether it 'corresponds'." Hence, Kaufman says, in metaphysics and theology "the ordinary truth-criterion of correspondence simply cannot be directly applied."[23] This means that metaphysical and theological beliefs are trapped behind a wall of ignorance. When Kaufman and most postmodernists imbued with a Continental heritage reject correspondence epistemologies, they effectively reject all strong epistemologies, for no longer do they permit choice to be explained or even contextualized by any account of how the subjects came to know what they know. Kaufman understandably revolts against the tyranny of tradition and its presumptuous determination of belief, as well as against a simple correspondence theory of truth and its naive realism. But because with that he has also revolted against all strong epistemological accounts, the intellectual choices of the subject must be seen as merely arbitrary and random.

What is missing, I am saying, is a strong epistemology that is not the conventional correspondence theory of truth epistemology. A candidate for such an epistemology might be that radical empiricism of William James, John Dewey, Alfred North Whitehead, and empirical theology. They argue that the full breadth of experience must include the experience of relations as well as of atomic entities, of value-realities as well as of fact-realities, of affectional senses as well as of the five senses. But even here Kaufman must not be faulted for oversight. He does not deny the reality and importance of noncognitive religious experience—at least not in the *Essay*, when he was still discussing epistemology. It is just that it cannot "provide the principal foundation for theological work." "The raw preconceptual and prelinguistic ground of religious experience is simply not available to us for direct exploration, description or interpretation, and therefore it cannot provide us with a starting point for theological work."[24] This is hard to disagree with; such adumbrative experiences cannot be the subject of "direct exploration," nor do they seem to offer any sort of viable "principal foundation." Nevertheless, the effect of this understandable move seems to be that after 1979 Kaufman abandoned all efforts to ask how such raw experiences might be accessed even indirectly and used. So, effectively, it is as though strong epistemology in all forms is simply rejected.

---

[23]Ibid., 254-55.

[24]Kaufman, *Essay*, 7.

But, again, Kaufman is not heedless. Even though he has no strong epistemology, he does all he can to reduce the arbitrariness of a theology without such an epistemology. He argues repeatedly that no good imaginative construct is reached except through interaction with tradition. In *The Theological Imagination* he insists that the good imaginative construct "is always a qualification and development of notions inherited from earlier worshippers and prophets, poets and thinkers."[25] In *Theology for a Nuclear Age* he argues that any imaginative reconstruction of Christian symbols "draws heavily, of course, on what these symbols have meant in the past."[26] And that inheritance, it must be remembered, has already been winnowed through earlier pragmatic tests. Consequently, imaginative constructs would seem not to be arbitrary, but to be reconstructions of a pragmatically tested religious history.

But does this really answer the problem of arbitrariness? For Kaufman what is crucial about imaginative construction is precisely that it moves beyond what tradition presents. The crucial religious moments, thus, are not those moments when quiet conditions permit the virtual reiteration of tradition but just those exceptional moments when cultural or natural changes require departure from tradition. It is exactly this movement beyond tradition which causes Kaufman to see "imagination" and "construction" as the very source of theology. Just in this movement imaginative constructs are so inexplicable by reference to tradition that they can appear to be arbitrary and random.[27]

My concern about the arbitrariness of theological concepts could not be dismissed by the claim that *any* free gesture must appear quite arbitrary—that if a free act were explicable, it would not be free. This improperly would equate freedom and arbitrariness, whereas free decisions are prompted by causes. Decisions have histories and use specific insights as significant responses to specific situations. That is, even free gestures can be explained to some extent epistemologically, by an account of how they are reached. But it is just this which is prevented by Kaufman's rejection of all strong epistemology.

Finally, it is true that after the imaginative construct has been ventured, experience might be used in order to test pragmatically the utility of that construct. But our point is about how the construct is first reached, not how it is later confirmed. This emphasis on timing can appear to quibble, but it does not. If experience, for example, can be used in the formation of the imaginative construct, then the construct is in part explained by reference to that on which it is contingent; if experience cannot be so used, then the construct to the extent that it is novel shoots

---

[25]Kaufman, *Theological Imagination*, 23.

[26]Kaufman, *Theology for a Nuclear Age*, 21.

[27]Further, even if tradition somehow could guide these imaginative constructs, the fact remains that tradition itself is made of nothing but imaginative constructs—even if those constructs are tested pragmatically after they have been introduced. (Kaufman, *Theology for a Nuclear Age*, 23.)

luckily or unluckily, with unmitigated arbitrariness into the historical dark. As Richard Rorty says of Galileo, he was not guided by something he understood; rather, when he reached his conclusion, "he just lucked out."[28] Chance, then, provides the only novel options that get to be tested or adopted; those novel options chance does not happen to put forth never get to be even candidates for truth. Further, explanations by chance leave unexamined the possible role that unwitting political or moral sentiments might play and leave unanswered the question, Why do academic theologians so regularly hit on liberal solutions to social problems?

There is a question of the philosophy of history here. The dichotomy between conventional epistemology and no epistemology at all might be put as a choice between a *deterministic historicism* and an *aleatory historicism*, a mechanistic historicism and a historicism of sheer chance, where luck alone can lead you out of problems. To these two options classical pragmatists and empirical theologians have wanted to add a kind of *contingent historicism*—where unpredictable choices are made, but for a cause, and where knowledge of the cause is requisite. Taking a view of history similar to this, Stephen Jay Gould, speaking as a paleontologist, says, "This third alternative represents no more nor less than the essence of history. Its view is contingency—and contingency is a thing unto itself, not the titration of determination by randomness.[29]

The classical American pragmatic tradition held out for contingent history, over against today's deconstructionists and neopragmatics, both of whom seem well on their way to affirming an aleatory history—in fact, if not in principle. The contingent historicism leaves some (perhaps small) role for experience, even religious experience. The classical pragmatic tradition did not require the abandonment of epistemology—although it did require the abandonment of direct epistemological justification. William James, for example, was a pragmatist, but he was also an epistemologist. That is, while he acknowledged that consequences make truths, he also insisted that knowledge contributes to the ideas that get to be a candidates for truth. The "that" received from the past is the seedbed for the "what" that we test. James put it this way: "The 'that' of it is its own; but the 'what' depends on the 'which'; and the which depends on 'us'."[30] Although James here stresses the subject's "which," in context it is clear that the subject's "which" depends to some extent on the experienced "that." Accordingly, James was deeply interested in experience as a source of truth, and his radical empiricism set forth his broad and original notion of how experience hooks onto the world external to the self.

---

[28]Richard Rorty, *Consequences of Pragmatism (Essays: 1972–1980)* (Minneapolis: University of Minnesota Press, 1982) 193.

[29]*Wonderful Life: The Burgess Shale and the Nature of History* (New York: W. W. Norton & Company, 1989) 51.

[30]William James, *Pragmatism* (Cambridge: Harvard University Press, 1975) 118.

When such questions are disregarded, there is no adequate account of the role of individuals in history. The proof, James said, is that Herbert Spencer (a pure environmental pragmatist, a predecessor to the neopragmatists, if there ever was one) was unable to explain great people and how they shape history.[31] Anyone, I might add, at the moment of forming an imaginative construct uniquely suited to his or her private history is in the position of the great person in public history, so that to neglect to explain how imaginative constructs are formed is to fail to account adequately for ordinary people as well as great people. Apart from such an account Jesus or an Albert Schweitzer are just statistical freaks; they just have this incredible lucky streak taking them from one stupendous spiritual insight to another in a quite inexplicable way. An Adolph Hitler is just extremely unlucky, going from one spiritual monstrosity to another, on and on. In neither case can we explain what's going on by introducing the religious individual's experience of environment and interpretation of that experience. Forget Jesus' Jewish upbringing; forget Hitler's personal history. Equally, if you take away strong epistemology, the genius moments in our personal histories become merely accidental—just lucky constructs or unlucky constructs.

I certainly agree with Kaufman that any conventional correspondence theory of truth makes no epistemological sense in metaphysics or theology. I also believe that empirical theologians sometimes have given voice to an evidentialism that appeared to be merely a disguised form of such an epistemology.[32] I also believe that there is no point in asking Kaufman to shake in a little objectivism and realism to spice his group subjectivism and projectionism with a little referentiality—for apart from an alternative epistemology and worldview, this would be a shallow and indigestible compromise between persisting contradictions.[33]

But I also agree with Sidney Hook when he protests extreme reactions to less-than-perfect knowledge. At a practical juncture in his political life Hook protested, "because nothing was absolutely true and no one could know the whole truth about anything, it did *not* follow that it was impossible to establish any historical truth."[34] In other words, because radical empiricism said that what is known—especially at the fringes—always is and will be vague and murky and because what is known cannot be empirically grounded in any direct way, it does not follow that there must

---

[31]William James, "Great Men and Their Environment" in *The Will to Believe and Other Essays in Popular Philosophy* (Cambridge: Harvard University Press, 1979).

[32]See my "Empirical Theology: A Revisable Tradition," *Process Studies* 19 (1990). This article is based on a paper given at Iliff School of Theology at a conference on methodology in process theology in February 1989.

[33]Such a compromise appears to be the approach taken by Kevin J. Sharpe, in "Theological Method and Gordon Kaufman," *Religious Studies* 15 (1979).

[34]Sidney Hook, *Out of Step: An Unquiet Life in the Twentieth Century* (New York: Harper, 1987) 219.

be no strong epistemology at all. Dewey, James, and Whitehead, along with Henry Nelson Wieman, Bernard Meland, and Bernard Loomer (the empirical theologians who took those philosophers most seriously) moved beyond the dichotomy between no epistemology and a bad epistemology and ventured an alternative epistemology. They posited an empiricist epistemology that gave status also to nonsensuous and affective perceptions: James called it "radical empiricism," Dewey call it "immediate empiricism," Whitehead referred to "causal efficacy," Wieman to a kind of mysticism, Meland to an "appreciative awareness," and Loomer (running out of time) said, finally, that he agreed with Meland. This epistemology was conjoined with the hypothesis that the world was just as spiritual as it was material, not because it was a compromise between the two but because it was a world based on relations between the known entities and, especially, between the known and the knower, rather than on a collection of material objects or spiritual subjects. Their empiricist epistemology described, usually indirectly, this relational world and its ways of prompting an experience that was religious.

IV. A Paradoxical Implication for the Concept of God

I have argued that epistemological considerations are important because they offer some guidance in the formulation of useful hypotheses. Beyond this, however, the sheer act of epistemological examination fastens attention, however inadequately, on the difference between experience and interpretation, between what is received and what is construed from what is received. This, in turn, can suggest ways in which the theological interpretation may outrun what it experiences. Specifically, attention to strong epistemology focuses on the individual's own creative contribution; this, in turn, implies that what is thought is more a function of the thinker than otherwise would be apparent. Paradoxically, this can lead to greater emphasis on the creativity of imaginative construction than is present even in Kaufman's own constructivism. Finally, this has unanticipated implications for the reality of God.

Kaufman and other constructivists may call the individual creative, imaginative, or constructive; but, while these characterizations give power to the subject, they often function as neoKantian caps on further inquiry, simply leaving it that, of course, structures emanate from subjects, their thought, their language, their conversation, or their cultural-linguistic workings. Leaving it at that, suggesting that the individual's creativity is sheerly groundless and unexaminable, leads in fact to the neglect of individual creativity. In other words, the impossibility of examining how individuals deal with their pasts leads nonepistemological theologians to emphasize the only thing open to discussion, which is the social context and social pragmatics. So those theologians who reject strong epistemology turn their real attention to social constructs, treating them as the new philosophical "givens," insulated now from the critical scrutiny once directed at the epistemological examination of how individuals deal with their past.

Unlike Kaufman, but using much the same constructivism, narrative theologians (cagey and postmodern people in most respects) can simply authorize the intratextual discourse of the Christian tradition, even if this means accepting an epistemologically problematic supernaturalist eschatology.[35] Equally, neopragmatic theologians or philosophers of religion can simply authorize the role of conversation, even if this means ignoring questions of the epistemological roots of that conversation.[36] This means, in effect, the authorization of group interpretations of God.

Gordon Kaufman has protested the authoritarianism of such procedures when they were seen to proceed from a scriptural or ecclesiastical tradition. But if Kaufman refuses to trace epistemologically the specific grounds of knowledge and simply posits the imaginative construction as the *terminous a quo*, he may indulge in his own Myth of the Given,[37] just as surely as if the construction had been required by ancient tradition.

Paradoxically then, the consequence of emphasizing the imagination's sheer constructivity is to diminish, not to augment, the creativity of the imagination. This bears particularly on the concept of God. While what I say applies as well to narrative and neopragmatic theologians, I concentrate on Kaufman. My point is that when he refuses to go behind the concept of God as the "cosmic movement" or the "hidden creativity" to ask at any length how, epistemologically, these imaginative constructs are reached, they work as ideas merely posited. His emphasis is not on how the God construct was produced by the individuals and historical communities that produced it, but on the only thing open to examination—the *ex post facto* pragmatic efficacy of the construct. The result is that the role of humans in creating God is underemphasized.

Thus, Kaufman can say: "There is a hidden creativity at work," and it "has made human life distinctively human, and it is only in hope of continuing positive effects of this creativity . . . that we today can take up the heavy responsibilities thrust upon us."[38] Kaufman here seems to make God creative, and the human task that of merely using God's creativity. Admittedly, Kaufman does sometimes clearly affirm that God is literally a human construct, that "ideas—including the idea of

---

[35]See, e.g., George A. Lindbeck, *The Nature of Doctrine: Religion and Theology in a Postliberal Age* (Philadelphia: Westminster, 1984) 62-63.

[36]For Stout, e.g., reasons arise not prior to but in conversation: "reason-giving is something *people do*, under historically *specific* circumstances, in conversation with their *contemporaries*." *The Flight from Authority: Religion, Morality, and the Quest for Autonomy* (Notre Dame IN: University of Notre Dame Press, 1981) 266; emphasis in original.

[37]See Wilfrid Sellars's strictures against the "Myth of the Given" in his "Empiricism and the Philosophy of Mind," in *Minnesota Studies in the Philosophy of Science*, vol. 1, ed. Herbert Feigl and Michael Scriven (Minneapolis: University of Minnesota Press, 1956) 253-329, esp. 293-300.

[38]Kaufman, *Theology for a Nuclear Age*, 41.

God—were *made*"[39] by humans for humans (although Kaufman is not the subjective idealist that Mark C. Taylor makes him).[40] Nevertheless, Kaufman focuses on the construct and not the constructivity, thus effectively neglecting how humans once literally created the construct in the first place. Kaufman readily states that the God construct originates in the human imagination and its effort to express an ultimate point of reverence, and he talks briefly about the evolutionary evidence for a creative God; but attention to human creativity stops far short of a close examination of religious experience or of evolutionary theory, for those already have been declared not the epistemological source of religious knowledge. The result of this closure has been to shut off appropriate scrutiny of imagination's creativity.

Let me be more specific. My concern is that when religious experience is cast into the outer darkness by, say, a Wayne Proudfoot,[41] then it is forgotten that every idea about God entered history only because it once sprang into the mind of an individual. The result is that the sociology of knowledge is beautifully stressed, but forgotten is the fact that individuals in their dark dialogues with their past have created the God ideas that eventually were polished under the sun of society. This forgetfulness did not follow logically; it just happened—due, perhaps, to preoccupations with overcoming bad epistemologies and stressing good social pragmatics. Nevertheless, in turning away from how we know, there is a temptation to forget that in knowing it is we who have created the world, including its God, in the first place.

Were we to go behind the giveness of God constructs and their fruits and to dig for epistemological roots, the notion of God might be enlarged in ways consistent with Kaufman's own already rich suggestions. Principally, this would show the extent to which God is a reality partially created by the world, just as the world is partially created by God. This is to say that imaginative construction creates not only the divine attributes and the inevitable metaphysical framework, both of which Kaufman recognizes. It would acknowledge that imagination partially creates also the very reality of God—not just the interpretation of God, but the divine reality itself; not just the apparent God, but the real God. Surely, some constructions about God remain apparent only, in the sense that they have no public chance of being made true. But other constructions that began as only apparent or only imagined do

---

[39]Ibid., 19; emphasis added.

[40]Referring to Kaufman's God, Taylor says, "What previously had been believed to be an objective reality existing independently of the mind, now is recognized as a construction of the mind itself." Mark C. Taylor, *Tears* (Albany: SUNY Press, 1990) 211. Taylor's two-option approach consistently misses the import of Kaufman's "directly" when Kaufman says, e.g., that religious images and terms "should not be understood as directly descriptive of objects" (quoted in ibid.). Kaufman's point is not to deny any and all reference to a world beyond the mind, but to deny direct reference.

[41]Wayne Proudfoot, *Religious Experience* (Berkeley: University of California Press, 1985).

become publicly useful and thereby real. The earliest source of this reality is the private imagination of the individual in dialogue with its past.

I should hasten to add that, while God may be partially created by interpretations, this does not necessarily limit God to what God is interpreted to be, for almost everything that begins as a construct usually takes on a life of its own, outrunning what it was interpreted to be. While God may be a chain of signs always interpreted into being in the course of nature and history, this does not necessarily make God utterly dependent; for God the signified can become a signifier with the world as its signified, a creator with the world, in part, as its creation. The significance of this proposal is that closer attention to how the self interprets experience leads to closer attention to how God begins as an imaginative construct, which in turn leads to closer attention to how God can become a real force in nature and history.

Admittedly, a point like this requires extensive elaboration, arguing how the interpreters of God include all those nonhumans going back to the big bang—when God and individuals began shaping each other. But such panpsychic proposals are not new to the American neonaturalist tradition. Equally, a nonfoundationalist and pluralistic realism and a nonsubjectivist relativism must be elaborated; but these too have their neonaturalistic precedents.

This proposal seeks to extend Kaufman's amalgamation of Continental subjectivism and American neonaturalism by emphasizing Kaufman's denial of God's sovereignty and his affirmation of human constructivity and responsibility. It does not opt for subjectivism, for this is not implicit in acknowledging that God begins in the imagination of the individual. It defends the reality of God, for this constructed, signified God is shown to become a signifier itself, much as biblical religions testify. Admittedly, it does make God a reality that begins as a construction within time. But then, so do we all. We were constructed largely by the interaction of our parents and by interactions within society, and yet we are real. As John Dewey noted, the locomotive is a construct of Stevenson's imagination, but now it is real.[42]

The sum and substance of this commentary is to acknowledge the persisting importance of experience, even after reading Gordon Kaufman's formidable theology, even after observing a culture rightly distrustful of authorization by reference to experience. It is apparent that experience can provide some minimal guidance to imagination, permitting a contingent historicism rather than an aleatory historicism. Paradoxically, to remember this role of experience gives more, not less, significance to imagination. It gives to imagination a role even in creating God.

---

[42]John Dewey, *A Common Faith* (New Haven CT: Yale University Press, 1952) 49

Salvation in the Theologies of Henry Nelson Wieman and Mordecai M. Kaplan

Emanuel S. Goldsmith

I

The concept of salvation, the heart of real religion, is often synonymous with religion itself and shares in religion's complexity.[1] Salvation may be this-worldly or other-worldly, individual or social, attainable once and for all or a process of growth, predominantly an escape from something or a positive achievement, conditional or absolute and eternal, and won by self-effort or with the aid of a savior. It may be attained through asceticism, ceremonies, moral effort, faith or knowledge.[2]

In the Hebrew Bible, the words for salvation (*y'shu'a*, *t'shu'a*, *yesha*) are derived from a root meaning to be wide and spacious. Their opposite, the word for trouble (*tsara*), denotes the state of narrowness. This implies that "the soul is wide when it develops without checking forces," and salvation is thus the development of the human soul. It signifies "unchecked prosperity, happiness in security under the protection of the strong God, [and] the abolition of all dangers." Despite the this-worldly nature of salvation in the Hebrew Bible, the demand that everything evil and everything hindering salvation be removed, extends it to the idea of "the confusion of death" which in the subsequent development of Judaism and Christianity evolves into eschatology.[3] The fact that God is the savior is an essential aspect of his divinity in both the Hebrew Bible and the New Testament.[4]

---

[1]Cf. Gerald Birney Smith, "Salvation," *A Dictionary of Religion and Ethics*, ed. S. Mathews and G. B. Smith (New York: Macmillan, 1921) 306.

[2]Cf. Charles S. Braden, "Salvation," *Encyclopedia of Religion*, ed. V. Ferm (New York, Philosophical Library, 1945) 683.

[3]Cf. Johs. Pedersen, *Israel: Its Life and Culture* (London: Oxford University Press, 1926) 2:330-34.

[4]Cf. Claus Westermann, *What Does the Old Testament Say about God*? (Atlanta: John Knox Press, 1979) 28.

The experience of salvation is universal. As Westermann explains, "it is something that everybody knows and which has occurred always and everywhere throughout the history of humanity up to the present day." The notion is based on the fact that "as long as human beings live they are in danger, assailable, and vulnerable. If they survive the danger, they know of the experience of being saved. This applies to the individual, any human community, and to humanity as a whole."[5] In our own day, according to Braunthal, despite secularization, "the quest for ultimate salvation by the historical religions has not subsided. . . . Moreover, the trend has accelerated toward bridging the gap between the religious yearning for salvation and the secular striving for higher degrees of societal perfection."[6]

Henry Nelson Wieman (1884–1975) and Mordecai M. Kaplan (1881–1983) were two outstanding twentieth-century theologians of salvation. One a Protestant and the other a Jew, they were both modernist theologians who worked within the traditions of American liberal theology, religious naturalism, religious humanism, pragmatism, empirical theology, and pluralistic process thought. The words theologian and modernist require explication. Wieman and Kaplan sought to defend what they considered to be the vital aspects of their respective religious traditions from the acids of modernity which included atheism and atheistic humanism. At the same time, they approached their religious traditions as twentieth century men who consciously embraced the achievements of modern science, philosophy and comparative religion and for whom the spiritual problems of their own time were primary and the insights of their inherited traditions secondary.

The religious liberals of the early twentieth century continued the work of the Enlightenment and led religion into the worlds of modern science, philosophy, and history. They domesticated modern religious ideas and carried forward, in Ahlstrom's formulation, the "confrontation between traditional orthodoxies, and the new grounds for religious skepticism exposed during the nineteenth century."[7] What Adams has written concerning the Age of Enlightenment is equally true of liberal religion in the first half of twentieth century: "Apart from this effort the religion of the West would be unable to elicit integrating commitment or to find vital points of contact with secularism and with the myths of other religions and cultures."[8] The liberal theologians sought to free religion from obscurantism and narrowness. They stressed human freedom and creativity and the ability of human beings to do good to their fellows. For them the establishment of the kingdom of God would be the

---

[5]Ibid., 28.

[6]Alfred Braunthal, *Salvation and the Perfect Society: The Eternal Quest* (Amherst: The University of Massachusetts Press, 1979) 348.

[7]Sidney E. Ahlstrom, *A Religious History of the American People*, (New Haven: Yale University Press, 1983) 783.

[8]James Luther Adams, *The Prophethood of All Believers* (Boston: Beacon Press, 1986) 122.

natural, this-worldly outcome of the historical process. As Ahlstrom writes, "their confidence in the future outran even that of the Enlightenment's apostles of progress."[9]

American religious liberalism, in particular, was characterized by ethical passion and a preoccupation with religious experience. As Williams argues, "there is a theological development peculiar to the American experience. . . . Americans are likely to have a distinctive sense of theological method. . . . all American religious groups have had to come to terms with the vitalities and structures of American society, and there are definite parallels in the Roman Catholic and Jewish theologies for the trends . . . described in the Protestant tradition."[10] According to Williams, five principal aspects of the incorporation of experience into American theology were: (1) "treatment of religious experience as a source of knowledge of God," (2) "use of religious experience as the sign of vitality in religious faith," (3) "emphasis on experience as the testing ground for moral character and for the achievement of moral goals," (4) "the viewing of experience as the field for cooperation among peoples of differing doctrinal persuasions," and (5) "modernist use of present experience for criticism and interpretation of traditional doctrines and practices."[11] Cauthen characterizes the underlying motifs of American religious liberalism as *continuity*, or emphasis on the immanence rather than the transcendence of God; *autonomy*, or the centrality of experience rather than the appeal to external authority; and *dynamism*, or the stress on evolution in nature and history rather than the appeal to static categories.[12]

While clearly within the broad stream of American religious liberalism, Wieman and Kaplan were critical of certain liberal presuppositions. As modernist liberals or radical modernizers, they took scientific method, empirical fact, and prevailing forms of philosophy as their point of departure.[13] Although aware of much in Judaism and Christianity that should be retained in modern times, they believed that their traditions had to be evaluated in the light of modern science, philosophy, psychology, and sociology. Nothing was to be adhered to unless its relevance could be made apparent.[14] As modernists they advocated "the conscious, intended adapta-

---

[9]Ahlstrom, *Religious History*, 780.

[10]Daniel D. Williams, "Tradition and Experience in American Theology," *The Shaping of American Religion*, ed. J. W. Smith and A. L. Jamison (Princeton: Princeton University Press, 1961) 443-46.

[11]Ibid., 448. Cf. Frederick Sontag and John K. Roth, *The American Religious Experience* (New York: Harper, 1972) and Randolph Crump Miller, *The American Spirit in Theology* (Philadelphia: Pilgrim Press, 1974).

[12]Kenneth Cauthen, *The Impact of American Religious Liberalism* (New York: Harper, 1962) 25.

[13]Ahlstrom, *Religious History*, 782-83.

[14]Cauthen, *Impact*, 29.

tion of religious ideas to modern culture."[15] For them, God was immanent in cultural evolution, and society was progressively moving toward realization of the kingdom of God, even if such a goal might never actually be attained.[16]

II

Wieman and Kaplan shared a deep concern with the concept of value. Religion is concerned with value in that it involves the choice, appreciation, and adoration of value or the source of value, and in that it posits a faith in the universe as hospitable to value.[17] Kaplan placed the term *God* in the category of value which is related to wisdom rather than in the category of fact which is related to reason and intelligence. Values, he insisted, are actually as real as visible and tangible facts.[18] "As psychic and social facts or realities, values are far more potent as fact makers or factors, in the sense of producing results."[19]

Wieman contended that, as a supreme value, God is a perceptible natural process.[20] The term *God* is a name for the growth of meaning and value in the world, and values are the data by which God is sought and found. Although God is always greater than "the specific objects of human desire and aversion," God and the highest human values are identical.[21] "The creative source of value must come first in man's devotion, while the specific values apprehended through the narrow slit of human awareness must come second, if we are to find the way of our deliverance and the way of human fulfillment."[22] Smith observes that Wieman's position rests on two central theses. "His claim that God is truly present in perceived experience is intended to avoid reducing God to a mere concept or ideal. His interpretation of God as the source of human good or value, on the other hand, seeks to avoid confusing God with the whole of reality."[23]

The approaches of Wieman and Kaplan were also soteriological. For them salvation is a this-worldly social, as well as individual, reality which must be under-

---

[15]William R. Hutchison, *The Modernist Impulse in American Protestantism* (Cambridge MA: Harvard University Press, 1976) 2.

[16]Ibid.

[17]Edgar S. Brightman, *A Philosophy of Religion* (Englewood Cliffs NJ: Prentice-Hall, 1940) 86.

[18]Kaplan, *The Religion of Ethical Nationhood* (New York: Macmillan, 1970) 48.

[19]Ibid., 23.

[20]James A. Martin, Jr., *Empirical Philosophies of Religion* (New York: King's Crown Press) 6.

[21]Wieman with Walter M. Horton, *The Growth of Religion*, (Chicago: Willet, Clark, 1938) 267.

[22]Wieman, *The Source of Human Good* (Chicago: Chicago University Press, 1946) 39.

[23]John E. Smith, "Philosophy of Religion," *Religion*, ed. P. Ramsey (Englewood Cliffs NJ: Prentice-Hall, 1965) 380.

stood in terms of human needs. The key to the Wiemanian and Kaplanian concepts of salvation is the notion of *openness* or receptivity to diverse individuals and cultures—an idea with deep roots in American religious liberalism. Salvation for both designates a natural, human, earthly activity which sustains and transforms and is synonymous with religion at its best.

As Loomer writes, "Wieman's concern has been soteriological throughout. His focus has been the relation between God and man as they encounter each other in the process of salvation."[24] For Wieman, salvation is the life of aspiration in which the deepest need of human nature finds fulfillment. This need is "the need of bringing to fulfillment that multiplication of responses which arise in a man over and above his established habits. . . . It is to interact with ever more of the world round about him."[25] Modern persons can find their salvation only through the social world in which they participate, and social reconstruction is the modern road to salvation.[26]

> [Psychologically, salvation is emergence] from inner conflict or stagnation to progressive integration of personality; from personal powers confined to personal powers released; from a disjunct personality to a conjunct one; from a sense of insecurity to a profound and indestructible peace; from specific objectives that imprison and perish to a total objective that is eternal; from bondage to an established social pattern of life, to a pattern that opens out into an illimitable realm of possible value and meaning.[27]

The salvation of society involves rearranging institutions, ideals, and customs in order to "restore mutual support and release growth of meaning."[28] The salvation of the individual and the salvation of society are interrelated. "The salvation sought is the salvation of man, psychologically, socially, historically. It is the salvation of human life in its total movement of history, society and individual existence."[29]

Religion's major responsibility is to point to the way of salvation.[30] The salvation that affords deepest satisfaction and maximum realization of human potentialities is found in a creativity that reconstructs personality, society, and history by generating insights and expanding horizons. It operates through creative intercommunication between individuals, peoples, and cultures. This creativity expands the

---

[24]Bernard E. Loomer, "Wieman's Stature as a Contemporary Theologian," *The Empirical Theology of Henry Nelson Wieman*, 395.

[25]Wieman, *The Wrestle of Religion with Truth* (New York: Macmillan, 1927) 123-24.

[26]Wieman with R. W. Wieman, *Normative Psychology of Religion* (New York: Crowell, 1935) 99-100.

[27]Ibid., 171.

[28]Ibid., 172.

[29]Wieman, *Intellectual Foundation of Faith* (New York: Philosophical Library, 1961) 169.

[30]Ibid., 80.

range of what an individual can know, control, and appreciate as good and distinguish as evil, and the depth and scope of what he can appreciate and understand about himself and about the unique individuality of other persons and peoples.[31]

Wieman reminds us that all the great religions have maintained that what happens after death depends upon the nature of our ruling commitment before death. Such a ruling commitment must enable us to control anxiety and increase the values of human existence. Anxiety must be controlled in a way that enables us to criticize and correct the evils of life and impels us to improve our behavior. When anxiety is not controlled in this manner, it becomes a source of fanaticism. The values of human existence are increased when the activities which maintain the living organism on the physiological, psychological and sociological levels support each other across wide areas of conflict and diversity.[32]

The concept of salvation formulated by Wieman is synonymous with the biological concept of homeostasis. Religion serves to promote commitment to what orders and directs the totality of sustaining and regulating activities so that they may sustain and promote each other instead of breaking down into inhibitions and frustrations.[33] Religion, moreover, reminds us that "human purpose cannot create or sustain homeostatic systems but can only cooperate with them."[34] Salvation is the process by which the individual person gradually becomes human and grows religiously, culturally, politically, scientifically, aesthetically, and socially, through the kind of dialogue and action that creates genuine community.[35]

Schulweis has noted the revolutionary character of Kaplan's interpretation of what constitutes personal salvation for every individual. Kaplan's "soterics" is based on two elemental and compulsive factors in human nature: the will to live and the will to maximum life.[36] "Just as the will to live testifies (in an intuitive, not in a logical sense) to the reality of life, the will to live the maximum life testifies to the realizable character of such life."[37] Kaplan characterizes the human being as a "salvation-seeking animal"—an animal that cares about maximum life.[38] Moreover,

---

[31]Ibid., 7-8.

[32]Wieman, *Science Serving Faith*, ed. C. Peden and C. Willig (Atlanta: Scholars Press, 1987) 181-83.

[33]Ibid., 182.

[34]Ibid., 183.

[35]Cf. Mary Minella, "The Echshatological Dimension of Creative Interchange," *Creative Interchange*, ed. J. A. Broyer and S. Minor (Carbondale: Southern Illinois University Press, 1982) 436.

[36]Harold Schulweis, "Mordecai M. Kaplan's Theory of Soterics," *Mordecai M. Kaplan: An Evaluation*, ed. I. Eisenstein and E. Kohn (New York: Jewish Reconstructionist Foundation, 1952) 266.

[37]Kaplan, "The God Idea in Judaism," *The Jewish Reconstructionist Papers*, ed. M. M. Kaplan (New York: Behrman's Jewish Book House, 1936) 98.

[38]Kaplan, "The Interdependence of Science and Religion," *Reconstructionist* 43/1

in the Hebrew Bible (where God is referred to as the "God of salvation" 273 times) salvation is described as acquired by wisdom, knowledge, and intelligence rather than by faith.[39]

According to Kaplan, being important to someone or being needed by someone is fulfillment or salvation.[40] "Salvation means to a person or a people being rescued from drowning in a sea of futility and meaninglessness."[41] Salvation is tantamount to continuous growth and gradual approximation to the ideal of perfection.[42] Kaplan approaches Wieman's definition of salvation as homeostasis when he describes it as "the maximum harmonious functioning of a person's physical, mental, social, moral, and spiritual powers."[43]

Religion is man's conscious quest for salvation or the achievement of his human destiny. [44] The proper task of religion is not to prove the existence of God but to assist people in their quest for self-fulfillment or salvation.[45] Salvation is "the achievement of such personality in the individual and of such society in the collective, as to augment the measure of integrity, responsibility and creativity in the world."[46] It is the maximum fulfillment of those capacities that entitle people to be described as created in the divine image.[47] It is the effort to improve oneself and one's environment and as such is prophetic of human destiny and a manifestation of the divine in human life.[48] It is the capacity to play a conscious role in the evolution of self, as well as the urge to transformation and metamorphosis.[49]

The concept of salvation is rooted in the objective psychological need to be needed, which is experienced as the need to be accepted and loved. To be needed, a person must be honest, creative, just, and ready to serve. Every person may be creative, because, insofar as one produces more than one consumes, one contributes to making life worthwhile for all.[50] The need to be needed applies to nations as well as to individuals. To achieve salvation, human beings must strive for world peace,

---

(February 1977): 9.

[39]Ibid.

[40]Kaplan, *Not So Random Thoughts* (New York: Reconstructionist Press, 1966) 162.

[41]Ibid., 158.

[42]Kaplan, "Religion in a New Key: An Introduction to the Science of Soterics," *Reconstructionist* 25/1 (19 February 1960): 17.

[43]Kaplan, "When Is a Religion Authentic?" *Reconstructionist* 30/11 (2 October 1964): 15.

[44]Kaplan, *The Future of the American Jew* (New York: Macmillan, 1948) 172.

[45]Kaplan, *The Religion of Ethical Nationhood* (New York: Macmillan, 1970) 21.

[46]Kaplan, "Religion in a New Key," 17.

[47]Kaplan, *Questions Jews Ask: Reconstructionist Answers* (New York: Reconstructionist Press, 1956) 126.

[48]Ibid., 480.

[49]Kaplan, "Religion in a New Key," 18.

[50]Kaplan, *Religion of Ethical Nationhood*, 49.

ethical nationhood, and individual happiness.[51] For the individual, salvation also consists of the satisfaction of the three primary needs: health, love and creativity. For society, salvation involves seeing to it that every person has the economic and cultural opportunities necessary for maximum self-fulfillment.[52]

III

For Wieman, the God of salvation is to be sought in growth, community, creativity, and creative communication among individuals and peoples. God is the infinitely rich, complex, and yet unified growth of community among people. God must not be thought of as an ideal or possibility of value that does not yet exist nor as a being existing in some other world outside nature. God is rather the concrete growth of community or the unlimited growth of individual personality, nation, culture, or historical or planetary epoch.[53] God is "creativity operating to transform destructive conflicts into creative conflicts and to bring diversities into that kind of interaction which transforms them into mutually sustaining parts of a more comprehensive system while retaining their diversity."[54]

The word *God* may become a device with which to conceal from oneself and from others the true character of one's faith.[55] For Wieman, the word *God* refers to a kind of communication,

> the kind which creates appreciative understanding of the individuality of persons and peoples when they allow it to operate in their lives, creating society, sustaining all these in their being and increasing the values in them, when required conditions are present. This operative presence creates in each individual his capacity to love and appreciate and understand the individuality of others.[56]

Such communication occurs between persons all the time to some degree. But to be radically transforming, it must rise to a high level and overcome the counter-processes which ordinarily obstruct and suppress it. When it rises to a level of power and dominance, it endows life with all of its great values.[57]

God is the process of creative good or creativity which, in the form of creative interchange and internal integration, operates to transform human life in a way that it could not do by itself. It delivers human life from evil and conveys it to the

---

[51]Kaplan with Arthur A. Cohen, *If Not Now, When?* (New York: Schocken, 1973) 80.
[52]Kaplan, *Future of the American Jew*, 206.
[53]Wieman, *Growth of Religion*, 478-79.
[54]Wieman, *Science Serving Faith*, 184.
[55]Wieman, *Intellectual Foundation of Faith*, 47.
[56]Ibid., 52.
[57]Ibid., 55.

greatest good which human life can ever attain.[58] God can never be a person or a personality.

> It is a logical fallacy to call God a person if any of his essential powers are different in kind from those essential to, and definitive of, the human being. This is so because the established meaning of the word "personality" is to designate the characteristics which are distinctive and essential to the human being.[59]

There is a creativity which personality may undergo but not perform. It is this creativity that progressively creates personality through community.

> Either God exercises the power of creativity progressively creating personality, in which case he cannot be a personality because he is then exercising the creativity no person can exercise but can only undergo; or else, if he is a personality he is himself a creature of this creativity. A God who is a creature of an ontologically prior creativity is properly called an idol.[60]

Creative interchange can be readily observed in the growth of young children where it creates mind, personality, and, through "symbolized meanings," a community with others.[61] In the form of symbolized meanings conveyed by language, values reach the human mind. Language may be distinguished from the signs to which lower animals respond by its ability to carry such symbolized meanings that can expand indefinitely in terms of values, knowledge, skills, and power.[62] Creative interchange may be said to create the universe, since it makes possible whatever experience of the universe people can have. "It creates the human mind and in that way creates the world relative to the human mind."[63] Because it creates us and sustains us at the human level and gives us all the values which human beings can have, creative interchange is the one basic and most precious good which all human beings share together.[64]

For Kaplan salvation is "durable happiness" and God is the Power or Process that makes for such salvation.[65] The central element in religion is not its idea of God but its idea of salvation since "whatever constitutes salvation for the religious

---

[58]Ibid., 53.

[59]Ibid., 58.

[60]Ibid., 66.

[61]Wieman, "Appendix," *Creative Interchange*, 447; see n. 35.

[62]Ibid.

[63]Wieman, *Man's Ultimate Commitment* (Carbondale: Southern Illinois University Press, 1958) 31.

[64]Wieman, "Appendix," 447.

[65]Kaplan, *Not So Random Thoughts*, 159.

community determines the idea of God which the religion of that community professes."[66]

> [God is] the correlate of the idea of a better and happier world, or of the salvation of man . . . the power or process of interdependence and creativity that enables society to fulfill itself. . . the creative, coordinating, integrative process of the universe, insofar as it makes for the salvation of man, both individual and social.[67]

Nature's God or Godhood is identical with the totality of creative processes in man and nature which make for self-transcendence and self-perfection.[68] "Divinity is that aspect of the whole of nature, both in the universe and in man, which impels mankind to create a better and happier world and every individual to make the most of his own life."[69] God is "the functioning in nature of the eternally creative process, which, by bringing order out of chaos and good out of evil, actuates man to self-fulfillment."[70]

Kaplan sought to divorce the God-idea from mythology, anthropomorphism, and supernaturalism, and identify it with "all human conduct that strives for the creative survival of the human species in a warless world."[71] Since we can now understand the moral aspect of social existence that impels us to fulfill ourselves as human beings, we can freely reject the supernatural elements of traditional religion.[72] We can find God in the urge to truth, honest, empathy, loyalty, justice, freedom, and goodwill.[73] Religion must be purged of (1) "an attitude of credulity which renders the mind susceptible to irrational and superstitious beliefs in luck, fate or sinister consequences"; (3) "intellectual fixation on some past stage in the history of one's religion as one of divine revelation, and the nostalgic hope for a return to that period"; (5) "inability to identify divinity with the natural processes of body or mind"; (6) "belief in divine reward and punishment not only for social sins but also for ritual transgressions and unbelief"; (7) "other-worldliness or the assumption that man cannot possibly achieve his destiny in the world"; (8) "the dichotomy of body

---

[66]Kaplan, *Religion of Ethical Nationhood*, 6.

[67]Kaplan, "The Meaning of God for the Contemporary Jew," *Tradition and Contemporary Experience*, ed. A. Jospe (New York: Schocken Books, 1970) 71.

[68]Kaplan, *Religion of Ethical Nationhood*, 109.

[69]Ibid. 75.

[70]Ibid. 10.

[71]Ibid. 82.

[72]Ibid. 70.

[73]Kaplan, "Between Two Worlds," *Varieties of Jewish Belief*, ed. I. Eisenstein (New York: Reconstructionist Press, 1966) 141.

and soul as a rationale for asceticism which is pleasing to God"; (9) "abnormal mysticism which is a perversion of normal mysticism."[74]

Although Kaplan emphasized moral responsibility and conscience as the principal manifestations of Godhood in human life, he sought to prove that ethical traits are the subjective expressions of objective process in nature.

> The theory of reciprocal responsibility is the conscious human manifestation of the principle whereby everything in nature is both cause and effect of everything else. It corresponds with the universal law of polarity whereby everything in the universe, from the minutest electron to the vastest star, is both self-active and interactive, independent and interdependent.[75]

"The cosmic process of universal reciprocity outside the human mind comes to be God only when it is experienced as cosmic interdependence, and, in the world, as moral responsibility."[76] Human nature is an extension of cosmic processes while conscience, which dictates to a person what he or she should do and induces remorse for failure, is actually the "semi-conscious intellectual effort to experience Divinity without recourse to anthropomorphic terms, rational propositions or mystic ecstasy."[77]

Kaplan stressed the significance of group or public religion as essentially an expression of response to human needs. Group religion is an aspect of wisdom or the concern with value, and, as such, responds to the need to be needed. The need to be needed is identical with the need to transcend oneself or to experience the holiness of life. Transcendence or holiness is the human equivalent of what in nature is known as organicity, or the process by which anything is more than the sum of its parts. God is the incremental plus of organic human society. "The process of organicity, functioning *self-consciously* in organic human societies, is God, as the power that makes for salvation."[78] The God of Israel "represents the power of salvation which the collective self-consciousness generates by means of its organic function, and which is inherently akin to that which makes the cosmos or nature as a whole, possible."[79]

To Kaplan, the idea of God is a correlate of the idea of salvation or self-fulfillment. It reflects awareness of the organicity of the universe and assumes that there is enough in the world to meet people's needs but not enough to satiate their lusts

---

[74]Kaplan, *Religion of Ethical Nationhood*, 86-87.

[75]Ibid., 34-35.

[76]Ibid., 48.

[77]Ibid., 71.

[78]Kaplan, *If Not Now, When?*, 38.

[79]Kaplan, "Our God as Our Collective Conscience," *Reconstructionst* 41/1 (February 1975): 14.

and greeds.[80] Historically, the term *god* denoted any value or good that answered a need. "The unique God denotes the fulfillment of all human needs."[81] Such fulfillment depends on the functioning of conscience and moral responsibility. Religion is not a response to an intellectual need but to the human need to be needed. "It is not a matter of reflection but a matter of responsibility."[82] The term God is not a substantive but a functional noun denoting something exceptional and therefore transcendental or transnatural. It denotes the experience of holiness, which is related to the functioning of conscience.[83]

IV

Related to the concepts of God and salvation, are those of evil and sin. By denying the traditional conception of divine omnipotence, Wieman and Kaplan were able to rescue divine beneficence without resorting to, and glorifying in, paradox. Wieman stated unequivocally that although creativity creates mind, culture, and history, it does not create the monstrous evils in the world. Evil results from counterprocesses and obstructions to creativity.[84] Creative interchange creates all the positive values of human existence, but the self-destructive processes result from what obstructs creativity and operates in opposition to it.[85] More important, whatever evil exists, people can always choose between better or worse. The responsibility to know what is better and to commit oneself to it devolves upon all of us. "Whether the good is mighty or weak over against the evil, it is the best there is and blessedness is found in living for it even in error and defeat."[86]

Sin results from not living solely for the hidden riches of God, from fearing things other than alienation from God, from conscious and subconscious interests corrupting singlehearted devotion to God.[87] At its deepest level, sin is inability to commit oneself to the creativity which saves and transforms.[88] Sin is defying "the imperative demand that men remove or fight the conditions obstructing creativity and that they relinquish what must be cast out of their life if the creative event is to have free way there."[89] Thus, "wherever the growth of community with fellow men and with nature takes hold of a man with life-transforming power, God's for-

---

[80]Kaplan, *If Not Now, When?*, 14.
[81]Ibid., 79.
[82]Ibid., 119.
[83]Ibid., 89.
[84]Wieman, "Appendix," 446.
[85]Ibid.
[86]Wieman, *Intellectual Foundation of Faith*, 120-21.
[87]Wieman, *Growth of Religion*, 268.
[88]Wieman, *Man's Ultimate Commitment*, 126.
[89]Ibid., 127.

giveness is accomplished."[90] Forgiveness is change "from a state of being in which one cannot enter into appreciative understanding with others" to one in which one can have this appreciative understanding "despite wrong done and wrong suffered."[91]

Kaplan spoke of evil as religion's worst quandary and the source of its crisis in the modern world. Theology's attempt to understand evil intellectually and to resign people to it actually contributes to the worsening of the human situation. Religion is too preoccupied with justifying "God's ways" and preaching resignation instead of actively seeking an end to exploitation and war. The various attempts to account for evil are erroneous because they derive from the incorrect notion that God is a being like a human being. Insofar as Godhood is the correlate of humanity's efforts to improve human life, God is a process. The creativity manifest in human responsibility, integrity, and loyalty or love, constitutes the Godhood or divinity of the cosmos. This perspective shifts attention from metaphysical speculation to man's inhumanity to man.[92] "If God, conceived as function, denotes whatever is of ultimate value to mankind, he cannot be represented as a personal Being infinite in power and goodness, which is a contradiction in terms."[93] Theodicies that attempt to justify God's ways are meaningless and replete with inconsistencies. "Nature is infinite chaos, with all its evils forever being vanquished by creativity, which is God as infinite goodness. . . . The power of God is inexhaustible but not infinite."[94]

Kaplan's position was based on his analysis of the empirically verifiable functioning of conscience. The function of conscience, the "pain of the human spirit," is not to promote speculation about God or reconcile humanity to man-made evil but to eliminate the causes of such evil and help bring about God's kingdom on earth. Conscience is thus also the revelation of God in the human spirit.[95]

Sin is the commission or omission of an act "that runs counter to the self-fulfillment of the individual as an integrated personality or of mankind as a fraternal cooperative society."[96] Sin is whatever thwarts the effort of life "to achieve and express unity, harmony, and integrity."[97] It is "the failure to live up to the demands of conscience for the exercise of moral responsibility, authenticity, loyalty or love, and creativity."[98] Moreover, every sin is at the same time a sin against ourselves,

---

[90]Wieman, *Growth of Religion*, 269.

[91]Wieman, *Man's Ultimate Commitment*, 132.

[92]Kaplan, "The Unresolved Problem of Evil," *Reconstructionist* 29/7 (17 May 1963): 11-16.

[93]Kaplan, *Religion of Ethical Nationhood*, 51.

[94]Ibid.

[95]Kaplan, "The Unresolved Problem of Evil," *Reconstructionist* 29/8 (31 May 1963): 15.

[96]Kaplan, *Questions Jews Ask*, 233.

[97]Kaplan, *The Meaning of God in Modern Jewish Religion* (New York: Behrman House, 1936) 167.

[98]Kaplan, *The Purpose and Meaning of Jewish Existence* (Philadelphia: Jewish Publica-

a sin against our neighbors, and a sin against God since "sins against the organic life of the individual prevent him from giving as efficient service as he might otherwise give, and, in frustrating the tendency of life to seek integration, they are sins against God."[99]

People overcome sin by engaging in repentance—the process of creativity that enables them to improve themselves as human beings. When a person engages in repentance, he is actually re-creating himself, so that his general behavior thereafter is transformed. The capacity to repent is derived from God, "the process of creativity in the cosmos, whereby chaos is transformed into order and nature is being continually renewed."[100]

V

Wieman and Kaplan did not fail to apply their approaches to the attitudes of their respective religions to other faiths. Wieman said:

> The value of the Christian message lies in what it can contribute to promoting creative interchange between parent and child, husband and wife, human associations of all kinds, cultures and peoples. When not applied to human living in this way, the Christian message becomes a tyranny of dogma, a barrier to creative interchange, and the source of great evil, as history demonstrates.[101]

Diverse temperaments, traditions, and regional interests require different forms of religion. The different forms of religion need not be reduced to one form only; but if conflicting interests are to be brought into greater interdependence, the various forms of religion must have a ruling commitment to creative interchange that can bring conflicts under control.[102]

Kaplan wrote of the *sancta* of a people or church as the persons, events, texts, places, etc., through which it helps those who belong to it achieve salvation. The *sancta* of each people or church naturally mean more to its members than to those of any other group. Whether the *sancta* of one group are more ethical or spiritual than the *sancta* of another group is beside the point. "The fact is that such comparison is not only odious but unwarranted, because the sancta of no religion or civilization are so fixed or static as to be incapable of development and revaluation."[103] Since every religion aspires to be a means of salvation to its own people or church,

---

tion Society of America, 1964) 151.

[99]Kaplan, *Meaning of God*, 172.

[100]Kaplan, *Purpose and Meaning*, 158-59.

[101]Wieman, *Religious Inquiry* (Boston: Beacon Press, 1968) 21.

[102]Ibid., 33-34.

[103]Kaplan, *Judaism Without Supernaturalism* (New York: Reconstructionst Press, 1958) 74.

the assumption that one's own religion is the only true religion is obsolete. No religion can be absolutely more or less true than another. "Though, at some particular time or place, one religion may be more helpful to its own adherents than another religion is to the adherents of that religion, that condition may be reversed before long."[104] Each religion exists in its own right and has no need to justify itself by asserting its superiority over other religions.

> If a devout Christian tells me that he finds in the adoration of the personality of Jesus all the inspiration that he requires for living a life that satisfies his spiritual needs, I cannot as a Jew say this attitude is not true, although I am so conditioned that I could not possibly find it true in my own experience. On the other hand, if I say to him that I can find in the Torah literature of the Jew the reflection of an attitude toward life more satisfying than any I could find in the New Testament or elsewhere, I, too, am speaking the truth, and my religion is as true as his.[105]

Each religion exists in its own right and should not have to justify its existence by any assertion of superiority.

Thus, for Kaplan and Wieman the future of interfaith goodwill depends on something other than tolerance between groups. The way to deal with diversity is for each faith to heed the voice of conscience and the dictates of moral responsibility, and to relate to other faiths in the spirit of creative intercommunication and mutual learning in depth. It is a tribute to the diversity and openness of American society that these two religious thinkers of diverse traditions could not only come to know and appreciate each other's work but also to acknowledge publicly their mutual admiration and respect. Kaplan was a diligent student of Wieman's writings and recommended them to his students. In the classes in philosophy of religion that he taught at the Jewish Theological Seminary, he sometimes utilized Wieman's books as texts. Wieman, for his part, said that he was certain that Kaplan's thought was on the right track and that, sooner or later, the dominant form of religion by which people find salvation would be developed along the lines indicated by Kaplan.[106]

VI

Further exploration into the theologies of Wieman and Kaplan will reveal similarities of view on such diverse topics as history, community, tradition, mysticism, worship, religious education, the Bible, comparative religion, civil religion, religion and government, religion and economics, etc. These similarities are even more striking when one takes into account that both thinkers also wrote much in defense of

---

[104]Ibid., 75.

[105]Kaplan, *Judaism in Transition* (New York: Covici-Friede, 1936) 282.

[106]Wieman, "Mordecai M. Kaplan's Idea of God," *Mordecai M. Kaplan: An Evaluation*, 210.

the specific differentia of their respective traditions. Thus Wieman wrote much about Jesus and the Church and Kaplan about the Torah-tradition and about the Jewish people and Zionism. They were both apologists of their faiths in the highest sense of the term as well as innovative and reconstructive theologians.

The ideological convergence of the Judaism of Kaplan and the Christianity of Wieman constitutes a significant development in American religious thought. The two thinkers remained remarkably loyal to the presuppositions of modernist liberalism during careers that extended beyond the emergence of crisis theology, neo-orthodoxy, existentialism, and death-of-God theology. While their thoughts continued to evolve and to absorb insights from new developments in philosophy and the social sciences, the two thinkers remained firmly rooted in the basic outlooks they developed quite early in their careers. Refusing to succumb to despair about human nature and the possibility of progress, they continued to affirm the interdependence of religion and culture and to require of their respective faiths both intellectual honesty and moral action consonant with belief.[107] In the tradition of a significant sector of American religious thinking, they were radical or "free theologians" seeking both self-understanding and insight into the issues of their day through creative thinking about God.[108] They grappled critically and imaginatively with human experience so that it might provide new religious vision and hope. Such reflection has often played a unifying and constructive role in the history of religion. The theologies of Wieman and Kaplan may indeed play such a role in the future.

---

[107]Hutchison, *Modernist Impulse*, 310.

[108]Cf. Sontag and Roth, *American Religious Experience*, 340.

The Normative Argument for a Valuational Theism

Charley D. Hardwick

In this paper I want to introduce readers to a new strategy for developing a theology on naturalist philosophical grounds. This strategy is worked out much more fully in my manuscript "Events of Grace: A Naturalist Theology of Creative Transformation." I have chosen a difficult issue which should be of interest to naturalists and religious empiricists; it is also one that serves nicely to introduce the framework of the book. The paper is divided into three parts. The first is a schematic presentation of the book's argument and of its philosophical basis in John Post's 1987 work *The Faces of Existence*,[1] which defends a physicalistic naturalism. Though highly condensed, this part will make clear what I mean by a "valuational theism" and show why such an approach to religion requires a difficult "normative valuational argument." In the next two parts, I shall take up some of the constructive issues posed by the necessity of the normative argument.

I

"Events of Grace" is basically an effort to wed existentialist interpretation to philosophical naturalism. If Rudolf Bultmann and Fritz Buri are really correct that faith is an existential self-understanding such that *every*, literally *every*, legitimate theological notion receives its content exhaustively from a mode of human being in the world, then in principle Christian theology ought to be neutral as between physicalism, naturalism, or any other conception of the world. To be sure, there is a problem with the divine anchor of the Christian self-understanding. How can "God" and "God's gracious action" be existential modes of being?

Wieman's naturalist conception of God, I argue, provides an answer to this question. Part of this comes simply from Wieman's naturalism whereby "God" is "a term used to designate that Something upon which human life is most dependent for its security, welfare and increasing abundance,"[2] combined with his empiricist

[1]John Post, *The Faces of Existence: An Essay in Nonreductive Metaphysics* (Ithaca: Cornell University Press, 1987).

[2]Henry Nelson Wieman, *Religious Experience and Scientific Method* (repr. Carbondale:

agnosticism about our ability, even our need, to determine anything about any "transcendent" or "ultimate" attributes of this "Something." More important, however, is Wieman's mature development of this idea as "creativity" or the "creative event." I attempt to show that "the creative event" is best conceived as "creative transformation," whereby "God" becomes that reality upon which we are dependent to do for us what we cannot do for ourselves. "Creative transformation" is then very close to the existentialist notion of God's nonobjectivity, for God, in both Wieman and existentialist thought, can only be known in the transformative events by which God is active upon us.

Creative transformation so construed becomes equivalent to the grace of God if such transformation has the structure of a release from bondage: if it is, to quote Wieman, a "reversing of the order of domination in the life of man *from* domination of human concern by created good *over to* domination by creative good."[3] The question is whether it is possible to give an account of bondage to sin that is phenomenologically and hermeneutically neutral as to any theologically loaded terms. Through a very careful analysis of Bultmann's description of St. Paul's "life after the flesh" and "the life of faith," I show that such a phenomenological account is precisely what Bultmann's conception of sin amounts to. If I am correct, then a fully naturalist account of the movement from unfaith to faith is possible. In sum, I try to show that Wieman's incipient but never developed theology is best conceived under the method of existentialist interpretation, and then that the troublesome concepts of "God" and of "God's action" in Bultmann can be rendered naturalistically by Wieman's "creative transformation." On these terms, a strong yet fully naturalist conception of justification by faith is possible on naturalist terms. Faith becomes "readiness for transformation" where "readiness" itself is an event of transformation.[4] "Readiness for transformation" thereby has an identical structure to Bultmann's existentialist notion of faith as "openness to the future."[5] "God," "the love of God," and "the event of God's grace" articulate the transformative event of openness to the future, the content of which is trust in being through which the giftedness of life is itself received, always ever anew, as a gift.

John Post's physicalism provides the philosophical scaffolding for this theological argument. Post's work is important for two reasons. First, *The Faces of Existence* is a very broad-gauged defense of a naturalist and physicalist metaphysics in which most of the current issues in the philosophical literature are addressed in

---

Southern Illinois University Press, 1971; orig. 1926) 9.

[3]Henry Nelson Wieman, *The Source of Human Good* (Chicago: University of Chicago Press, 1946) 269.

[4]Cf., Charley D. Hardwick, "Faith in a Naturalist Theology: Henry Nelson Wieman and American Radical Empiricism," in *Religion and Philosophy in the United States of America*, 2 vols., ed. Peter Freese (Essen: Verlag der Blaue Eule, 1987) 1:379ff.

[5]Cf., Ibid., 384-85.

an extremely artful fashion. In this sense, Post simply provides a powerful and respectable philosophical framework for my argument. Second, his originality lies with his arguments in favor of an alternative physicalist ontology. Classically, physicalism has been taken to require term-term reductionism. Most philosophy today is fundamentally sympathetic to physicalism, but there are widespread doubts about the possibility of a coherent physicalism because of difficulties in conceiving the identity conditions thought necessary for reductionism. Post places physicalism on a different footing by arguing that term-term reductionism is unnecessary and that an ontological monism is achievable through what he terms a "physical determination relation." Physical *determination* is sufficient to achieve what reduction cannot. Physical determination can be shown to hold across different domains of discourse through "connective theories" and "bridge principles," the logic of which are well understood and fairly noncontroversial in the philosophy of science, and reduction is not required. Post's physicalism is attractive because the determination relation permits him to be noneliminative and extremely open to explanations and domains of discourse outside the physical sciences.

Physicalism is normally hostile to religion, and certainly to theism, because God as an ontologically absolute subject/person is not to be found in a physicalist inventory of what exists. Significantly, however, Post appeals for a potential renewal of a type of theism on physicalist terms through a valuational approach to religion. Such an approach is made possible by Post's argument that the determination relation permits physicalism to overcome the fact\value gap. The argument is intricate, but it hinges on accepting, as all value subjectivists seem to, what J. L. Mackie has termed "the argument from queerness," namely, that "objective values would have to be very queer sorts of things" because their relation to objective facts cannot be conceived intelligibly, hence the fact/value gap which reigns supreme in contemporary philosophy and theology.[6] From the queerness argument, it follows that subjectivism can be defeated in principle simply by showing that value objectivity can be coherently conceived, and this can be achieved with the physical determination of value. Physical determination permits us to claim that across any set of mutually conflicting moral values one and only one set of truth values is correct, and the correct one is determined by the world (rather than belief about what is morally correct, coherence, the longrun convergence of ideal inquirers, etc.).[7]

This argument for value objectivity now permits Post to make extremely interesting proposals in the philosophy of religion. One of the problems a naturalist philosophy of religion has always had is that "God exists" is false if "God" is taken to be the value of a variable, that is, is taken to be in the inventory of what exists. But "God exists" can be true, indeed objectively true, if "God exists" can be construed as a meta-assertion for articulating a "seeing-as" that expresses a set of

[6]Post, 254.

[7]Cf., Ibid., 256-67, 274-83.

values, a "complex valuational matrix," that is itself true. Now, what is significant is that Christianity existentially and naturalistically interpreted as I have argued is just such a valuational matrix, and Wieman's naturalist conception of God as creative transformation, suitably qualified, provides just the linkage to conceive "God exists" as a meta-assertion for expressing a complex valuational matrix. It makes possible, in other words, a "valuational theism" on the basis of a physicalist naturalism in which "God exists" is cognitively true.

At this point, however, Post poses a demanding constraint upon a valuational theism. With it we turn directly to the topic of this paper. Given the objectivity of valuational truth, the *truth* of "God exists" could only be established by a normative argument for the truth of the valuational matrix that "God exists" expresses. We can easily see, I think, the theological cogency of my argument for construing the claims of the Christian witness of faith since, apart from the extremity of its naturalism, this argument in favor of an existentialist interpretation stands directly within major strands of contemporary theological discussion. But how could we make the normative argument for the truth of such an existentially interpreted valuational matrix? This is the form of the truth question for a valuational theism, but it is not at all easy to see how such a normative argument could be constructed. Despite his sympathy for redeeming the truth of "God exists" within a physicalist ontology, Post is skeptical about any such argument succeeding.

Actually the normative argument breaks down into two different normative issues. We would have to show, first, "that the theistic values and form of life are indeed among the true ones." Then we would still have to show that such values require a "theistic complex of experiencing and seeing-as."[8] In the remainder of this paper I want to explore some of the issues involved in this two-stranded normative argument, and I want to do so by challenging the way Post formulates one important part of the argument. This issue concerns the second part of the argument, the necessity for a *theistic* seeing-as. I shall devote most of my attention to this question, but first let me make some brief comments about the first issue.

II

With Post we can agree that the only way to justify language about God from within an austere naturalism is to show that "ultimately its truth consists in or at least is based on the objective correctness of certain values and a way of life." Granted, according to the determinacy of value, that there is a fact of the matter "as regards values and forms of life," then, necessarily, there is "a fact of the matter as regards the kinds of seeing-as entailed by them," but "one would still have to argue that the theistic values and form of life are indeed among the true ones."[9] Now, I

---

[8]Ibid., 347.

[9]Ibid.

think it would be naive to think that this challenge posed by Post of showing the truth of a valuational matrix is anything but formidable. Furthermore, I believe that nobody knows how such a task might be addressed. Though the emergence of a one-world civilization is producing thinkers who are attempting to address such issues, our resources are still quite meager.

A first step is to make the obvious distinction between strictly moral values and values of a more comprehensive sort. So divided the problem would admit of three more modest justificatory issues. (1) We would have to justify the strictly moral values, something well within the purview of contemporary philosophical discussions. (2) There is the problem of justifying the valuational stance of a theistic seeing-as in its own right. (3) And finally we would have to justify that there is a relationship between the strictly moral values and the values of a theistic seeing-as. I suggest this threefold division because it seems evident to me, though I shall not defend it here, that moral values must receive their justification through reason alone, and this is a strictly philosophical undertaking.[10] It is also one that has been generally accepted among theologians since Kant's arguments that moral values cannot be grounded *directly* in God. This position, of course, leaves open the question whether religious values or other values of a more comprehensive sort may illumine, enrich, deepen, and perhaps even transvalue moral values grounded strictly in reason. Theologically, one can presume that they will since the Christian valuational stance entails a form of life. But an engagement with this issue would still presume a successful defense of the strictly religious or more comprehensive valuational stance itself.

Regarding this question about a more comprehensive valuational stance, it seems to me that the most important thing for the theologian to recognize, certainly at least the naturalist theologian, is that he or she is no more disadvantaged by the question, stands in exactly the same position, as the nontheist or nonreligious person. Once the question is posed about a wider valuational framework for our lives, it becomes evident that it simply cannot be addressed by moral considerations alone, so that every thinking human being will be confronted by more or less the same normative requirements—even if, as Post suspects, the theistic version of the normative argument is doomed.

These reflections now provide a clue concerning how a religious or theistic version of the argument might be made. Once we recognize the entirely general character of the problem, it becomes evident that any solution will involve a valuational matrix grounded in a broad conception of human being in the world. In the case of my own argument, for instance, the summary term for the Christian valuational stance is "openness to the future." Yet this conception and the way it

---

[10]This case has recently been made with unusual power in Jeffrey Reiman, *Justice and Modern Moral Philosophy* (New Haven CT: Yale University Press, 1989).

enables us to interpret "God exists" is deeply embedded in an account of human being in the world that involves bondage to a self-defeating order of living, what the theological tradition calls sin. This account, in turn, arises out of the theological tradition itself. In my case, for instance, it arises from the prophetic tradition, the critique of idolatry, the letters of St. Paul, and the works of Augustine, Luther, and Bultmann and Buri.

The point is that *any* defense of the normative status of a wider valuational matrix will require some such broad conception of human being in the world. Once this is recognized, the theological resources for addressing the normative question may suddenly appear refreshingly rich in contrast to the more or less impoverished resources of the nontheistic or nonreligious person. This is especially true if the resources of the theistic tradition can be exploited naturalistically as I have argued. In any case, I want to claim that a closer examination of the elements involved in Post's challenge make it appear less formidable for the valuational theist who is a naturalist than at first seemed to be true. Let me turn, then, to the second part of Post's challenge.

III

What precisely is the nature of the "requirement" involved in connecting the objective correctness of a valuational matrix to a theistic seeing-as? Post suggests that it must be quite tight. He assumes, that is, that if a valuational matrix and a form of life are constructed theistically, they will simply take up the language of the theistic tradition. This assumption emerges, for instance, in the following statement where he is proposing how the theologian might defend the necessity for a theistic seeing-as in reference to a normative conception of moral value: "A correct and sufficiently subtle morality requires a certain sort of 'seeing-as,' according to the theologian, a seeing-as that involves, among other things, seeing us and the world as created, for a purpose, by a loving and transcendent God."[11] The problem is that these formulations block any direct critical reflection on the theistic terms of a theistic seeing-as. As naturalists, we want to know precisely what all the crucial terms in "seeing us and the world as *created*, for a *purpose*, by a *loving* and *transcendent God*" mean. Questions about such terms are especially demanded by the method of existentialist interpretation, for I have argued that all such terms must be translated into structures of human existence. Furthermore, existentialist interpretations of at least some of these and related terms are already widely accepted in contemporary theology by antinaturalist theologians, even when they do not accept the rigorous and thoroughgoing existentialist method upon which I insist. So, it cannot be that we must merely appropriate and defend a theistic seeing-as. We must also give attention to precisely what makes such a seeing-as theistic as such,

[11]Post, 344.

and this requires a more critical and revisionary approach to what the content of a theistic seeing-as is than Post envisions.

The way to focus this issue is to see that a fully naturalist theology requires us actually to rethink the very question to which the religious response is an answer. This is because a naturalist theology qualifies or even eliminates many of the ontological terms of absoluteness and ultimacy which traditional theism, both classical and revisionary, has assumed were necessary to anchor the language of faith. In this sense, it amounts to a radical revision of what "God" means in human life. I believe that Wieman should be seen as engaged in just this enterprise. He is not merely redefining God by the source of human good but, in effect, trying to recast the entire religious question to which God is an answer. Thus, the plausibility of a significant number of my proposals depends upon a willingness sympathetically and imaginatively to entertain a revisionary reflection on this question.

It is true that many of the ontological references theologians have wanted to make are compromised by this effort. But the day is very late for Western theism, and those references are already deeply compromised anyway. Furthermore, the method of existentialist interpretation is widely accepted among theologians today, such that much of the "ultimacy" language of the witness of faith is already best understood existentially and thus valuationally, not ontologically or cosmologically. Even Ogden agrees with much of this, as is evident in his interpretation of the language of creation, which, whatever else he takes it to mean, has a strong existential footing and is certainly not what a great deal of the tradition meant.[12]

Once one sympathetically embarks on rethinking the religious question itself, then it is quite significant that a valuational theism readmits much from traditional theology but from a different angle of vision. Take, for instance, the conception of religion itself. It is widely assumed that the question of religion requires answers that place our lives against the widest ontological and metaphysical background, and this is often the way the issue of "ultimacy" in religion is construed. This would certainly be the case with Tillich's definition of religion as ultimate concern, perhaps the most influential conception of this sort in recent theology, for despite the existential force Tillich gives ultimacy, he also means that an authentic ultimate concern must concern what is genuinely ontologically ultimate.[13] Distinguishing between "faith" and "religion," Ogden has been extremely helpful with this issue because this distinction permits him more clearly to root the issues at the level of an existentialist interpretation. Thus, by "faith" he means the ultimate confidence in the worth of life that all human beings express understandingly in their existence. By conceiving the "religious" issue as a question of faith in this sense, he is able to distinguish between authentic and inauthentic forms of faith. "Religion," in

[12]Cf., e.g., Schubert M. Ogden, *The Reality of God* (New York: Harper, 1963) 178-79.

[13]Cf., Paul Tillich, *The Dynamics of Faith* (New York: Harper and Row, 1957) 8-12.

contrast, he understands as one form of culture among others by which this basic faith, presupposed by all cultural forms, seeks expression in beliefs, ritual, and forms of social organization. At the same time, however, Ogden never doubts that the sole adequate expressions of this "basic faith" must be conceived in terms of "the ultimate nature of reality as it presents itself to that faith."[14]

The entrenched character of such assumptions about religion militate against the possibility of a naturalist theology from the outset, for, from the perspective of naturalism, the ultimate *ontological* unifiers probably do not support the values religious affirmations otherwise express. But note that, apart from their ontological ground, those religious issues are entirely valuational in character, as Ogden's distinction between "faith" and "religion" has the merit of identifying. If we change the angle of vision from which we ask what the religious question is and cease simply assuming that it can only be satisfied by a universal and ultimate ontological ground, then the questions of ultimacy return in valuational dress. This is the virtue of Wieman's attempt to understand God valuationally in terms of the source of human good. The religious question becomes the valuational question of the direction of a final devotion or loyalty. Since it admits of being interpreted in terms of an existential self-understanding, it also may be rephrased exactly in terms of Ogden's conception of faith, but it does not beg the question about what satisfies our ultimate confidence in the worth of life.[15]

Admittedly, some of the human needs by which religion has been understood for the last two millennia may be disappointed by such a change in angle of vision, but it is also evident that such changes are by no means uncommon in the history of religion and account for some of its most profound alterations, as is made evident, for instance, by Santayana's distinction between "natural" and "ultimate" religion or Bergson's between "static" and "dynamic."[16] After all, Christianity's naming Jesus the Messiah was itself just such an alteration in the question a "Messiah" was taken to answer. All that is required is a willingness to entertain the question with a sympathetic imagination (along with an admixture of the courage that high religion has always required). And as I mentioned earlier, the day is late for Western theism.

---

[14]For this entire discussion of Ogden, cf., "The Reality of God," in Ogden, *The Reality of God*, 21-43, and "On Religion," unpublished, mimeograph version of a paper presented to the Dartmouth College seminar on "Religion, Myth, and Reason," 2-4 May 1972. The last quotation is from the latter, 2.

[15]Cf., Charley D. Hardwick, "Theological Naturalism and the Nature of Religion: On Not Begging the Question," *ZYGON: Journal of Science and Religion* 22/1 (March 1987): 21-36.

[16]Cf., George Santayana, "Natural and Ultimate Religion" in his *The Birth of Reason and Other Essays*, ed. Daniel Cory (New York: Columbia University Press, 1968) 67-70; and Henri Bergson, *The Two Sources of Religion and Morality*, tran. R. Ashley Audra and Cloudesley Brereton (New York: Holt and Company, 1935).

Another such alteration concerns the predicates of absoluteness that are applied to divinity but are eliminated by an austere naturalism. They reappear in a valuational theism, but from a changed angle of vision. Wieman's argument for the "absoluteness" of the creative event is a case in point.[17] This argument has been almost entirely neglected by students of Wieman, perhaps because it has seemed artificial, more a "term of art," developed against the background of classical theism, than something integral to his position. But when Wieman's thought is viewed as an attempt to redefine the religious question itself, then this argument becomes much more relevant.

The claim is that God, creative good, is absolute good. The argument depends on transforming absoluteness from an ontological to a valuational concept. In this sense, absoluteness means that the creative event is good "under all conditions and circumstances." Its goodness is not relative to time or place or to human need, desire or belief. It "remains changelessly and identically the same . . . so far as concerns its goodness." It would continue as good even if human beings ceased to exist, and it remains good even when it "runs counter to all human desire." Yet it is also good "when desired and when working in the medium of human existence." A second mark is that it is unqualified good. From every standpoint, its goodness remains unchanged and self-identical, unlike created good for which there is always some standpoint from which its value can be qualified.

Three final features are more specifically religious and bring God's absoluteness close to the Bible's "living God of history," as this is especially qualified by the Biblical critique of idolatry. Thus, the third mark is that demands of the creative event are unlimited. Its goodness is absolute because "it is always good to give myself, all that I am and all that I desire, all that I possess and all that is dear to me, into its control to be transformed in any way that it may require." Closely related, fourth, is the infinite value of creative good. "Its worth is incommensurable by any finite quantity of created good," for "the created good of the past sinks into oblivion when not continuously revitalized by the recurrent working of the creative event." It is also, fifth, entirely trustworthy. "We can be sure that the outcome of its working will always be the best possible under the conditions, even when it may seem to us otherwise."[18]

These last three features become especially helpful, I believe, in clarifying how an existential interpretation of Wieman's transformative event as openness to the future is to be understood theistically. Openness to the future is itself indeterminate as to value. But when openness to the future is interpreted as God in reference to God's transformative gracious action and, thus, understood as readiness for transformation, then readiness for transformation can be understood valuationally in terms of the absoluteness of God's goodness. Openness to the future, readiness for

---

[17]Cf., Wieman, *Source*, 79-82.

[18]Ibid., 80-81.

transformation, is the formal valuational structure appropriate to the absoluteness of God's goodness. The absoluteness of God's goodness thereby permits us to shift our angle of vision and understand trust in being valuationally, not ontologically. In Ogden's terms, our basic faith in the worth of life is made normatively transparent by the absoluteness of God's goodness. Furthermore, again in the terms of Ogden's analysis, our need for *reassurance* about this basic confidence, which the symbolic expressions of religion serve and which are the object of normative theological reflection,[19] are also addressed by Wieman's conception of God's absoluteness, though from an altered, valuational angle of vision, and thus much differently than Ogden would have it. It is evident, for instance, that Wieman's argument here can readily support Ogden's statement that "religious assertions can serve to reassure us only because they themselves are the re-presentation of a confidence somehow already present prior to their being made." But the changed angle of vision on what kind of question the religious question is is crucial. Otherwise we are straightaway driven into thinking that a naturalistic conception of things has no resources for addressing these most profound religious issues of human living.

A final example concerns the issue of monotheism. Wieman has been criticized for having an insufficiently determinate way of identifying the unity of God.[20] The implication is perhaps that Wieman's conception of God is henotheistic. The criticism is certainly well taken if the issue is understood ontologically. God for Wieman is *whatever* events or processes it is in nature that produce value, and he remained blithely unconcerned about their ontological identifiers. From the standpoint of physicalism, these processes seem certainly not to share an ontological unity since they are differently determined physically in different domains of nature and since at the level of intentional states and other emergent properties, the same states and properties can be determined by nonidentical physical states, especially by different brain states.[21] Thus, it would seem that in Wieman monotheism is compromised. But again, the angle of vision on what question religion addresses is crucial. Once we see that the question is a valuational one, then the problem disappears, for the question of God is the question of an absolute devotion. Valuationally considered, it has the same unity that monotheism has always affirmed, and existentially conceived, it permits an equally powerful criticism of the worship of false gods.

The purpose of these comments is to try to show, contra Post's suggestion, that a theistic seeing-as appropriate to a naturalistic theology must undertake a revision in the nature of theism itself. It cannot uncritically appropriate the traditional language of theism. Once such revision is justified, however, then a major barrier

---

[19]Cf., Ogden, "The Reality of God," 29-34.

[20]Cf., John B. Cobb, Jr., *God and the World* (Philadelphia: Westminster, 1969) 51-59.

[21]The latter, for instance, is a deep problem in neuro-physiology and the philosophical problem of mind.

is lowered for making the normative case for a theistic seeing-as in connection with a normative case for a particular valuational stance. Once the religious question is itself transformed, as it must be on naturalist grounds, then the normative defense of theism is quite similar to its defense on traditional grounds. A claim is advanced that theological statements are simply the appropriate way to render the normative valuational stance fully transparent. In this way Wieman's attempt to transform the religious question into a valuational one supports the argument in favor of a theistic seeing-as. The latter makes possible a cognitively strong theology on entirely naturalist terms. Though "God" is not in the *ontological* inventory of what exists—not really new for naturalists—"God exists" can be cognitively true because it expresses the truth of a valuational matrix, articulated as a seeing-as. If the Christian witness of faith may be appropriately interpreted existentially, then a new way is opened to conceive the cognitive *truth* of Christianity that is entirely consistent with an austere physicalistic naturalism.

's Naturalistic God

Tyron Inbody

Meland's thought about God is ironic. On the one hand, he says, "thinking about the meaning of God has occupied a major portion of my professional life."[1] On the other hand, he never provided an argument for the reality of God or a clearly formulated doctrine of God. The reason for his reticence is clear. The limitations of the human structure make any clarity and certainty about the ultimate mystery of existence impossible. The principle of limitation implies more than a methodological caution based on the disparity between language and reality. Uncertainty about "the nature of the affirmation" itself implies a "reverent skepticism accompanying belief" and causes him to "move very close to the skeptical attitude."[2] Yet he is "emboldened by some effort at a minimum designation of deity."[3] His focus is on "the fact of God" empirically located and described,[4] on what in the environing reality the term God points to, on how this reality works, and on the character of God.[5]

I. God as a Constructive Idea

Meland's empirical approach to God, however, should not be read as a naive assumption that the reality and character of God can simply be read off experience and nature. His empirical description of the reality and nature of God, like the empirical description of anything whatsoever, occurs within of a set of assumptions, images, and perspectives. What Meland offers is a description of what God means

---

[1]Bernard Meland, "In Response to Loomer," *American Journal of Theology & Philosophy* 5/2 and 3 (May and September 1984): 144. For two other essays on Meland's view of God, see Bernard Loomer, "Meland on God," ibid., 138-43; and Edgar Towne, "God and the Chicago School in the Theology of Bernard Meland," ibid. 10/1 (January 1989): 3-19.

[2]Bernard Meland, "Prolegomena to Inquiry into the Reality of God," *American Journal of Theology & Philosophy* 1/3 (September 1980): 77, 76.

[3]Ibid., 77.

[4]Meland, "In Response to Loomer," 144.

[5]"I have recoiled from trying to envisage or to define God in any complete, metaphysical, or ontological sense, preferring instead to confine attention to such empirical notions as the creative act of God and the redemptive work of God in history." Bernard Meland, *Fallible Forms and Symbols* (Philadelphia: Fortress Press, 1976) 151.

within a naturalistic framework. In his *American Philosophies of Religion* he identifies himself with the empirical theists who offer "a theistic interpretation of the universe along the empirical and naturalistic lines" of Ames, Dewey, Mathews, and Smith. "The key insight into this mode of thought lies in the idea that man has been produced by the natural universe, and that through healthful relations with its environing processes, he may fulfill his life."[6] The appeal is to what deity means as experienced in immediate awareness within a naturalistic perspective.

His is a constructivist idea of God in a dual sense. It is constructive in the sense that it moves beyond a strictly methodological preoccupation to an interpretation of the given realities within which the human structure exists. It is also constructive in the sense that God is a construct of the human imagination. In the latter sense his thinking is similar to the current interpretation of the idea of God among postliberals, historicists, and deconstructionists.[7] What is distinctive is that his constructivism is set within the perspective of empirical realism instead of neo-Kantian dualism. This orientation marks his as both similar and distinctive among contemporary imaginative and constructivist doctrines of God.

The similarity between empiricist and neo-Kantian constructivism is the common sense of mystery.[8] To the degree constructivists hold that the reference of the term God is something more than a construct of the mind, they offer a strong sense of the mystery within which the notion of God is set. However, most constructivism is based in a Continental neo-Kantian dualism in which the split between mind and mystery is thorough. Mystery remains remote, beyond the immediacies of experience. As a result the mind constructs an idea of God, but the dualistic assumption of the bifurcation between mind and reality locks out assurance of any correlation or even connection between the construct and reality. Mystery is something which supervenes the world, is cast like a shadow from beyond the world into this world, and so is itself a "reality" inaccessible to the mind. All we have access to is a construct of the mind. Although this claim about mystery is presumed to amount to more than a strict subjectivism, the assertion rests on the assumption which the framework cannot underwrite either empirically or rationally that somehow the supervening reality breaks into the world and provides some access to itself through the imagination.

---

[6]Henry Nelson Wieman and Bernard Meland, *American Philosophies of Religion* (Chicago: Willett, Clark & Company, 1936) 272.

[7]For one of the most thorough explorations of a constructivist concept of God, see the work of Gordon Kaufman. *An Essay on Theological Method* (Missoula: Scholars Press, 1975) chap. 2; *The Theological Imagination* (Philadelphia: Westminster Press, 1981) chaps. 1, 4, and 10; *Theology for a Nuclear Age* (Philadelphia: Westminster Press, 1985) chap. 2.

[8]Bernard Meland, "'Ultimate Mystery' and Structured Thought," *American Journal of Theology & Philosophy* 10/3 (September 1989): 153-57.

Meland, too, has a strong sense of how thoroughly any concept of God rests in ultimate mystery. However, the mystery of which he speaks is not a dualistic supervening reality but rather ultimacy within the immediacies of experience. This understanding of mystery, too, is a construction, a reading of reality within a certain interpretive framework. He recognizes "empirical realism as a metaphysical interpretation of human existence."[9] It is no more an objective, certain mirror of reality than neo-Kantian constructivism offers. However, since ultimate mystery is set within the framework of an empirical realism instead of neo-Kantian dualism, ultimate mystery as it traffics with immediate experience is given more empirical meaning.

Thus Meland's understanding of ultimate mystery and the notion of God combines both constructivism and realism. He moves beyond both subjectivism and objectivism in his notion of God. The imagination is free to construct subjective variations on the reality of God, and the concept of God is derived from and determined by environmental realities outside the subject. One might call his viewpoint a "constructive realism" or "soft realism." Any concept of God is a construct of the mind, but that concept, although it is not "read off" of experience directly and unambiguously, can nevertheless be shaped, revised, or even vetoed by the ultimate mystery of the environing realities in which we are set.

II. The Religious Meaning of the Concept of God

The most compelling evidence for how thoroughly Meland understands God as an imaginative construct is his claim that the primary meaning of the term God is religious, and that its religious meaning is its capacity to gather certain realities into an object of devotion. "God, as a religious concept, is a collective representation of certain sustaining relations having cosmic implications."[10]

There are two approaches to reality, the contemplative and synthetic, on the one hand, and the theoretical and analytic, on the other. The primary meaning of God rests in the former. God is primarily a religious notion for contemplation, not for reflection. It has to do with our adjustment and devotion to the forces which sustain us. Thus, God is primarily a synthetic concept.

In an early discussion with John Dewey, "Is God One or Many?" Meland claims that "the term God is essentially a religious or contemplative concept."[11] In worship the mind synthesizes the multiplicity of experience into a oneness and is devoted to that vision. To make a single object of devotion the many sustaining activities of the universe is to believe in God. Even though empirically experienced and analytically considered, the reality of God may not be One or a personality, the term God has its primary meaning as a synthetic concept and as an idealized and synthesized feature of the pluralistic reality of behaviors of the universe. Thus God

---

[9]Meland, *Fallible Forms and Symbols*, 123.

[10]Ibid., 176.

[11]Bernard Meland, "Is God One or Many?" *Christian Century* (31 May 1933): 725.

is "a collective term," meaning those important conditions upon which life depends. It is used primarily not as a theological term but for purposes of devotion and address.[12] God is a regulative notion synthesized by the religious person for religious purposes.

III. The Realistic Meaning of the Concept of God

Although the primary meaning of the term God is a collective term of devotion to the most important conditions upon which human life depends, the meaning of the term is not exhausted by purposes of devotional commitment. When the concern is about practical adjustment to these conditions and theoretical reflection upon them, the language of worship, including an unambiguous and confident use of the term God itself, must be set aside and in its place a more empirical language used. The method is clear.

> In reflective tasks, where the objective is avowedly that of discerning the empirical nature of sustaining reality; and in practical tasks, where the objective is that of adjusting to those empirical conditions of supreme importance, the preliminary method at least would seem to be analytic, and would therefore call for terms expressive of the empirical phenomena thus encountered.[13]

In his earliest writings it is clear that Meland shared the view of the early Chicago School that the function of the religious concept of God was adjustment to objective reality. Countering the themes of subjectivity and mentalism in liberalism, he says, "The distinctive religious dimension, then, is awareness and appreciation of reality. Religion is reality-centering."[14] This objective sense of reality of which he speaks is the larger environment which supports the human venture and prompts the creatural response of mystery and devotion.

The term God, then, also is an empirical concept. The term has some correspondence to the mystery and depth of the environment, and thus has some "realistic" reference as well. When viewed analytically, that is, in terms of the kind of language which seeks some margin of intelligibility within an empirical and naturalistic framework for understanding the world, not only does the singular focus and focused meaning of the term God dissipate; the meaning of the term becomes more vague and ambiguous than either traditional theism or the process-relational doctrines of God suggest.

When empirically approached from the point of view of what a rich view of experience offers and what a naturalistic construction of the world permits, God as an empirical and realistic concept refers to particular behaviors or structures of reality in the total environment that sustain us.

---

[12]Bernard Meland, *Modern Man's Worship* (New York: Harper, 1934) 171-74.

[13]Meland, "Is God One or Many?" 726.

[14]Meland, *Modern Man's Worship*, 185.

In his earliest discussion of the idea of God, which was primarily a critique of the christocentric description of the character of God in terms of personality, Meland argued that to understand the idea of God in terms of the analogy of personality overstates the case. The "cosmic reality" cannot be understood in terms of personality, for personality is itself an emergent synthesis so is not of absolute or even ultimate significance. The mystery cannot be reduced to a Oneness. Instead, all behaviors must be included in any concept of God. "The very assumption, in fact, that there is a single organic tendency at work in the universe which may be designated God, seems an over-simplification of the facts. . . . The richest reality may not be the One, but the Many."[15]

When approached empirically, then, the term God has a pluralistic meaning. Finally, he stands with Ames, Dewey, and Mathews, against Wieman, acknowledging pluralistic elements which, taken together, describe God.[16] The "certain sustaining relations having cosmic implications" are not One, simple, single, unified.

Empirically apprehended and reflectively comprehended their relations are pluralistic. Religious conception cannot reduce objective reality to an empirical Oneness. The full experienced reality vetoes any assumption that reality can be so conceived as one in any direct or indirect way. Instead of designating this activity as One or one aspect of this activity as God, as did Whitehead and Wieman, he opts for an explicit pluralism on the grounds of what is empirically required.

> It would seem to me, however, that these many sustaining activities, so important to life, attain synthesis in each individual event, person, or concreted object. These many activities so work together as to produce events in synthesis and to sustain them, just as associated activities in any system, organization, or institution work together to sustain the good of its members. But that *working together* in the cosmos cannot be abstracted as a single behavior and term God any more than the working together in organizations and institutions may be abstracted and termed the head of the system or the initiator of the system. The many activities come to synthesis in specific events, and there is this working together of the many activities which issue in the synthesis of the many; but the empirical character of these sustaining realities, when theoretically conceived or practically approached, is pluralistic, even though these pluralistic elements be correlated into harmonious operations. To state it simply, reality thus conceived gives the effect of a *community of activities*, rather than a single behavior.[17]

---

[15]Bernard Meland, "Toward a Valid View of God," *Harvard Theological Review* 24/3 (July 1931): 202-203.

[16]Wieman and Meland, *American Philosophies of Religion*, 274.

[17]Meland, *Modern Man's Worship*, 179.

God, then, designates "a reality in the creative process" bent on qualitative attainment, "winning the creative passage for qualitative emergence."[18] This reality, empirically described, is particular behaviors and structures within the creative passage. Earlier, when emphasizing the pluralistic character of the forces within the environment which produce and shape us, he speaks of God as a "community of behaviors," an efficacious complex of forces or powers within the natural world which produces whatever meaning emerges out of the sheer ongoingness of nature. In a later credo statement he speaks of God as "a structure of infinite goodness and incalculable power," and of "the transcendent structure of meaning which is beyond our comprehension" and says that "God stands to man as one structure of meaning stands to another."[19]

Meland's pluralism stands between Wieman's monism and Loomer's pantheism.[20] Unlike Wieman, he is unable to designate God as one behavior or structure.

> The very assumption, in fact, that there is a single, organic tendency at work in the universe which may be designated God, seems an over-simplification of the facts. The concern to reduce all spiritual reality to a Oneness, and to define this ultimate in terms of a single tendency or behavior, may of itself be misleading.[21]

The richest reality may not be the one but the many. On the other hand, he "will not make a devil out of God"[22] by identifying God with sheer ongoingness or creativity. By identifying God with the world instead of with behaviors or structures of sensitivity which have some correspondence to human interests, one has no basis on which to select devotion to or even to identify the good.

Meland's empirical realistic approach to God, also, stands between a strictly constructivist and a strictly objectivist interpretation of God. He does not treat deity either as an objective being which is singular or a subjective construct which is illusion. On the grounds of his wider theory that experience and language even though disparate nevertheless interpenetrate,[23] Meland insists, on the one hand, that the con-

---

[18]Bernard Meland, "The New Language in Religion," in *Bernard Meland, Essays in Constructive Theology*, ed. Perry LeFevre (Chicago: Exposition Press, 1988) 141; and *Faith and Culture* (London: George Allen & Unwin, 1955) 126.

[19]Ibid., 195-96.

[20]A critique of Loomer's pantheism in the light of Meland's thought will come later in this essay. For a critique of Wieman's monism in a similar light, see Tyron Inbody, "How Empirical Is Wieman's Theology?" *Zygon* 22/1 (March 1987): 49-56.

[21]Meland, "Toward a Valid View of God," 202-203.

[22]The phrase is Meland's, from a taped conversation between him and Loomer at a conference at Purdue University in October 1982 on "Bernard Meland and the Future of Theology."

[23]Nancy Frankenberry, *Religion and Radical Empiricism* (New York: SUNY Press, 1987) 136-44; William Dean, *History Making History* (New York: SUNY Press, 1988) 142; Tyron

cept of God is a linguistic construct both in the broad sense that it is a strictly functional or linguistic concept of devotion and in the narrower sense that all of experience, including realism, is interpretation from within a perspective. On the other hand, the surrounding mystery proffers behaviors and structures which veto certain constructs as abstractions or inadequate and suggest other constructs as worthy of pragmatic exploration. "The nexus of relationships that forms our existence is not projected; it is given. We do not create these relationships; we experience them."[24] Meland's view of God is as Bill Dean describes: "God, like any entity, is the creature of current interpretation; equally, God is historically creative just as any historical force is creative."[25] Meland himself is quite explicit about this dual movement of constructivism and realism. "From one angle, we might say that what the organismic philosopher designates God, namely the integrating process, is part and parcel of the very activities which are so integrated."[26]

As noted earlier, Meland's caution if not skepticism about the possibility of developing a doctrine of God causes him to focus most of his discussion on the character and operations instead of the existence of God.[27] Thus, one never finds an "argument for the reality of God" in the writings of Meland. Insofar as he ever approaches anything like an argument, it is from empirical evidence.

> Gushing out like a stream of turbulent water, is the brute process of creativity. It is without form and void. It is a ceaseless ongoing of coming into being and perishing, coming into being and perishing. Presumably this endless creativity could go on indefinitely as a formless void having no meaning, no purpose, no end in view; but it does no such thing. Instead, it issues in events of meaning, in beauty, in concrete objects with character and pattern, in cycles of history, in a drama of triumph and tragedy. Whence all this character and meaning rising from the formless void?[28]

This is an argument for God as the principle of concretion. Creativity itself is sheer brute process, coming into being and perishing. However, because of the ultimate solidarity of existence, existence has this character "because God, like a presence in every event of emergence, stands over the brute process with tenderness

---

Inbody, "Meland's Post-Liberal Empirical Method in Theology," in *God, Values, and Empiricism: Issues in Philosophical Theology*, ed. W. Creighton Peden and Larry E. Axel (Macon: Mercer University Press, 1989) 99-108.

[24]Meland, "How Is Culture a Source for Theology?" in *Essays in Constructive Theology*, 3.

[25]William Dean, "Pluralism and the Problem of God," in *God, Values, and Empiricism*, 49.

[26]Meland, *Modern Man's Worship*, 180.

[27]Meland, "Seeing God in Human Life," *Christian Century* 53 (April 1936): 491-93.

[28]Meland, *Seeds of Redemption* (New York: Macmillan, 1947) 59.

and patience, holding up to it all possibilities of meaning and value." One has to distinguish between what is brute force in creativity and what gives to creation meaning and character. God is that necessary gentle working. The empirical datum is the abundance of concrete good that is in each situation which is beyond each individual's perception and even apprehension.[29]

IV. God as a Designative Image

Instead of offering a doctrine or definition of God, Meland provides a series of images in his effort to point to what within the surrounding mystery of existing the term God designates. God is both an imaginative construct which focuses the religious devotion and a reality within the creative passage.[30] Since that reality is a mystery deeper than we can think, we can designate that structure only through images which suggest what within the creative passage the religious term designates. One can also trace the development of Meland's thought about God as a structure within his empirical realism by examining the primary images he uses to designate this structure.

In *Modern Man's Worship* the primary image is "sustaining process."[31] In *Write Your Own Ten Commandments*, the final chapter on "The Supreme Reality" designates this sustaining activity as a Silent Process. He speaks of God as "a growth in our midst, a Silent Process making us what we are and shaping us into what we shall become."[32] In *American Philosophies of Religion*, this community of activities which sustains and promotes human life is designated as "a Creative Order in the universe." "Wholly apart from its wider implications, it is clear that it fulfills human ends. This Creative Order, the mystical naturalist calls God."[33]

Clearly, however, the predominant two images are "the sensitive nature within nature" and "depth and ultimacy within the creative passage." The former of these

---

[29]Ibid, 51, 53, 57, 59; also *Faith and Culture*, 180.

[30]A similar argument has been made by Gordon Kaufman. In his earlier writing about God as a constructive idea, the term *God* was discussed almost exclusively as a "regulative concept" analogous to "world" or other strictly Kantian metaphysical ideas. In his most recent writings, the term comes close to referring to (at least certain) cosmic forces at work within the evolutionary process for relativizing and humanizing purposes. See, e.g., *Theology for a Nuclear Age*, 35, 37, 42-44. He even speaks of his emerging concept of God as "conceived in this narrowly naturalistic way," 40.

[31]Meland, *Modern Man's Worship*, chap. 12. There also appear here images such as "wealth of sustaining activities and relationships," "the portion which is sustaining," "many sustaining activities," "those most important conditions upon which life depends," "sustaining reality," "the system of progressive integration," and "the integrating system."

[32]Meland, *Write Your Own Ten Commandments* (Chicago: Willett, Clark & Company, 1938) 140.

[33]Wieman and Meland, *American Philosophies of Religion*, 294. See also "Seeing God in Human Life," where "Silent Process" and "Silent Force" are used, p. 491.

two dominant images appeared when emergent evolution, the new physics, and organismic thinking forced his reconception of nature.[34] The new cosmology provided a new set of imagery for thinking about God.

The significance of the cosmology for his image of God is most apparent in *Seeds of Redemption*.

> The distinctive turn of the new metaphysics lies in the fact that it has distinguished between that which is brute force in creativity and that which gives to creation meaning and character, a gentle working that is the redemptive influence upon force. This is the thesis we return to again and again, which gives metaphysical ground for the assertion that a situation is right, religiously right, only when force and process yield to the shaping of a sensitive working which can issue in meaning and character.[35]

Creativity as sheer ongoingness, as brute force, is modified by a structure of sensitivity within nature. In *The Realities of Faith* he speaks of "a matrix of sensitivity in which all life is cast."[36] What this sensitive nature within nature reaches for is qualitative attainment.

> Creativity is, on the one hand, the tragic process of dissolution. It is made good only as its perishings are transmuted into meaningful events. . . . On the other hand, bare Creativity is advance into novelty. . . . Creativeness, or the creative act, issuing in event, implies turning the reproductive process toward meaningful ends by transmitting to each event the burden of actuality, which is to make it, in some sense, the bearer of attained value. God is on the side of qualitative attainment, pressing its demands upon the impulse toward novelty.[37]

Sensitivity rather than mind or will is a better designation for God, for what gives significance to mind is precisely its capacity for sensitiveness.[38] The sensitive nature within nature is the ultimate efficacy. Countering Loomer's dissociation of sensitivity from causal efficacy and his implication that sensitivity is weakness and impotence, lacking efficacy, Meland stresses that sensitivity is a mode of being attentive and that caring is a form of efficacy within nature.

Following his arrival at the Divinity School at the University of Chicago, Meland broadened his images of God. He added the notion of depth and ultimacy

---

[34]Meland, "In Response to Loomer," 145.

[35]Meland, *Seeds of Redemption*, 57.

[36]Bernard Meland, *The Realities of Faith* (New York: Oxford University Press, 1962) 184.

[37]Meland, *Faith and Culture*, 105-106.

[38]Meland, *Seeds of Redemption*, 60.

within the Creative Passage as the proper designation.[39] The context for the talk about the sensitive nature within nature became Ultimacy as a Creative Passage within which our immediacies transpire. Creative Passage is Meland's term for being. It is his term for envisioning ultimate reality processively and for expressing the depth and ultimacy that pervade and sustain every moment of our immediacies. "On its subjective side I see existence as a stream of experience; in its objective aspect, as a Creative Passage."[40] The term Creative Passage talks about both being and becoming in their interplay. It is the most fundamental characterization of existence. Although he does not identify God and the Creative Passage, he did "come to see the reality of God as being of a piece with the Creative Passage."[41] So designated, God is the ultimacy efficacy within relationships. This sensitive working and efficacy inheres in the creative passage.[42]

V. The Ambiguity of God

Toward the end of his career the theme of dissonance or ambiguity within the creative passage and thus within God began to appear more prominently. "It has become increasingly insistent in my own reflections during recent years that the creative matrix itself inclines to suggest that coherence, taken by itself or comprehensively, tends to be a false motif."[43] The creative matrix is ambiguous.

Part of the problem in understanding the subtlety of Meland's concept of God focuses on his use of the term *ambiguity* in relation to God. The term itself can mean either conceptual imprecision or conflict within and between commitments. Clearly God is an ambiguous idea in the former sense. The issue in understanding Meland is the use of the term *ambiguity* in the moral and aesthetic sense.

Here again Meland stands between Wieman and Loomer. He rejects, on the ground of empirical evidence, Wieman's devotion to a structure or behavior of singular goodness abstracted from the rich range of sustaining behaviors or structures in experience within the creative passage. On the other hand, he is not about to worship nature or to make a devil out of God, as Loomer's pantheism permits by

---

[39]Meland, "In Response to Loomer," 151. "The path in between has been to broaden the base of inquiry by viewing the dimension of ultimacy not simply as being terminal, nor exclusively as a dimension of depth in the sense of earlier conceptions of immanence, but as being processively present and immediately operative within our immediacies as a Creative Passage. Within that broader conceptualization of a processive depth of ultimacy, I have envisioned the impelling efficacy of a Sensitive Nature within Nature effecting its qualitative attainments."

[40]Meland, "How Is Culture a Source for Theology?" 2.

[41]Ibid., 3.

[42]Meland, *Fallible Forms and Symbols*, 151.

[43]Ibid., 65.

making nature in the widest range of its creative power God. In one of his earliest book he wrote,

> To those who are not committed to an either-or doctrine—either a perfect world, or a chaos of demonic intent—this growth of the ages gives evidence of an emerging organic reality; not inevitable and omnipotent, but persistent and potent, as mighty as the growth of the fields and of the higher creatures of the earth; a Silent Process of unfathomable scope and possibility, shaping the course of our days in so far as we are able to yield intelligently and effectively to its shaping.[44]

Because God is of a piece with the creative passage, the reality of God is ambiguous to the extent that the creative passage is itself rugged and hazardous. This means the power of God is tragic. "We do not understand this silent working of a creative God in our midst if we think of it as wholly beneficent. Growth involves destruction if it is to be creative."[45] Growth as the creative advance of life means also suffering. Indeed, in a footnote reminiscent of much scripture, of some themes in classical theism, and of Gordon Kaufman's discussion of the complexity of the love of God in his essay in this volume,[46] Meland rejects the notion of the evil God but advances the notion of the ambiguous God, if ambiguity be defined as a power which is more complex in moral and aesthetic character than singular goodness or singular unity abstracted from the richness of the creative passage. Referring to these counterthemes, Meland says, "These reveal sensitiveness that knows wrath and justice as well; but the wrath of a patient, long suffering deity differs from the ruthless deity revealing its power."[47]

This does not make God evil, nor does it make ambiguity something to be celebrated or worshipped. Meland accepts the naturalistic theists' point that the term *ambiguity* as applied to God can only assume the term *God* has meaning with reference to human interests, for nature is not ambiguous in itself but only from the point of view of the commitment to the human good.[48] Nor does ambiguity require pessimism. "Religious pessimism, in short, is not simply required by the fact that there may be no omnipotent, unambiguous, extrahistorical, and evil-eradicating historical

---

[44]Meland, *Write Your Own Ten Commandments*, 143.

[45]Meland, *Seeds of Redemption*, 63. See also "The Tragic Sense of Life," *Religion in Life* (1941): 212-22; and "The Breaking of Forms in the Interest of Importance," *Criterion* (Winter 1971): 4-11.

[46]Kaufman, "Empirical Realism in Theology: An Examination of Some Themes in Meland and Loomer," below, in this volume.

[47]Ibid., 147.

[48]Marvin Shaw, "The Romantic Love of Evil: Loomer's Proposal of a Reorientation in Religious Naturalism," *American Journal of Theology & Philosophy* 10/1 (January 1989): 40.

process."[49] Ambiguity does permit religious devotion to what increases the surplusage of good in existence.

But God is implicated in the ambiguity of the creative passage in the sense that God as the structure of sensitivity within the creative passage is interdependent, and so shaped and limited by the creative passage. Meland's idea of God, then, is closer to the concrete complexity of the historical creativity and love of God in scripture than to the monopolar unity of God and the singular goodness of God which speculative metaphysics has ascribed to God as a cosmic individual or as a discrete entity or transcendental force. This means that tragedy and ambiguity stand at the very heart of God as well. This tragedy is not what we worship. Religious and ethical commitment should not be given to the ambiguous whole but to sustaining concrete behaviors or structures within the creative passage. Meland is a naturalistic theist in the sense that we are devoted to what increases meaning. But any empirical accounting of the meaning of the term God requires that the situation within God is more ambiguous than most theisms admit.

VI. Evaluation

Meland is a theist in the sense that the human imagination does not create the latent possibilities of value but discovers them, and human effort does not contrive the relevance of natural conditions but responds to them.[50] He is a naturalist both in the sense that he hypothesizes no extrahistorical reality and that he assumes a naturalistic construction of experience. He is a *naturalistic theist* in distinction from a pantheist in that he sides with the priority of human interests instead of nature as a whole and with the ways human effort itself is undergirded by the grace of nature. In that fundamental sense, then, Meland's use of the term God is a term of selection and places him among such naturalistic theists as Ames, Mathews, and to some extent Wieman.

As a *naturalistic constructivist*, he carves out a place to stand between the fallacy of the extreme options of objectivity, where there is a permanent matrix or framework and God is an objective being or force to be discerned and described, and relativism, where there is no higher appeal than a language scheme and God is only a regulative notion of the imagination. His position may be described as "contextualism" or "weak realism," in which the human mind constructs reality but in which those constructions can be vetoed by nature. As William Dean describes his own contextualism, it is one in which the imagination "is both free to construct subjective variations and is derived from and determined by environmental possibilities outside the subject."[51] This viewpoint means that the religious person may have "a

[49]Dean, "Pluralism and the Problem of God," 51.

[50]Shaw, "The Romantic Love of Evil," 35.

[51]William Dean, *History Making History: The New Historicism in American Religious Thought* (Albany: SUNY Press, 1988) 142.

vague, indistinct, unclear, groping sort of empiricist apprehension"[52] of God as the Sensitive Nature within Nature and as the depth and ultimacy of the Creative Passage.

In order to evaluate the adequacy of his concept of God, one must evaluate it in relation to his basic purpose. His concern is not the logical necessity or irrefutable proof for the existence or reality of God. Nor is it clear knowledge of a transcendental absolute which casts its shadow upon finitude. Nor is his goal to salvage theism from the trilemma of evil. His primary interest is the religious life and whether, to what degree, and how its sensibilities can be supported and nurtured within a naturalistic vision of the surrounding environment.

The adequacy of his concept of God, then, is not its logical necessity, or conceptual coherence, or accurate description but its religious serviceability, namely, its capacity to enhance sensitivity and meaning within the mystery of our surrounding environment.[53] If one begins with a naturalistic vision of the world, with the assumption that reality and meaning are confined to the experienced world and not superimposed upon the experienced world from a more ultimate reality, then the truth in the term God must be measured by its success in increasing meaning within the confines of the experienced world. Meland's constructivist-realistic concept of God, it seems to me, better serves the religious needs than alternative concepts. His naturalistic God stands between Wieman's singular and undifferentiated goodness as an object of devotion and Loomer's undifferentiated power of nature. His more subtly constructed God seems both more adequate to account for the experienced complexities of the surrounding environment and to support the humanizing needs of religious sensibilities and practice.

---

[52]Ibid.

[53]For a similar argument about the religious criteria for evaluation, see David Conner, "A Functional-Empirical Approach to the 'Whitehead without God' Debate," included in this volume. See also Tyron Inbody, "Paul Tillich and Process Theology," *Theological Studies* 36/6 (September 1975): 472-92.

Mythic Logic: Theological Implications of a Melandean Epistemology

Jennifer G. Jesse

This essay is a proposal for constructive theological methods grounded in a Melandean epistemology. It is offered in an experimental spirit, seeking not a particular new kind of method or structure as much as an expansion of the ways in which we conceive our theology. Since Meland's method of inquiry is heuristic, an "existential groping" toward new ways to express the depths of creaturely experience theologically, his theory of knowledge is especially conducive to this project. It is the grace and subtle sensitivity of Meland's way of doing theology which makes it possible to conceive of genuinely new ways of thinking and speaking about God, humanity and creaturehood. His empirical realism engenders a construal of the divine reality and human existence which transcends—or rather, undermines—the reductive tendency of modernity toward oppositional thinking.

In our context, where theological dialogue has become not only desirable but vital, I am presuming our agreement that simple binary forms of logic are no longer sufficient for our need. And I suggest they never have been adequate to our experience. Admittedly, ways of thinking outside this cut-and-dry logic are much less manageable, as Meland would say. And as these twilight areas are the realm in which his thought comes into its own, I find it especially illuminating here. Meland presents a theory of knowledge which manifests one complex world of sense through distinct but interrelated modes of discernment. In this world, causality cannot be reduced to a natural/supernatural dualism, nor knowledge to a material/spiritual contrariety.

This essay is an investigation into the *variety* of logical patterns which can communicate our lived experience theologically. It also addresses the implications of this for the matter of authority in regard to religious expression. It is my intention: (1) briefly to summarize Meland's epistemology in the context of his empirical realism; (2) to discuss his epistemology by way of its construal of the relation between philosophy and theology, expression and experience, logos and mythos; (3) to suggest broader structural changes in the constructive enterprise implied by Meland's thought; and (4) to elucidate the understanding of the authority of religious expression that results.

I

Throughout Meland's work we find his concern about the relation between concrete experience and our aesthetic and rational expression of that experience. He notes the continuing displacement of myth by science and philosophy, and questions how we can attend adequately to the "unmanageable intimations of meaning" arising from the depths of experience (Meland 1987, 112).

Meland proposes two different modes of knowing: rational inquiry which strives toward definition and closure of meaning; and "appreciative awareness" which is by nature open-ended. Both are necessary to the enterprise of knowledge. For Meland, rational certainty is by no means the preeminent good. Nor is it to be considered supersessionist in relation to myth. We always can reach further into the depths of our elemental realities through appreciative awareness.

However, all cognitive expression—both rational and appreciative—is provisional when considered in view of the concrete depths of experience out of which those structures arise. The focal point of empirical realism as Meland articulates it is that we are in touch with a reality Other than creaturely, though it is expressible only in creaturely forms. There is no basis for dualism between the human and natural, or the human and divine reality, or even between subjective and objective knowledge. (If the object of one's knowledge is internal to one's subjective becoming, where can such a boundary be drawn?) In the depths of our immediacies we come face to face with ultimate reality. This perspective clearly transforms materialistic notions of knowledge.

II

It is this philosophy of empirical realism that informs Meland's theology. His view is that philosophy serves to make theology intelligible, and that it must do so in a way that does not profane religious experience, but "preserves a sense of dignity and restraint in our approach to what is holy" (Meland 1976, 168).

This method offers "a margin of intelligibility"[1] by illumining one's witness of faith without confining all its meaning to any particular rational framework. Keeping in mind the limitations of our creatural stance, a discrete distance must be maintained between what can be thought, what can be experienced, and the source or real referent of our experience. The theologian is to avail herself of the philosophical system as analogy only, as a thesaurus or lexicon, and to be aware that she speaks only within the limits of that provisional system. But theology cannot stop

---

[1]The "margin of intelligibility" connotes both the marginal status of intelligibility within the context of lived experience, and that Margin of experience itself which lies beyond intelligibility: "Intelligibility is marginal to the vast fringe of existing meaning, just as the fringe of consciousness will always appear marginal to what is clearly in focus" (Meland 1976, 115).

with philosophy: the theologian is compelled to reach beyond those bounds to address the witness of faith.

For Meland, though we live in the depths of the Creative Passage, only so much of that plenitude of experience can be translated into expression. Nevertheless, just as experience and expression are not discontinuous for Meland—"we live more deeply than we can think, but not beyond our awareness"—neither are mythic and rational forms of expression. Myth addresses the depths of existence "as being a horizon of data and efficacy *relevant to inquiry*; though it may be inaccessible or unmanageable within modes of inquiry prescribed by the various recognized disciplines" (Meland 1987, 118; my emphasis). Experientially concrete forms of awareness cannot be communicated at all outside of the logical structures of language and symbol; and rational forms of expression hold no inherent meaning outside of the mythic construal of experience within which they function.[2]

Meland further describes the difference between our experience of reality, and our understanding of that experience by saying "knowing always occurs within a context of unknowing" (Meland 1976, 115). He distinguishes between "mythos" as the deeper level of imaginatively projected patterns of meaning, and "logos," the conscious expression of as much of that meaning as the rational faculty can grasp. The wider experiential context of "unknowing" gives all expression a marginal character. And it gives rise, in Meland's thought, to a gradation of epistemological forms. We can conceive of "knowing" in different ways, and mythic forms penetrate deeper into experience than rational forms.

Meland portrays the relationship between mythos and logos as one of "alternation" and "correlation,"[3] suggesting the possibility of a less rationalistic alternative, exercising a logic of meetness, analogy or congruity. Nevertheless, alternation and correlation are both dialectical movements of thought, and never resolve completely into any ideal synthesis. For him, the abstract and the appreciative modes always remain both oppositional and correlative (Meland 1984a, 136). An experiential gap or margin remains between what most essentially is and our expression of it, and a procedural gap remains between our mythical and logical modes of expression. In such a creatural situation, where there may be an incalculable variety of connections within this gap, what could be more appropriate than the generating of a variety of logical models of construction?

I suggest this emphasis on correlation—as a variation of the notion of alternation[4]—involves a more integral interrelatedness between mythos and logos than Meland himself has been comfortable with addressing too explicitly. He continually focuses on the need for the logical structures of theology to become more sensitive

---

[2]See Meland 1976, 111. We might say, in Kantian fashion, that the mythos without logos is blind, and the logos without mythos is empty.

[3]See Meland 1953, 35, 125, and 179; 1976, 105; 1984d, 90-91.

[4]E.g., Meland, 1984a, 137.

to mythic forms of expression (e.g., Meland 1953, 96), yet he does not himself make any tangible proposals as to the effects of this on the shape of those logical structures themselves. He is concerned rather with the logos claiming too much for itself and usurping the place of the mythos. This falls into the realm of "mysticism" and as he understands it, this too often results in an illusory overreaching "which issues in definitive, cultic expressions," a closure different than the usual rationalistic kind, but nonetheless a closure (Meland 1984c, 114). Waiting for us in the Margin beyond intelligibility is a forgetfulness of our creatural stance, for Meland. In striving to name it, we forget that we cannot name it.

For now, I want to bracket his concern about mysticism and take the risk I believe is implied in his epistemology. As I see it, Meland's writing not only invites us to travel into the Margin, but commands it. We cannot name it, yet we must name it. We are driven ineluctably to name experience. (This paradox does not resolve itself but is an essential aspect of the efficacy, the perpetual motion, within our lived experience as Meland has conceived it.) If we refuse to enter the Margin, we transmogrify it into a Kantian limit-concept. We substitute positing for interpretation, ethical imperative for knowledge. This is just what Meland hopes to avoid—the separation of expression from experience. I wish to take up the logos and carry it further in the direction Meland has indicated, that is, into the deeper responsiveness of rational thought to mythic forms of awareness. All the while however, we must qualify our movements by the safeguard Meland has provided, which is a creatural awareness that all expression of our experience remains partial and provisional: we recognize that we are naming what remains unnameable.

What I am proposing from within this Margin is a correlational interaction of mythos and logos which generates an elemental mode of rationality conceived at a mythic or viscous level. I suggest that the structure of reason has become unnecessarily solidified in our conceptualization of it: the efficiency with which any one pattern of reasoning functions for us tends to preempt alternate patterns readily available in our experience, patterns which could offer us geniune choices in the ways we reason. In actuality, reason is itself a "structure of experience" in the Melandean sense, and partakes much more profoundly of the elemental processes of our existence than we have recognized.[5] What this yields is an imaginative reason, a mythic logic; which also could be called a reasonable imagination, i.e., a mythos with variously identifiable logical structures. This emphasizes reason's *formal* nature, its ability to generate a variety of logical systems, as well as its universal structure of criteria. That is, it judges the credibility of *any* system according to

---

[5]Meland himself makes overtures in this direction with his descriptions of reason in *Fallible Forms and Symbols*: "Logos implies the level of rationality *implicit in experience* which is available through an overt inquiry into conscious experience" (1976, 102-103, emphasis mine). Cf. 1976, 128, and *Higher Education and the Human Spirit* (Chicago: University of Chicago Press, 1953) 171-83.

internal criteria of coherence and consistency, and external criteria of relevance and appropriateness.

Again, rational forms can never be free of ambiguity. We must be aware of the tragic proclivities of reason and be constantly self-reflexive. I do not mean in any way to put aside Meland's warnings about the concupiscence of reason into claiming for itself a discrete "intellectual intuition," a concupiscence that is inevitable and irresistible. To dwell very long in this Margin is a profound risk, but this is where we find Meland. The whole of *Fallible Forms and Symbols* takes place there, on the narrow ledge between the Mystery of Existing and the Mystery of Not Existing. And in my experience of Meland, it is from the place of this risk that the redemption of reason comes. So while there are important qualifications about the necessary tensions between mythos and logos, there clearly is also a neo-Romantic intention of reconnecting, of correlating, these different dimensions of expression (Meland 1953, 211).

This is not to say there can be any exact parity of the two in Melandean thought. It is clear the mythos is prevenient. Reason can never arrive at any genuinely new knowledge without imagination. Creativity resides in imagination, in the mythic depths of our culture. But it is for reason to decide whether our imaginings are true or false, good or evil. Meland calls rationality to be a steward of the mythos. It can never account *for* the origin of mythic revelation—its own existence is partially conditioned by such revelation. But it must be enabled to take account accurately *of* revelation, to test it by the consistent criteria of its various systems of logic.

III

What are the implications of this epistemological insight about the essential interrelatedness of mythic and rational expression for constructive theology? One implication is the possibility of an internal relatedness between these modes of expression in the very method and shape of theology—for example, the replacement of rationalistic coherence with a metaphoric or symbolic logic.

To speak of a poetic principle as "logic" is confusing because it has a different quality than the usual discursive connotations of the word. Reason always must operate in a logical fashion, but a poetic logic would be characterized by the mode of relatedness that inheres in the world which the poetic image forms.[6] I am using the word logic formally as "order," and am maintaining that reasoned inquiry can embody different forms or styles of logic.

---

[6]"The kind of intelligibility that is sought is one that coheres with the internal ordering of experience" (1976, 115). For Meland, experience does not wait upon rationality to give it order: "Structure is somehow given in the reality experienced" (1976, 111). Its apprehension is what needs clarification (1976, 111).

In his book *The Burning Fountain*, Philip Wheelwright describes alternate styles of logic by distinguishing between literal or "steno-language," and "expressive" or "depth" language pertaining to poetic, mythic and religious statements. He identifies ways in which we may allow our language to be more sensitive to experience by recognizing the characteristic "traits" of expressive language, such as referential congruity (an organic relation between signifier and referent); contextual variation (meaning that is flexible between shifting contexts); plurisignation; soft focus; and assertorial lightness (statements which, by consisting in associations of softly focused plurisigns, assert with varying degrees of weight).

Poetic logic should not be judged as irrational: "We cannot ask whether one type of language is *more* precise than the other, we can only try to understand and accept their different *kinds* of precision" (Wheelwright 1968, 88). The poetic or mythic system is likely to appear somewhat disorganized—unmanaged and unmanageable—if viewed condescendingly by philosophy. But it is a complete and harmonious organization of a different style. The system itself would not be built primarily upon unilinear and binary connections of rational thought (such as causality and temporality as we now think of them); it would be an holistic organic image, organized by imagination and explicated by reason. It is the recognition of truth-value in metaphorical language that enables coherence in theological thinking. It is this which empowers our theology to take account of our experiences of wonder that are so essential to the Melandean worldview. Whenever we imprison those experiences within a narrow logic, we can only distort them. We see the effects of this in the classic "problem" of evil, created by the logic of excluded middle: either (1) God must have caused what we experience as evil (or must have permitted it, which is the same thing for an omnipotent being); or (2) God could not have controlled it, which is to say God is not omnipotent. But if we allow ourselves to look into what has been excluded, we will be venturing into the Margin of intelligibility. (Indeed, if we do not venture in, we will be in danger of making the Margin itself into the middle we exclude, which would be a refusal of the Melandean project.)

What about, for instance, a causality of meetness or congruence, by which we could reasonably conceive of human suffering as of one piece with a loving God, without having to choose between the oppositions above? Might God even have caused this suffering and still be a loving God? Or might God not have caused this suffering but still be omnipotent? And if God is forgiving, may not God also be just? What happens when we conceive of God as forgiving because God is righteous, and not in spite of that righteousness?[7] The possibilities for a middle way

[7]Meland makes intimations in this direction when he suggests that the structures of gracious love and forgiveness transmute the logic of causality and morality (1953, 220-21).

become actual when we seriously consider how power, love and justice are experienced within alternate worldviews.

This is not to say that these alternate forms of logic will always seem completely coherent to us.[8] And it is not illegitimate in a Melandean view to resort to the argument that such things may simply be beyond our cognitive understanding: his theology relies on the belief that we do *not* understand, in articulate terms, *most* of reality *most* of the time. All we really need do is look to the cultural mythos out of which our theology rises to see how often the essence of the Christian message is expressed in paradox. When a rationalistic logic is permitted to throw out these poetic systems as contradictory, it is simply a distortion of the subject matter of its inquiry.

Finally, we could say that metaphor may be the only way language can apply accurately to God. To recognize metaphor as not only a primary but a secondary mode of language as well[9]—indeed sometimes the only mode of theological expression—*and* as having truth-value, raises the possibility of systems of coherence quite different from a strictly philosophic logic, systems constituted by the mythic disclosure of entirely new structures of meaning. That capacity to contain within itself complexity beyond rationalistic expression is descriptive of the Melandean mythos. The possibility of such mythic logic, operating according to the coherence of multidimensional images rather than binary ratios, could expand immeasurably the methods and styles of constructive theology and the expressive possibilities of its fallible forms.

If we give rein to this intimation of an internally related mythic logos as a form of theological discourse, one of the main questions with which we must contend is that of authority. Can metaphoric statements function authoritatively? What is the truth value of "fiction," if you will?

IV

This becomes the paramount issue for faith: is it true for us? What is the reality of imaginative constructs? I have chosen to define truth signification as an authority issue. While it can be approached in other ways philosophically and semiotically, I believe the matter of authority is most relevant to the theological issues at stake. It also is most appropriate to a Melandean epistemology because to approach

---

[8]"Coherence, taken by itself or comprehensively, tends to be a false motif; or at least a misleading one" (1976, 65; cf. 112, 198).

[9]Marjorie Suchocki also entertains this notion; metaphor "may be, oddly enough, both primary and secondary at the same time. . . . Its primary nature stems from the sense in which it is closer to the matrix, nearer to the ambiguity and complexity of raw experience. But its secondary nature comes from its possibly prior dependence upon the factual language of abstractive and creative use" (Suchocki 1984, 83).

authority theologically is to focus on matters of consent, trust, and meaning, rather than certitude.[10]

Religious authority is a difficult thing to analyze. It operates at the level of our deepest assumptions, conditioning the ways in which we perceive and experience the world. It is a mysterious thing arising out of the deep past of our lives, and far beyond us to the past of our communities. It arises both from our nature and our freedom. It can never be fully accounted for by our cognitive explanations. Yet we can acknowledge differences between the kinds of evidence by which it manifests itself—personal experience, the testimony of others, logical coherence, or consensus. All these, however, are qualified in regard to the worldview within which they are experienced. They are interpreted with varying weight depending on the cosmological system within which they are defined.[11] In other words, they are all relative to one's prior presumptions about reality.

Strictly speaking then, within human existence there is no possibility of an absolute authority. Authority as such does not exist independently of the experiencing subject. Thus, I am defining authority broadly in functional terms as the commanding of consent. It is a matter of meaning. It is not an external principle of truth, but the internal principle of truth-as-relevant, as trustworthy. It is essentially a matter of response—a conferral of authenticity—because the essence of its power is relational and consists in being *recognized* as such.

If religious authority is constituted by human receptivity, how are we to ground the authority of imaginative constructs? Where is the "objective" validity which evokes our consent?

Inherent in a Melandean ideology of organicism is the most fundamental ground of validity, the one mystical creaturely body of which we are all members. I find Meland's organicism to be essentially a Romantic concept of "individuality," meaning not isolated autonomy, but indivisibility. As members of this one universal individual, we are essentially interconnected. By sharing the same mystical body, we share the same objects, the same valuations, the same structures of perception. And since every entity is partly self-determining, there is objective valuation already inherent in our experience. This Creative Passage includes God, which is, again, the focal point of Meland's empirical realism: God is not only present in experience, but is the very condition of experiencing.

---

[10]Meland addresses the issue of truth in myth in chap. 7 of *Faith and Culture* and concludes that "truth as applied to myth or to the structure of experience can have only the force of intelligibility" (1953, 118). It is a presumption about as much of actuality as can be accomodated by the intellect.

[11]E.g., compare an idealist's and a materialist's valuation of their own thought experience. For one, ideas condition all other experience; for the other, their reality is highly contingent.

And yet, in spite of this essential unity, it is expressible only through creaturely means which can never do so adequately. We may be concretely united as one organism, but what about our historical existence which is ruled by a partial and selective consciousness? What about the mundane world in which we are constantly forced to adjudicate between paradoxical contraries? Given this, the Melandean theologian's logic must proceed symbolically. How else is the infinite whole to be presented in the finite particular? There always will be diversity in our knowledge of this one organic reality because every entity will reflect it synecdochally, in the guise of one unique aspect. And further, each will see every other reflection only partially, from a different perspective. This aspect of finitude is every bit as essential as the organic worldview which it characterizes.

The most graceful passages of Meland's theology arise from his profound sensitivity to human finitude. Mythic expression may reveal "eternal" truth, but it cannot do so flawlessly. It is inexorably affected by the finite, historical culture from which it has arisen and which it has itself partially created. We cannot pretend that we can have the mastery of, or infallible access to, anything which is so wholly beyond our world that it is untouched by the vicissitudes of human life. Just because the mythos is our closest connection to the ultimacies in our immediacies does not render it infallible. As a result, no particular imaginative system ever can be free of the risk of being wrong (which is why the place of reasonable inquiry is such an indispensable part of any responsible theological system). The bottom line of finitude, for the matter of authority, is that nowhere can we be certain—on any cognitive level, mythic or rational—that we are getting the straight scoop, the way it "really" is.

But as Meland continually reminds us—and as is appropriate to a mythic logic—the ambiguity within which any theological statement is framed does not invalidate its claim to ultimate significance. Just because it is fallible does not mean it is not able to grasp and communicate our redemption. What enables this significance is precisely its provisionality. Because *we* are always grounded in a specific time and place. Since we are defining authority as the commanding of consent, it is precisely that experiential realism (in virtue of its ambiguity) that *is* the authority of this perspective. It is through this quality of particularity that the ultimacies of our existence incarnate themselves in forms relevant to us.

This particularity of time and space is also the source of the dynamic quality of all human knowledge. It is our assurance of freedom and growth. What faith communicates now is empowered with ultimate significance, without having to—indeed, without being able to—carry the same weight once other relations and connections become part of one's awareness. Meland's empirical realism keeps us aware that there always exists more than we can think. There will always be a remainder, an anomaly, to our systems. And it is this which also keeps us aware of our creatural stance and of our proclivity for missing the mark.

By recognizing the fundamental ambiguity of both mythos and logos, a Melandean epistemology defines religious expression and belief as human, constituted not by infallible doctrines or transcendent truths, but by variable mythicological constructs within a changing cultural ethos. Consequently, religious authority is a matter of meaning, of truth-as-relevant, and as such, it remains a finite standard of judgment, yielding provisional norms, whether those norms are pragmatic, ethical, aesthetic, or dogmatic. It functions by a rhetoric of ambiguity which defines religious belief as "invincible surmise."[12] Here, where binary logic fails, plenary inspiration and the provisionality of belief are two dimensions of a single reality. At the experiential and mythic levels, there is undeniable confessional conviction. But at the level of theological expression, there is always a reasonable doubt which must never be denied its validity, though it must be denied absolute sovereignty. The mythic character of our faith claims us by the sheer power of its beauty and translucence. But the authority of faith lies partly in the reasonable credibility of testimony to its reality. Faith, while it need not be rationally discernible, must be reasonably defensible. Conversely, while reason cannot account *for* the origins of faith, it must be able to take account *of* faith, or neither will offer up any meaning for human existence.

This theological vision is not merely "idealistic." Nor is it cynical or fatalistic. It is painfully, empirically, realistic. It is our everyday life of hope in the midst of despair.

Reference List

Meland, Bernard E.

1953 *Faith and Culture*. Carbondale: Southern Illinois University Press.

1976 *Fallible Forms and Symbols*. Philadelphia: Fortress.

1984a "In Response to Frankenberry." *AJT&P* 5: 130-137.

1984b "In Response to Inbody." *AJT&P* 5: 72-79.

1984c "In Response to Miller." *AJT&P* 5: 107-116.

1984d "In Response to Suchocki." *AJT&P* 5: 89-95.

1987 "Myth as a Mode of Awareness and Intelligibility." *AJT&P* 8: 109-19.

Suchocki, Marjorie.

1984 "The Appeal to Ultimacy in Meland's Thought." *AJT&P* 5: 80-88.

Wheelwright, Philip

1968 *The Burning Fountain: A Study in the Language of Symbolism*. Bloomington: Indiana University Press.

[12]My source for this phrase is George Buttrick's *The Christian Fact and Modern Doubt* (New York: Scribner's, 1934).

Empirical Realism in Theology: An Examination of Some Themes in Meland and Loomer

Gordon D. Kaufman

Certain limitations of this paper should be brought to the reader's attention right at the outset. I am not attempting here to present a well-rounded interpretation of the wide-ranging and rich theological writings of either Bernard Meland or Bernard Loomer. My intentions are much more limited than that. I want to scrutinize carefully certain crucial texts in the work of these two men in which it appears to be held that a direct *empirical* grounding is available for theological reflection and that only such a grounding can make accessible to theology the *reality* with which it is (should be) concerned.[1] It shall be my contention in this paper that the arguments offered for these claims are faulty in various respects, that they are not persuasive as stated, and that they probably could not be reformulated in any way that would make them more convincing. It may be, moreover, that the failure of Loomer and Meland to notice the problems to which I shall call attention was itself due at least in part to their overly optimistic belief that some sort of "empirical" access to what is "ultimately real" is available to humans. If this is the case, then one would have to conclude that whatever else might be said about epistemological "realism" in theology, from a methodological point of view it is in important respects a counterproductive stance: the strong conviction that one is dealing with what is *really the case* can all too easily allow (or lead to) reification of the metaphors, images and concepts that seem to us most precious or important, that is,

---

[1]I shall be working almost entirely with texts drawn from Bernard Meland, *Fallible Forms and Symbols* (Philadelphia: Fortress Press, 1976), and Bernard Loomer, *The Size of God* (Macon GA: Mercer University Press, 1987). Hereafter these titles will be referred to as FFS and SG, respectively. This paper was written in response to a request that I prepare a critical analysis of these particular texts from my own methodological and theological perspective. Consequently, it is quite selective in the issues discussed, and (taken simply by itself) gives an unbalanced picture of the overall contents of these works and is far from presenting an adequate assessment of the theological work of these authors as a whole.

to our taking them as concrete *realities* rather than recognizing them to be the imaginative constructs which they in fact always are. Meland is more alert to these dangers than is Loomer, and he tends to be, therefore—at least on some occasions—more guarded in his claims. But at other times he slips into surprisingly unnuanced formulations. The rhetoric of "realism," it seems, may blind us to fallacies of "misplaced concreteness" in our work, rather than open our eyes to the limitations of our language and thought; it can thus diminish our powers to be rigorously self-critical with regard to our claims about matters of ultimate concern—a cardinal sin, I would say, for theologians.

My intention in this paper is to examine carefully certain of these (largely methodological) problems in the programs of "empirical theology" as developed by these two writers. This paper deals, therefore, with only a few relatively small—but important!—texts in the work of Meland and Loomer, and it does not pretend to give an overall assessment of their contributions to the contemporary theological conversation. I have the highest respect for the theological work of both of these men—if I did not, I would not be willing to engage it so intently at these points where I think there are serious problems—and I am in large agreement with the positions that they take on a number of major material theological issues, for example, respecting the complex interconnection of religion and culture, the thoroughly historical character of all human faith, the relational and processive character of all reality. In this paper, however, I have limited myself to identifying and discussing the points where I find myself most dubious about the theological program(s) in which they are engaged.

I

In the opening chapter of his book on *Fallible Forms and Symbols*, Bernard Meland argues that a wide consensus developed in the mid-twentieth century with respect to what he calls "The New Realism in Religious Inquiry." His survey of the most influential theological writers of the first half of the century—ranging from Barth, Tillich and the Niebuhrs to Wieman and other theologians influenced by Whitehead—reveals a consensus that rejects "the idealism that underlay liberal-modernist theology" and replaces it with a "clear sense of *otherness* beyond the human world" (FFS, 9).

> Despite dissimilarities between various modes of postliberal theology, stemming either from a phenomenological orientation of thought or from that of a process metaphysics, an underlying ground of new realism pervades them. . . . In both wings of the new realism ultimacy is seen to inhere in a ground of otherness to which man, in his subjectivity, relates himself. (FFS, 21)

I think in these pages Meland has correctly characterized the epistemic attitude expressed in much of the theological work of the middle third of the twentieth century. In view of that consensus it is not surprising that he felt he could quite properly take his own epistemological realism largely for granted as he pursued his theological work. We shall turn in a moment to some of the difficulties that followed from this somewhat uncritical assumption; before we do that, however, let us briefly call to mind three issues which *prima facie* might lead many theologians today to be somewhat wary of moving forward too quickly with this assumption of realism.

The first of these increasingly prominent issues to which I wish to call attention is our growing consciousness of the significance of religious pluralism. It is well known that the many religious traditions around the globe present very different pictures and conceptions of human being, of the world in which we humans live, and of the "ultimate" realities or powers with which we humans must come to terms. Serious consideration of the significance of this fact may force us to ask questions about the claims of these various traditions—including our own—to knowing what is *true* about *reality*. Perhaps such truth is not as straightforwardly available to us humans as we have supposed? Perhaps it is not available at all? Perhaps the very quest for such truth is based on misunderstandings? I am not arguing any of these points here, nor do I maintain that there is no way in which epistemological realists in religion can deal with them. I mention them only to point out that our growing consciousness of significant religious diversity on these matters suggests that it would be naive simply to take for granted that we are in direct epistemic touch with some sort of "religious reality" (what Meland, for example, refers to repeatedly as "ultimacy"). The problem of religious truth may well be much more complex than that sort of easy assumption suggests.[2]

The emergence of feminist theological reflection during the past two decades similarly poses hard questions for epistemological realism in theology. Feminist critics have argued that many of the most fundamental images and concepts of our western religious traditions—God (as lord and creator), the human self (as individual agent or ego), freedom and autonomy, rationality and truth, good and evil, history, ultimacy, power, life and death, maleness and femaleness, etc.—are sociocultural and linguistic constructions which patriarchal cultures have used to suppress and oppress women and to sustain patterns of order deemed desireable and proper by dominant male groups. In what respects and to what degree, then, are these symbols

---

[2]Loomer does not consider the question whether the diversity of religions opens up important issues for religious truth-claims; Meland, however, appears to be aware there may be some sort of problem here, but this does not significantly affect his basic epistemological realism. He seems to take for granted the reality of "a depth of ultimacy embracing all faiths and cultures, in which each of them participates with varying degrees of relevance and revelatory power" (FFS, 198; cf. 122ff., 155ff.); hence the principal question that religious pluralism poses for him epistemologically has to do with disagreements in *interpretation* of this "ultimacy," not with its reality. He seemingly never raises this latter issue, even though the very idea of this sort of "ultimacy" is not consistent with, e.g., Buddhist teaching—or, for that matter, with modern secularism and positivism.

also vehicles of *truth* about *reality*? Who is to say, and on what grounds can such judgments be made? Once again, I am not arguing here that there are no defensible answers to these sorts of questions; I am suggesting, however, that the issues they raise—when taken together with what we have been taught by Marx, Nietzsche and Freud, Foucault and Derrida, on the one hand, and by developments in the history and philosophy of science since the publication of Thomas Kuhn's work on *The Structure of Scientific Revolutions*,[3] on the other—are deep enough and disturbing enough to shake any easy confidence in the direct access of human experience and reflection to any sort of "ultimate reality." The closest and most careful scrutiny of all claims to truth in matters as broad and far-reaching as those considered in theology now seems, therefore, absolutely necessary.

An awareness of the difficulties about matters of truth in theology and religion is, of course, nothing new—and this brings me to the third point I want to make in this connection. From the time of Pseudo-Dionysius and before, apophatic theology has called into question all positive affirmations made of God; and from the Middle Ages on it has been emphasized that our knowledge of God is at best only analogical. God's reality and being have always been understood to be matters of profound mystery, going beyond human comprehension: at best, with regard to all such things, we can only look "through a glass, darkly" (1 Cor. 13:12 KJV). For many centuries virtually all theologians have known they were attempting to deal with questions at the very limits of human understanding. Most theologians, however—and this certainly includes both Meland and Loomer—have balanced their references to mystery with certain very definite claims about God (or "reality"), God's will for humankind, the nature and problems of human existence, and the like; so the emphasis on mystery did not seriously weaken their claims to genuine knowledge about "how things are."[4] In that respect, almost the entire theological tradition has been committed to epistemological realism. I suggest, however, that a too-easy commitment of this sort belies the acknowledgement that ultimately that of which theologians are attempting to speak is truly *mystery*. If we take this

---

[3]First published in 1962 (Chicago: University of Chicago Press). For a convenient summary of the new constructivism that has been developing in the philosophy of science, and some of its implications for theology, see Helmut Peukert, *Science, Action, and Fundamental Theology* (Cambridge MA: MIT Press, 1984). Many other related works could be cited. It is noteworthy, I think, that neither Meland nor Loomer seems aware of this work of Kuhn and others in the history and philosophy of science.

[4]Loomer and Meland express this consciousness of the limits of our experience and/or knowledge of God (or of Reality) in rather different ways. Loomer occasionally emphasizes the importance of the symbol of "mystery"; but he never really comes to terms with the radical questions which this concept puts before us (see below, 147ff.). Meland speaks freely of mystery (see, e.g., FFS, chaps. 4 and 5 on "the mystery of existing" and "the mystery of not existing," respectively), and sometimes his profound consciousness of mystery leads him to call into question any and all claims to certainty in either knowledge or faith (see, e.g., 134-42). On other occasions, however, his use of the concept of mystery seems to have the opposite effect: "the mystery of existing, as an inescapable depth and overtone of our understanding, intrudes a persisting horizon of awareness which somehow gives new dimension to understanding, itself, along with intimations of resources which cannot readily be dismissed or ignored wherever critical inquiry is ventured. . . . The mystery of existing, with its experiences of joy and sorrow, fulfillment or defeat, is the vivid empirical datum which evokes inquiry" (42, 44). Here the concept of mystery, instead of calling our knowledge about Reality radically into question, seems to have an epistemologically positive meaning.

acknowledgement seriously—as the two points made above (as well as others one might mention) suggest we must do today—then we dare not adopt a standpoint of epistemological realism without very careful scrutiny and argument. For "mystery"

> implies and requires an acknowledgement of our *unknowing* with respect to God, an acknowledgement, that is to say, that we do not know how the images and metaphors in terms of which we conceive God apply, since they are always our own metaphors and images, infected with our limitations, interests, and biases.[5]

We theologians face complex and daunting problems today. To come to terms with these issues, we shall have to be willing to put into question and carefully scrutinize some of our most cherished symbols and concepts, values and meanings, attitudes and approaches. Regularly reminding ourselves that, in the last analysis, we are seeking in theology to address ourselves to matters of the profoundest mystery, may help to keep us honest.

II

With these considerations in mind, let us turn now to an examination of the way in which Bernard Meland presents the "empirical" data to which he believes theologians should make themselves accountable. I will be able to examine only a few texts here; therefore, some of Meland's nuancing and qualifying of his assertions will necessarily be omitted. However, I think the texts at which we will be looking are representative of the main bearings of his thinking on the issues we will be considering.

There seems to me to be a deep tension in Meland's thinking between his commitment to epistemological realism, on the one hand, and his profound awareness of the powerful cultural shaping of all our experiencing and reflection, on the other. When he is arguing his realist and empiricist convictions, he often tends to emphasize what he calls

> the primal disparity between language and reality . . . [the] stark contrast between the language we use in attending the religious realities, of whatever faith, and the realities themselves. . . . since we live more deeply than we can think, no formulation of truth out of the language we use can be adequate for expressing what is really real, fully available, fully experienced, within this mystery of existing. (FFS, 23-24)

I want to call attention here to two claims made in this passage: (1) "Reality" and "language" are utterly distinct from each other. (2) The "really real" is directly and completely available to us in "experience," but it is only indirectly and incompletely represented or expressed in language; it is to experience, therefore—not our expressions in language—that we must turn in order to gain a significant relationship to what is real. Despite his repeated emphasis on human fallibility, Meland seems utterly convinced of this second point; fallibility apparently applies only to our symbols and concepts.

Each of these two points, in my view, needs to be much more carefully nuanced than they are here and in much of Meland's writing. "Lived experience"

---

[5]G. D. Kaufman, "Mystery, Critical Consciousness, and Faith," in *The Rationality of Religious Belief. Essays in Honour of Basil Mitchell*, ed. W. J. Abraham and S. W. Holtzer (Oxford: Clarendon Press, 1987) 67.

and "reality" are bracketed together closely in Meland's thought, but "language" is something essentially external to both. In fact, I shall argue, experience is largely structured by language, and the "reality" to which it gives us access, therefore, is never some sort of reality-in-itself-wholly-independent-of-language. (As we shall see, Meland sometimes also seems to take a position of this sort, but when he is discussing issues of epistemological realism, he does not bring these considerations into play.) Because Meland does not attend here as carefully as he should to the way in which experience is actually constituted by language, he fails to see how heavily dependent his own analysis of experience is on the particular words and concepts he uses. This leads to an unwitting reification of his own concepts—just the opposite of what he intends by his emphasis on "lived experience."

If we look closely at some further texts in this chapter of Meland's book, we shall see, I think, the kind of mistakes into which he is led by his consistent downplaying of the importance of language and thus his failure to see how it has affected his own work. No one, of course, will disagree with Meland in his claim that theology must not "understand itself to be . . . an enterprise of words for their own sake" (FFS, 27). Who, one wonders, would ever take such a position? This sort of rhetoric only serves to distract both Meland and his readers from attending to the actual role of language in experience and knowledge. But before I take that matter up directly, let me make it clear that I am not about to attack Meland's view of the importance of experience for theology. I do not want to take anything away from his basic claim that theology is

> a discipline in course with . . . lived experiences, sensitive to the depth of meaning they body forth in every moment of living; sobered and heightened, both with anxiety and anticipation by the very mystery of existing in which we are involved; and forever open to the intimations of reality as they come into focus through the structured thought we may tentatively formulate; through the sense of wonder and apprehension that may seize us when . . . we ponder the mystery of existing, the mystery of being and becoming. (FFS, 27)

From this thoughtful characterization of (certain major features of) the business and stance of theology, however, Meland goes on to sing the praises of experience in a quite uncritical and misleading way. "Reality," he says, "in all its vastness meets us in each and every succeeding present moment of lived experience" (ibid.). This is an amazing claim, one which is, in fact, hardly intelligible as it stands. Let us observe how heavily this apparently simple sentence about "lived experience" is actually directly informed by theory. The phrase, "reality in all its vastness," calls to mind for most of us, I would think, a universe millions of light years across and billions of years old. Do we "meet" anything like this "in each and every . . . moment of lived experience"? Our modern notion of "reality in all its vastness" is in fact an enormously complex construct of the scientific and philosophical imagination, put together—in the course of many generations of reflection, experimentation and theorizing—in *words*, *numbers*, and *equations*. Moreover, what we today mean by "reality in all its vastness" is something quite different from anything known or imagined—certainly anything directly experienced—before the twentieth century.

Meland's claim that all of this is present to us in every moment of experience is, I suspect, actually derived from Whitehead's conception of "actual occasions" (which are said to "prehend" their entire past); it certainly could not have been formulated simply on the basis of direct inspection of the "moments" of his own experience—that is, it is a product of twentieth-century theorizing. However *real* we may take the "reality" referred to here to be, it can hardly be something directly experienced; it can only be present to us *in concept*, that is, as represented in enormously complex configurations of words and other symbols. Our sense of the "realness" of this reality must be, then, connected more with our conviction of the validity and appropriateness of the concepts we are using than with the contents of our "lived experience" at particular moments. The sharp distinction which Meland has made between our words, on the one hand, and our "lived experience" of "reality," on the other, turns out to be much too simplistic. Our words and other symbols penetrate and form our actual experiencing in ways that Meland seldom acknowledges, and it is in and by means of these symbolical/experiential patterns, and reflection on them, that we construct *imaginatively* what we take to be reality (more about this last point as we proceed).

We cannot here engage in detailed analysis of all the passages in Meland's book which betray misleading oversimplifications of the sort to which I have just called attention, but I should like briefly to examine one more, a sentence in which he sums up his basic position: "reality," he says, "is in the immediacies of these lived experiences which are of a piece with and participate in dimensions of ultimacy within the Creative Passage" (FFS, 31). On the face of it, this seems straightforward enough: reality—indeed, the reality of "ultimacy"—is to be found directly given in the "immediacies" of "lived experiences." This suggests that "lived experiences" are something clearly and directly announcing themselves as such (cf. FFS, 54ff.), that their "immediacies" are evident to anyone who cares to look, and that within these immediacies "dimensions of ultimacy" which lie within "the Creative Passage" are clearly apparent. When we break the sentence down like this, however, it becomes clear that much more is going on here than a simple and direct "reading" of "experience." All of the key words in this passage—"reality," "immediacies," "lived experiences," "dimensions," "ultimacy," "Creative Passage"—are abstract, highly technical, philosophical terms, some of them peculiar to Meland's own thinking; *none of them name anything directly and immediately present in ordinary lived experience*, though Meland's way of expressing himself suggests that they all do. Probably none of these words would occur to any of us if we were asked to say what it is that we are experiencing just now. I am not claiming here that Meland's sentence has nothing to do with our experience, or with matters of ultimate importance to us humans. I am pointing out that it is composed of words that have been developed only on the basis of much sophisticated reflection over many generations, and that to the extent that we understand our experience in terms of these particular words, it is in fact *informed by them*—shaped by them in decisive ways, and interpreted through them. Our "lived experience" is, thus, not a pure-something-or-other which simply is-what-it-is, independent of and unaffected by the words and other symbolic patterns we use to understand and interpret it: *what* we experience at any given moment, the content we find in experience and the meaning we assign to it, is heavily shaped by the symbols we are using to focus our attention and to connect this present "lived experience" with wider reaches of our lives.

These symbolic patterns through which our experience comes to us are never "innocent," simply calling attention to "what is there." They have their meanings only in complex webs of relationship, contrast and comparison; so when they are used to identify and interpret for us items of experience, they do so by relating that item to a wide linguistic network in and through which each word's place—and thus its *meaning*—in our overall vocabulary is defined. This is true whether the word we are using in connection with our immediate experience is an ordinary one like "chair" (which has its meaning within a configuration that includes also "table," "furniture," "sitting," "writing," "eating," etc.) or a more unusual and technical term such as "ultimacy" (the understanding of which is tied to its connections with "last," "farthest," "conclusive," "most important," etc. and its contrast with "immediacy," "presentness," "commonplace," and the like). Our lived experience is in fact always a *construction* in which language plays a constitutive role; it is never a bare given from the fullness of which we create language by making impoverishing abstractions of various sorts. Meland's inattention to this (in his epistemological discussions) leads his texts to suggest that his theological and philosophical positions are justified by direct appeal to "experience," when in fact what we need to examine here is the pattern of *concepts* with the aid of which he is analyzing and interpreting experience. His actual interpretations are often very illuminating, but they are framed in a way that may seriously mislead us. It is certainly not as evident as Meland believes it to be that "lived experience" provides us with some kind of direct access to "reality."

Let us look a little further into the interconnections of language and lived experience. On the one hand, our words and other symbols are not, in fact, mere "empty" forms that have to be "filled" with experience in order to have meaning; they gain much of their meaning from their place within the wide symbolic network which imagination uses to connect this present moment of experience with our memories and dreams, our long forgotten experiences and our hopes, our intimations of value and fulfillment and our fears of suffering, failure and disaster. This whole symbolic network is brought—by the symbols and words that come to mind as we grasp an experience and its meaningfulness to us—into relationship with what is being experienced in each new moment. On the other hand, it is important to recognize that (in linguistically proficient human beings) there is no such thing as "raw experience," experience completely free of all symbolic and linguistic coloring and interpretation and thus the real locus of "realities" to which our words and symbols can only lamely and abstractly "point." It is a mistake, therefore—and one that can be seriously misleading—to regard theological work as grounded essentially in some sort of simple movement *beyond words* to the "lived experiences" within which the "realities" of theological interest can be directly apprehended. It is simply not true that "the grounds for awareness, common awareness, of the realities to which we seek to give recognition through language *precede our speaking*, our expressiveness through language" (FFS, 29, emphasis mine); language is in fact one of the principal grounds of our "common awareness"—as humans—of everything that we find to be of significant religious (and theological) import and meaning.[6]

III

It is somewhat puzzling that Meland made such a sharp distinction between language and experience in the first part of his book, since later he seems to admit (at least by implication) the interconnectedness which I am emphasizing here. The "mythos" of a culture, he says,

---

[6]This inescapable structuring of all experience by language—well known already to Hegel—is acknowledged today by many philosophers, psychologists, and others. It has been most thoroughly investigated and convincingly articulated in Ludwig Wittgenstein's later work; see especially *Philosophical Investigations* (Oxford: Blackwell, 1958).

> by its persistent shaping of the complex of feeling, along with other precognitive influences, generates a structured reality within experience in any given cultural history. The structure of experience is the most elemental level of meaning in any culture; this is so in contrast to the highly focused level disclosed in critical reflection and inquiry in which cognitive awareness is sharpened to its maximum degree. Yet it is also the most inclusive and, conceivably, mature, insofar as it bodies forth distillations from critical thought which have been assimilated to the lived experience of a community. . . . it is the distillation of all that has happened as actual event within the lived experience of a people. (FFS, 187)

In this quotation the "structured reality" that is available to us directly in lived experience is clearly not the underlying ontological structure of things, but rather the historical sedimentation of many generations of experience, reflective thought, and symbolization—what Meland is calling the "structure of experience." Our actual lived experiences always fall within the context of this historically developed structure of experience which, as "the most elemental level of meaning in any culture," gives them their basic symbolical patterning and meaning; and it is this deep structure, therefore, from which all reflective thought abstracts, on which it depends for its significance, and which it must ultimately illumine if it is to be sufficiently convincing to be taken as true.

This position seems to me much subtler than the one articulated in the earlier parts of Meland's book. It suggests that this deep "structure of experience," provided by the mythos, is what gives us our most basic access to whatever "ultimate reality" we may come to assume or accept; but, of course, "ultimate reality" of *this* sort—since it has been constituted significantly by generations of historical experience and reflection, and elaborate patterns of symbolization—must be regarded as at least a step removed from *ontological reality*, that to which we ordinarily seem to be referring with our phrase "ultimate reality." This latter ultimate-reality-as-it-actually-is-in-and-of-itself would seem always to remain beyond not only our conceptual, but also our experiential, grasp; though intended in our thinking, it is never actually reached in either experience or thought. Within this perspective, then, "ultimate reality" should be understood as a kind of "limiting idea." For this reason it would be more accurate to characterize what we are speaking of here as "ultimate mystery" rather than "ultimate reality"; for the latter term too easily identifies this ultimate object of our intentions and thought with the sorts of "reality" we encounter in our lived experience (this slippage, as we have been observing, occurs in Meland's own work), and it does not well enough preserve the ultimacy of the mystery with which we humans have to do in life. We can begin to see now that what is set out in Meland's analysis in much of *Fallible Forms and Symbols* as two sharply distinct epistemic "levels"—experience/reality, and language/thought—should actually be thought of as (at least) three levels (though he never seems expressly to acknowledge this point): mystery (or reality), experience, and language/thought; and all three of these are complexly interconnected with each other. We are moving here into a more sophisticated interpretive scheme than Meland has offered us, and one that does not so easily lead directly into the theological "empirical realism" which he wishes to promote.

Our scheme is still not sophisticated enough, however; we need to develop a four-level (or better: "four-dimensional") schema in order to do justice to the complexities with which we are here concerned. It is just as important that we make a clear distinction in the "upper level" of Meland's scheme (language/thought) as it is to make one in the lower (between "experience" and the ultimate mystery or reality). We have already noted the intimate connection between experience and language (the two "middle levels"), experience being given its most fundamental structure and meaning—as something which can be directly sensed and grasped, and understood and responded to, as real and significant—by language. We must now observe that there is also a very intimate relation between the two "levels" which Meland often seems to imply are most distant from each other, thought and reality (here Meland's metaphor of "levels," with its linear implications, is no longer serving us well).

Although all our thinking occurs within the medium of language (and other modes of symbolization), it involves much more than just speaking: it is speaking (or reflecting) carried on with the express intention of identifying what is real and what illusory, what is true and what false, what is good and what evil, what is important and what trivial, and so forth. That is, it is speaking and reflection oriented toward and guided by certain specific *criteria* which humans have found to be of value and importance—indeed indispensable—in dealing with the extraordinary complexities of historicocultural life. In our *thinking*, with the help of various criterial patterns of these sorts (themselves developed historically in distinctive and sometimes quite different ways in different societies), we make distinctions in our language and reflection—as well as in our experience itself—that are of importance to us; these distinctions help us identify that which is indispensable, or at least very valuable, to human life, enabling us to organize our world and orient ourselves in ways that promote human flourishing and other objectives. It is in thought, thus, that we identify what we take to be *real*, and seek to distinguish it from the many sorts of illusion which so often deceive us; it is in thought that we seek to distinguish what is reliable and trustworthy from that which is undependable; it is in thought that we sort out the true from the false. It has been in and through thought, of course, that we have been grasping the distinctions which I have just now been sketching—between reality (or ultimate mystery) and experience, between experience and language, and between language and thought—and have come to perceive the significant interconnections of each of these with the others; it is, therefore, at least as much through *thought* that we grasp the ultimate reality (or mystery) with which we have to do as through our lived experience. ("Mystery," "ultimacy," "experience," "reality"—these are all key *words* with which thought makes certain discriminations very important to theology.) It was thus, we may note now, in *thought* that Meland also worked out his own two-level epistemic pattern, and it ill becomes him to be so disparaging of "thought" and its "abstractions" as he often is. Perhaps it was just this failure to take "thought" sufficiently seriously that led him to set forth (as we have just been observing) an oversimplified two-level scheme which does not provide an adequate place for the very thinking that was required to produce it.

I am suggesting, then, that we must distinguish at least four major "levels" or "dimensions" interpenetrating each other in complex ways, if an adequate analysis of our theological epistemic activity is to be provided. (It should be understood that the scheme I am proposing here has been developed solely for the heuristic purpose of advancing our understanding of the issues under discussion; no claims are made for its overall epistemological validity.) As nearly as I can see, Meland confines most of his explicit epistemological analysis almost entirely to two levels, experience/reality and language/thought, maintaining the absolute priority of the former over the latter. This makes his realist epistemological program insufficiently nuanced and seriously misleading: on the one hand, he often overlooks the radical implications of the mysteries with which we have to do in theology, calling all of our meanings—and our experiences as well—into question; on the other hand, he fails to give adequate attention to the fact that everything in theology more specific and clearly defined than mystery is (in significant part at least) produced in and through the constructive activity of our own minds and imaginations. Indeed, this activity figures constitutively even—perhaps especially—in our giving the names "mystery" or "reality" to the deepest epistemic level to which we refer. Only as we become aware of the constructed character of *all* of this, do the full implications of the mysteriousness of human existence come fully into view, thus enabling us to enter into a truly critical assessment of all four aspects of our epistemic activity—as well as to be critical of this heuristic scheme itself (by means of which we are seeking to understand and interpret that activity). And as the ultimate inscrutability of the mystery(s) with which life confronts us gradually dawns on us, all our claims about the religious *realities* with which we have to do are put increasingly into question.

In these remarks about certain features of the epistemological and methodological dimensions of Meland's work, I have barely scratched the surface of his rich theological reflection. Much could and should be said about the "realities of faith" which he has done so much to illuminate, about the "appreciative consciousness" which he insists is required if we are to discern those realities adequately and to interpret them sensitively, about his important notion of mythos, about his sensitivity to the wider (secular) culture as a theological resource, as well as other matters. I find all of these emphases illuminating, and I do not want my critical remarks in this paper to be interpreted as in some way implying my disparagement of them. In particular I want to identify myself directly with much that he says about the appreciative consciousness: I certainly agree that in theological work, addressing itself as it does to the ultimate mysteries of life,

> an orientation of the mind [is required] which makes for a maximum degree of receptivity to the datum under consideration on the principle that what is given may be more than what is immediately perceived, or more than one can think. . . . The full meaning of the datum is not given. . . . Patterns, categories, criteria, useful as they may be for pursuing definitive meanings, are . . . approximate, tentative, subject to revision as the creative passage continues its route toward possible ends. . . . Whether one is speaking of some happening, a person, an institution, the living community, or of God, one is dealing with an inexhaustible event, the fullness of which bursts every definitive category. . . . The appreciative consciousness, then, takes as its starting point the mystery of what is given in existence.[7]

If I had space here to examine it carefully, there would be much I would want to applaud in Meland's emphasis on the appreciative consciousness; to develop such a consciousness is certainly an important discipline for every theologian. However, I should have to point out also that Meland sets out his view of the appreciative consciousness largely in terms of his oversimplified two-level epistemic scheme which we have found seriously misleading. In consequence, he fails to note that this very notion (of the "appreciative consciousness") is itself a kind of interpretive

[7]"The Appreciative Consciousness," chap. 5 in *Higher Education and the Human Spirit* (Chicago: University of Chicago Press, 1953) 63-64.

category—a *concept* generated by *thought*—by means of which he hopes to lead us to attend more sensitively to certain important features of experience, and our ways of apprehending and examining it. His epistemic scheme, however, (as we have noted) fails to call attention to the conceptual character of this (and other similarly) important notion(s); it is not surprising to discover, then, that he is not sufficiently guarded in his use of it, and upon occasion, unhappily, he even appears to *reify* it—thus falling into the very fallacy of misplaced concreteness which this consciousness is itself intended to protect us against (see, for example, pp. 61, 63, and esp. 78). It would be redundant here to undertake the detailed analysis of specific texts which would be required to sustain this claim, however, so I shall move on now to an examination of some themes in the work of Bernard Loomer.

IV

In the opening pages of his essay on *The Size of God* Loomer presents a magnificent vision of the world and God, a vision in which the abstractions and absurdities, and above all the metaphysical dualisms, of the theological tradition are to be overcome as we embrace a contemporary (ecological) understanding of all that is as "a web of interconnected events . . . [a] societal web of interrelatedness" (20). Like Bernard Meland, Loomer holds that the theological position he intends to sketch is grounded fundamentally on "the depths and immediacies of concrete experience" (SG, 21).

> Within the fundamental pluralism of this position there is the inherent claim that the heights and depths of existence, including the qualities of profound religious encounters and the resources for living an abundantly meaningful life, are to be experienced within the concrete realities of this world. This contention conjoins the sense of ultimacy in meaning and the immediacy of experiencable actualities (to borrow Bernard Meland's language). . . . I have described this stance elsewhere as a . . . "discerning immersion in what is most deeply present at hand and concretely at work in our midst." The cultivation of this commitment is the elemental reason for an empirical emphasis in theology and philosophy. (SG, 29)

One might suppose from these introductory remarks that Loomer attempts, like Meland, to examine "lived experience" with great care, showing what is apprehended directly in it, how it is constituted, how theological reflection can be based upon it and a program which is primarily accountable to it thus developed; however, this is not the case, as I shall argue in a moment.

Before I turn to that I want to point out that although (as I have attempted to show above) Meland's two-level epistemic model is not sufficiently sophisticated to carry his program of empirical realism, I have not argued against his principal theological intention: to develop an empirical theology attentive to the mysteries of existence. That objective seems to me reasonable and sound, provided its implications regarding the thoroughly *constructive* character of theology are fully recognized and acknowledged. (By a theology's "thoroughly constructive character" I am referring to the fact that at every point it is a product of what I call "imaginative construction," and should not be understood as a more or less straightforward "reading off" of data given directly and immediately in either "revelation" or "experience.")[8] Although Meland often describes his theological work as "construc-

---

[8]My principal argument supporting the conception of theology as "imaginative construc-

tive," I have tried to show that he does not recognize as clearly as he might all that this implies. An expansion and reconception of his epistemic scheme in terms of four distinct aspects or dimensions (as I have proposed) would help clear up these difficulties, and would also equip Meland to address more adequately the sorts of issues (mentioned in section II) with which theologians must today deal. Certainly it would bring his work and mine into fairly close convergence in many respects.

With Loomer, however, despite his attempt to identify himself with Meland's interest in lived experience, a very different kind of "empirical" approach is in fact presented. Instead of grounding his work (like Meland) on an examination of the relations of experience, mythos, language and thought, Loomer proposes "to take a set of ideas, the best that one has, and unflinchingly . . . explore experience with [their] aid" (SG, 23). This is an interesting and useful approach, suggesting that Loomer is more aware than is Meland, that "bare experience" is not directly accessible to us, and that to do truly "empirical theology" adequately we will need to be guided in our work by theory and concepts of the right sort (cf. SG, 36). Unfortunately, however, Loomer does not say much about how the "right" scheme of ideas is to be developed or chosen; instead, he simply appropriates what are basically Whiteheadian metaphysical definitions and categories, apparently taking these to be virtually self-evident and unquestionable "basic empirical, methodological principles" which do not require "an independent justification [since] they are of a piece with the accompanying ontological stance" (SG, 23). He freely admits that his principles "are in fact the methodological expression of this ontology" (ibid.); but he does not seem to see that for precisely that reason they should be carefully inspected and argued for in order to ascertain the ways and respects in which they might shape and color our understandings of experience, knowledge, reality, and so forth. (This lack of critical self-consciousness about his own preferred ideas, was also a problem in Meland's work, as we have noted.) Instead, he dismisses all such concerns with the sweeping self-confident pronouncement that the "spirit of these principles exemplifies the methodological and ontological humility characteristic of much of modern thought since the time of Hume and Kant" (24); and for this reason (presumably) we are simply to accept all the basic definitions that will largely determine the character of his program!—a rather far cry, I might say, from "the methodological and ontological humility" that characterized the painstakingly careful critical work of Hume and Kant.

Loomer actually moves, thus, on an entirely different track than Meland: his program claims to be "empirical" through and through, but it is in fact largely a constructive—*imaginative*, in the best sense, I would say—development of a particular metaphysical scheme. Had he been aware of the thoroughly imaginative-constructive character of his work, indicating openly that he was presenting a vision of God and the world which he hoped would enable his readers to see some important matters in a new light, one could only applaud his insight and achievement. But he seems to have regarded his Whiteheadian set of ideas not simply as one proposal among many, to be meditated on cautiously, tried on for size and workability, com-

---

tion" is to be found in my *Essay on Theological Method* (Atlanta: Scholars Press, 1975; rev. ed. 1979); see also *The Theological Imagination* (Philadelphia: Westminster Press) esp. chaps. 1 and 10, and *Theology for a Nuclear Age* (Manchester: University of Manchester Press; Philadelphia: Westminster, 1985) chaps. 2-4. An attempt to work out a full constructive theology on the basis of the method of imaginative construction will be found in my *In Face of Mystery: A Constructive Theology* (Cambridge: Harvard University Press, 1993).

paratively assessed in relation to other quite different proposals—one does not sense that sort of tentativity in this essay. Instead, Loomer writes as though he were setting out the metaphysical truth about the world and our place within it, a truth to be believed in and built upon but which no longer needs to be subjected to ongoing radical criticism. It is interesting to note that Meland had warned against precisely such attitudes in theology. The "process thinker," he said, often

> tends to fall into the habit of assuming that what he expresses at [the] ontological level is, in fact, not only intelligible but true in a definitive and adequate sense of that term. And because of the seductive nature of this habit of mind, . . . soon speak[s] theologically within this framework as if the framework itself were normative of meaning for ultimate reality itself. (FFS, 134-35)

This can only lead, he goes on to argue, into very serious problems, for theologians in fact undertake "a less manageable task" than philosophers and therefore "must assume a more difficult and precarious stance with regard to the disclosure of meaning." A theologian may employ "a philosophical notion for tentatively offering some possible meaning to the mystery to which the act of faith bears witness," but at most this notion will suggest

> what this reality could mean, not what it does in fact mean. . . . The theologian is thus compelled . . . to live on a frontier continually bordering his clearly formed structure of existence with an unmanageable depth of grace and freedom that . . . exceed[s] his conceptual reach. (136-37)

Passages like these show that Meland takes very seriously the methodological implications of the fact that, as I have put it, ultimately it is mystery with which theologians have to do. Though Loomer also speaks of mystery (see, for example, SG, 25-26, 42), he shows none of Meland's cautiousness and humility in face of it. Instead of addressing directly the questions of the ultimate mystery of things (as did Meland), he proceeds immediately to set out a number of major metaphysical claims which his readers are expected to accept without question, if they are to understand his (supposedly "empirical") program. First he boldly tells us what constitutes the world: "occasions of experience are the fundamental actualities of the world, the concrete individuals that constitute the successive moments in the historic lives of *all forms and levels of existence*" (SG, 26; emphasis mine). He then proceeds to explain to us just how these "occasions of experience" are themselves constituted:

> These occasions are the subjects of their experience. Their subjective experience is a synthetic process of unifying the several forms of vectorial energy derived from past occasions. Their subjective individuality, their self-creativity, and their freedom consist in the manner of their response to what they have received. This is their "howness" of becoming, or the style and spirit of their life: How they become determines what they become. (SG, 26)

Loomer goes on to tell us about other features of the world—"events," "enduring individuals," "material objects," "nexus," "societies," and so on; these are all well-known Whiteheadian metaphysical notions (with a few modifications in details), and I will not summarize further what he has to say about them.

The important point which we must note is that Loomer appears to regard these metaphysical definitions and expositions as setting forth the actual *concrete realities* with which we humans have to do; in his view these notions are to be sharply contrasted, therefore, with the "abstractions" with which, for the most part, other theological positions have concerned themselves. As we shall see, this accusation of "misplaced concreteness" will be Loomer's principal weapon against his theological opponents; it is important, therefore, that his claims about these "concrete realities" be well argued and persuasive, not simply dogmatic assertions—above all, not dogmatic assertions that fly in the face of the experience and usage that might seem especially cogent to readers of perspectives different from Loomer's. But Loomer takes no precautions with respect to such matters. By "concrete reality" he invariably means what is specified by the dogmatic definitions with which he begins his essay, rather than what might be suggested or implied, for example, by ordinary usage or a phenomenology of everyday experience: "concrete occasions and events," he emphasizes, "should be distinguished from material objects that we see, such as bridges, trees, and people" (p. 27). I have no problem with this as a metaphysical *proposal* that demands serious consideration—Loomer is certainly correct that there is much to be learned from Whitehead's work, and I am in agreement, in fact, with much of his interpretation of the world—but Loomer (unlike Meland) seems to take these metaphysical claims so much for granted that he is led into a stance which can only be characterized as basically dogmatic and almost completely devoid of self-criticism. This is really quite sad, since the material theological proposals he presents are interesting and important, and it is unfortunate that his manner of presentation probably precludes them from getting wide attention.

V

A quick look at some of Loomer's arguments against opponents will make clear just how he proceeds. The main thesis of his essay "which identifies God and the world," as he tells us, "grows out of a devotion to the concrete nature of God, which, in turn, is grounded in a conviction concerning the inadequacy of an abstract God" (36). The issue of concreteness vs. abstractness is, then, the fulcrum of his discussion of the adequacy of various conceptions of God. The compact scope of his essay prevents him from taking up a wide range of conceptions of God, but he does consider the positions of several fellow process theologians; and invariably his argument is that in their understanding of God they have mistaken abstractions for concrete reality.[9] The principal mistake of all of these writers is that they desire an "unambiguous" God (we will consider Loomer's notion of "ambiguity" below)—for example, a God of perfect goodness—but all "concrete realities" are ambiguous, so in all these cases an "abstraction" must have been identified as God.

Charles Hartshorne, for example, develops an a priori argument for God's perfection and existence in which "both ontological necessity and the meaningfulness of life are grounded on an idea, a meaning" (37). His philosophy, thus,

> tends to be a philosophy of abstractions. The religious stance of a theology of God's necessary existence harbors the impulse to become the worship of an idea of God. It acknowledges the reality of mystery, but it subsumes its sense of mystery under the structures of its metaphysics.
>
> The empirical philosophy of attachment [i.e. Loomer's position] attempts to think and live in terms of holding its ascertained structures of experience subject to the dynamic presence of mystery. (SG, 38)

---

[9]Though Loomer's discussion here focusses on process theologians, he attributes to the Christian tradition generally a similar attachment to misleading abstractions (SG, 43-44), and in this connection he discusses Reinhold Niebuhr briefly.

> [I have already suggested that Loomer himself makes the error which he here attributes to Hartshorne, of too quickly subsuming the ultimate mystery of things under his metaphysical categories; we shall have occasion to consider this problem further as we proceed.]

Whitehead takes a different alternative, but one just as abstract as Hartshorne's. He "defines the unity of the world abstractly in terms of a universal order. God is then identified as the abstract source or principle of this order" (*ibid*). And Wieman goes yet another way in which "God is identified with one aspect of the world or one kind of process . . . the process of creative transformation." But "a God . . . identified with an aspect of the world . . . is an abstract and not a concrete God" (40). In contrast with all of these views Loomer holds that

> God as a wholeness is to be identified with the concrete, interconnected totality of this struggling, imperfect, unfinished, and evolving societal web [which is the world]. As this universal society God includes all modes of temporality; God also operates through all the Aristotelian causes. God's action is not wholly or even primarily identified with the persuasive and permissive lure of a final cause or a relevant and novel ideal. . . . An exclusive or even a primary emphasis on final causation is abstractionism. God is also physical, efficient cause that may be either creative or inertial in its effects. . . . God is . . . the organic restlessness of the whole body of creation. . . . God is not only the ultimate end for which all things exist; God is also the shape and stuff of existence. (SG, 41)

I cannot discuss in detail here Loomer's criticisms of these various theologians with whom he disagrees; I have presented these examples only to show that his objections to their positions turn entirely on his claim about the inappropriateness of "abstractionism" when it is God we are attempting to identify and characterize, for God must be concrete actuality. But how do we decide what is *concrete actuality*? Surely Wieman did not regard his "creative event" as a mere *abstraction* in contrast with the "created goods" of the world; as the "source" of these goods it is much more real—it has qualitatively greater actuality—than they. And Hartshorne did not regard "perfection" as any "mere abstraction": the whole point of his argument is to establish its *necessary existence*, its reality. Nor is the "primordial nature" of God a "mere abstraction" for Whitehead. It is not at all clear from these examples on just what grounds we are to choose among these diverse claims about concreteness: it would seem that one person's highest degree of actuality is another's abstraction. Traditional Christian reflection has long insisted on God's "being" or "existence" or "reality," and this has always been intended to make precisely the point that however incomplete and tentative and otherwise abstract are the characterizations of God that are offered, it must be understood that it is *concrete actuality* of the highest degree—"ultimate reality"—that is being discussed. The fact that *from Loomer's point of view* Wieman's or Hartshorne's or Niebuhr's God seems abstract actually proves nothing more than that he has a different point of view. One could easily show that from their several perspectives similar accusations of abstractionism could be made about the metaphysical ideas Loomer outlines in this book as the basis for his conception of God; his position also—like every characterization, description or definition of God—is constructed out of "abstractions."

This point can be quickly confirmed if we look back again at the quotation above in which Loomer gives a brief characterization of what he takes to be God. The entire passage is composed of abstractions—to what else, after all, could

Loomer (or anyone else) turn, in trying to speak of "absolute" or "ultimate" "reality" (three very vague and general abstractions themselves!)? Many of these abstractions are of an extremely high order—"wholeness," "interconnected totality," "imperfect, unfinished, . . . evolving societal web," "physical, efficient cause . . . either creative or inertial in its effects," "the organic restlessness of the whole body of creation," "the shape and stuff of existence," and so on. The rhetorical effect of these accumulated phrases may give the impression of an ultimate and unsurpassably great concrete actuality—the entirety of the world, the totality of all that is—and that is certainly Loomer's intention; but every one of these phrases is itself a high order abstraction. Why should we prefer Loomer's abstractions to Wieman's or Reinhold Niebuhr's, or for that matter, to Anselm's or Augustine's? We need here (as we did with Meland) a much more sophisticated understanding of the way in which our symbolizations bear on, are related to, and themselves interpret the "reality" to which we take them to refer; it obviously begs all the important questions about what is "abstract" and what is "concrete reality" if we simply take for granted in our discussion a whole catalog of uncriticized metaphysical definitions, since these definitions are themselves all composed of abstractions of a high order. To presume that *my* abstractions refer to "actualities" but everyone else's are specious and misleading, evidences a much too unself-critical and dogmatic stance.

Why does Loomer take up such a stance? Is it the case, perhaps, that persons who make forthrightly "realist" claims in epistemology tend too easily and uncritically to identify their own definitions and conceptualizations with the Real? We need a methodology in theology (and also in philosophy) that calls attention to the fact that *all* our words and other symbols are *our own constructions*, and that therefore—however meaningful, illuminating, persuasive, true, they may seem to us—they must always be regarded with some suspicion: the more the "knowledge" they convey seems to us self-evidently certain, the more we should beware that we are overlooking some important issues and may be deceiving ourselves. Epistemological realisms, especially when strongly held, do not encourage the wariness that is necessary for truly sensitive theological work—concerned, as it must be, with what always remains ultimately mysterious. (Meland seems much more aware of this problem, as we have noted,[10] than does Loomer.)

The type of argument, thus, that Loomer offers in favor of his conception of God—that he presents us with a God of *concrete actuality* in contrast with others who give us only "abstractions"—appears to be, I am sorry to say, bogus (as other arguments of this sort have been in the past); one's concept of God is always an imaginative construction out of abstractions—something simply not susceptible to direct proof of any kind.[11] Despite this serious methodological problem with his work, however, and his own (mis)understanding of what he is doing, it is important that we look closely at the conception of God which Loomer presents, for his imaginative construction is both interesting and important, and it will repay our efforts to examine it with some care.

---

[10]See n. 4, above.

[11]For some discussion of my position on this matter, see the previously cited *Essay on Theological Method* and "Mystery, Critical Consciousness, and Faith"; see also " 'Evidentialism': a Theologian's Response," in *Faith and Philosophy* (1989) 6:35-46.

VI

"The thesis of my essay," he tells us at the very beginning, "is that God should be identified with the totality of the world, with whatever unity the totality possesses" (SG, 20). This is an unusual proposal, and Loomer himself asks why we should "deify this interconnected web of existence by calling it "God"? Why not simply refer to the world and to the processes of life? . . . what is gained by this perhaps confusing, semantic identification" (SG, 41-42)? He presents an interesting answer to this question:

> In our traditions the term "God" is the symbol of ultimate values and meanings in all of their dimensions. It connotes an absolute claim on our loyalty. It bespeaks a primacy of trust, and a priority within the ordering of our commitments. It points the direction of a greatness of fulfillment. It signifies a richness of resources for the living of life at its depths. It suggests the enshrinement of our common and ecological life. It proclaims an adequate object of worship. It symbolizes a transcendent and inexhaustible meaning that forever eludes our grasp.
>
> The world is God because it is the source and preserver of meaning; because the creative advance of the world in its adventure is the supreme cause to be served; because even in our desecration of our space and time within it, the world is holy ground; and because it contains and yet enshrouds the ultimate mystery inherent within existence itself. "God" symbolizes this incredible mystery. The existent world embodies it. The world in all the dimensions of its being is the basis for all our wonder, awe, and inquiry. (SG, 42)

This is a powerfully suggestive answer to the question posed. It implies that the central issue for theology is not, Does God exist?—a question which presupposes that the meaning of the word "God" is clear, and the important issue is whether any actuality corresponds to that meaning. In contrast to that more or less traditional theological approach, Loomer seems to be suggesting that "God" is a symbol looking for a referent. Our symbol "God" does not of itself *identify* that which we should worship and devote ourselves to; rather it poses for us important questions such as: what can properly make "an absolute claim on our loyalty"? what is really "an adequate object of worship" because it is "a transcendent and inexhaustible meaning that forever eludes our grasp"? Just what reality meets these specifications has always been unclear and fiercely debated; and the candidates that have seemed plausible and proper have changed much with time and circumstance—a "mighty warrior," "creator of the heavens and the earth," "our father in heaven," the "first cause," the "ground of being," "the creative event," "the infinite Person," "the ultimate mystery," and on and on. It is Loomer's contention that no particular reality within the world—or "outside" it for that matter (whatever that might mean)—can properly meet the specifications laid down by the symbol "God" (that is, those specifications mentioned in the above quotation). For reflective persons today it will be the world-as-a-whole, or "whatever unity the totality possesses" (SG, 20)—both of these being high order abstractions, we should note—that must be regarded as the only possible referent(s) to which the depths of meaning carried by this symbol could properly be directed.

This is an important theological proposal, especially for our time of methodological self-consciousness and ecological concern. Methodologically, Loomer is correct, I think, (a) in suggesting that the symbol "God" performs certain important functions in human life (at least in the West), and principally for this reason (quite properly) demands our attention; and (b) in insisting that theologians must be open to a thorough reconception of the reality to be called "God," if our theological analysis shows this to be warranted. However, these important contentions are not clearly and straightforwardly put. They are, in fact, so mixed up with Loomer's confused discussions of the "abstract" and the "truly concrete"—that is, with what are essentially his dogmatic metaphysical claims—that their real methodological force does not come through as clearly as one might wish; and it is possible for a reader easily to be misled into supposing that the importance of Loomer's program is to be found principally in his idiosyncratic metaphysical contentions instead of in methodological insights of this kind (Loomer himself seems to have believed this). From the point of view of modern ecological consciousness (and the consequent forced change from substantialistic patterns in our thinking to relational ones) Loomer also has much to offer. We must today learn to think of ourselves as embedded in, and a part of, the web of life on earth, instead of as occupying some sort of exalted position above and independent of that web, a position which frees us from continuous responsibility to it and care for it. Religious feeling and devotion need to be redirected in accord with this newer understanding of our human existence and situation; and reconceiving the referent for the symbol "God" will be an essential part of the profound reorientation that this requires.

Loomer does not, however, work out these methodological and ecological insights and proposals with care, showing what devotion to the world-as-God might mean in contrast to devotion to God as traditionally conceived, in what respects it would call for a reorientation of human personal life and human social institutions and patterns, and so on, and in this way showing its profound religious and human meaning. Instead he presents an argument which he believes will conclusively establish that a God-identified-with-the-world will be *concretely actual*, in contrast with the "abstractions" to which women and men have heretofore always devoted themselves. But by developing his position in terms of this contrast between "abstractions" and "concrete actuality," Loomer brings us back once again to the old question of the "existence of God": when speaking of God are we speaking of something "concretely actual," or only of an idea in our heads? Instead of following the new directions suggested by his methodological insights he thus returns to the traditional problem, a problem which, he thinks, he has found a way to resolve.

The problem of God's actuality, he believes, has historically been so painful and so insoluble because

> Christian theology has been obsessed with God as embodied perfection. From its beginning down to the present, theology has taken it as axiomatic that God is unambiguous in character. (In this tradition only the unambiguous can be perfect. Or, conversely, only the perfect is unambiguous.) God's goodness has been conceived as pure and unmixed, the personification of unambiguous love. (SG, 43)

This concern with the unambiguous, Loomer urges, has been a mistake, not because "ambiguity for its own sake" is something to be especially valued, but because—and here we return again to the problematical theme on which so much of Loomer's argument has rested—unambiguity is always necessarily abstract.

> The quest is for a living, dynamic, and active God—in short, a concrete God. An ambiguous God is not of greater stature simply because He is

> ambiguous. His greater size derives from the concreteness of His actuality in contrast to the reality of a nonliving, undynamic, and inactive abstraction. The concretely actual is ambiguous; only the highly abstract can be unambiguous. Thus, the conclusion, and the thesis, that an ambiguous God is of greater stature than an unambiguous deity. (SG, 43)

The identification of God with the world will assure God's existence (God's "concrete actuality") since there is no question about the existence of the world. The world, however, contains all manner of good and evil, imperfection, incompleteness—in short, "ambiguity"—so if this move is to be made, we will have to be prepared to acknowledge God's ambiguity as well as the world's. This means that the traditional divine "perfection" will have to go. But since that notion was only an a priori dogmatic postulate anyhow, Loomer (taking himself to be developing an "empirical" theology) finds little difficulty giving it up in the name of the "greater stature" of this concretely actual God to which he is directing our attention.

VII

There are many issues here worth exploring, and we cannot begin to consider them all. I want to argue three points in particular: (1) In its central contentions Loomer's proposal is no less aprioristic and dogmatic than the ones he leaves behind; it is not based on a straightforward empirical argument at all. (2) Loomer's idea of ambiguity is itself shot full of "ambiguities" and really adds nothing of significance to his argument; it may, in fact, have misled him in a number of significant ways. (3) On closer inspection, it becomes clear that the concept of the world cannot perform the functions in human life for which the symbol/concept of God is ordinarily employed, and therefore the straightforward identification of God with the world is quite problematical.

With respect to the first point, we shall see that it is precisely the dogmatic aspects of Loomer's position that are most decisively determinative with respect to what he regards as its distinctive "concreteness." Loomer's argument, it thus becomes clear, is not "empirical" in the sense he intends at all.[12] This conclusion should hardly be surprising in view of earlier contentions in this paper—above all, that God is never an object given directly in experience, but is always (at best) the supposed referent for an exceedingly complex construct of the imagination, a construct built up out of metaphors and concepts and definitions (all of them "abstractions") of various sorts. Necessarily, then, there will always be a number of significant "a priori" and "abstract" components in a conception of God; and Loomer's case is no exception (as we have been observing all along). Our task now is to pursue one step further the identification of the a priori ingredients in his notion of God, so that we will be in a better position to assess what is really going on here.

Several matters must be noted. In the first place, as the above quotation makes clear, Loomer's conception of God rests foursquare on his definitions of "abstractness" and "concreteness," and these, as we have already seen, are arbitrary. Virtually every writer in the Christian tradition has insisted that God must be thought of

---

[12]Although Loomer might find this remark devastating if true, I do not intend that conclusion to be drawn. I have argued throughout that "empirical theology," in the sense Loomer is using this term, is more a matter of metaphysical dogmatism than of concern for what is actually given in human experience; in my view Meland is a much more reliable guide than Loomer regarding the questions *qua* "empirical" to which theology must address itself.

as "living, dynamic, and active . . . in short a concrete God." Whose position, then, does Loomer think he is rejecting when he suggests that he alone—in contrast with others who present only "a nonliving, undynamic, and inactive abstraction"—is interested in a "concretely actual" God? The distinctive thing about Loomer's position is not his concern about the sharp contrast between the concrete and the abstract but rather the particular understanding he has of *what* it is that is concrete and what abstract; and this understanding derives directly, as we have seen, from his unargued metaphysical definitions. We need not discuss that matter further here.

Further dogmatic a priori elements (drawn in this case from more traditional Christian reflection) appear at the very heart of Loomer's conception of God. Christian theologians, as I have just suggested, were long concerned with the general question of whether God was concretely actual or merely an idea in our minds, but it was not until the time of Anselm that a specific argument was formulated which directly addressed precisely this point: Anselm's so-called "ontological argument." Major features of this argument seem to lie behind Loomer's conception of God, though he nowhere manifests awareness of this. Loomer's insistence on the greater reality and significance of "concreteness" over "abstractness" is clearly foreshadowed in Anselm's argument that a God who exists in reality is "greater than" a God who exists only in thought; and Loomer's emphasis on "size" or "stature" as a proper criterion of true deity was directly anticipated by Anselm's well-known definition of God in terms of "greatness" (God is that "than which nothing greater can be conceived"). These central operative concepts in Loomer's essay on God, thus, are not empirically derived at all; they are, in fact, heavily dependent on long-standing Christian conceptual claims. In this connection it is interesting to observe that some of Loomer's very sentences echo Anselm's *Proslogium*: "the thesis asserts that the unambiguous has at best the status of an abstraction, and that consequently an ambiguous God is of greater stature than an unambiguous deity" (SG, 43). Loomer nowhere mentions these matters, perhaps because he thinks his disagreement with Anselm about God's "perfection" means that he has left Anselm entirely behind. But it would have been wise for him to look a little closer at this point, for it was precisely Anselm's reflection on the idea of perfection that led him to his notion of "greatness." Is this, then, the real origin and basis for Loomer's concept of *size*? This notion surely is not, as he seems to suggest, a straightforward empirical concept, the evaluation and interpretation of which is merely "a matter of evidence" (SG, 42): what kind of empirical evidence could bear clearly and directly on a matter such as this?[13] Major components of Loomer's argument seem to be, in fact, heavily dependent on Anselm—and Anselm was the greatest apriorist in Christian history!

There are, then, major unargued dogmatic premises underlying Loomer's proposals in *The Size of God*, some deriving from his metaphysical commitments,

---

[13]It appears that Loomer is himself a bit uneasy with regard to this claim about "evidence," for he follows it immediately with qualifications that suggest he actually has in mind something much more like what is ordinarily called "intuition" (though for obvious reasons he prefers not to use that word): "With respect to the deepest questions, the search for evidence becomes the quest for self-evidence. The ultimate manifestation of self-evidence occurs at the level of embodied valuations. And stature, wherever found, is the most impregnable and incontrovertible form of self-evidence. Beyond it there is no court of appeal. On this hangs all the law and the prophets—and all the revelations" (SG, 42)—an utterly dogmatic claim, for which neither evidence nor argument is offered!

some from the theological tradition. To these general a priori premises of his argument, Loomer adds one more which, he believes, bears directly on the actuality of God: "the concretely actual is ambiguous." This contention, however (I want to suggest), far from being well argued, actually involves a failure to carry through careful consideration of his (and Anselm's) notion of "stature" as a criterion of deity; moreover, it rests on yet another fallacy of misplaced concreteness. Let us take up this latter problem first.

If one looks up the words "ambiguous" and "ambiguity" in the dictionary, one discovers that they are always used with reference to our *cognitive relation* to objects, never with reference to qualities inherent in objects themselves. Something is *ambiguous* if it is "doubtful, questionable; indistinct, obscure, not clearly defined . . . admitting more than one interpretation, or explanation; of double meaning, . . . equivocal."[14] All of these characterizations refer to *our* inability to get a clear and distinct view or understanding of something; in no case do they indicate some quality or characteristic of an object in itself. But Loomer appears to treat "ambiguity" as just such an *objective quality* which an object of experience or thought may or may not possess; consider the following quotations: "an ambiguous God is of greater stature than an unambiguous deity"; Jesus Christ has usually "been conceived as unambiguous in His being" (SG, 43); "ambiguity . . . [is] an inherent characteristic of the created world"; "our world . . . is filled with evil and ambiguous elements" (SG, 44); "Ambiguities derive from the basic characteristics of individuals and societies" (SG, 45); etc. In his discussion of "ambiguity" Loomer has objectified and reified what in fact is a characteristic of certain (cognitive) relationships, insisting that all "concrete actualities" have "ambiguity" as a property;[15] from

---

[14]*Oxford English Dictionary* 1:270.

[15]Loomer's reified use of "ambiguity" led him to make a number of rather strange claims, which, if he had had clearly in mind the word's proper use, he would surely have avoided. A couple of examples will make the point. Loomer states that in Christian thinking generally, "God's goodness has been conceived as pure and unmixed, the personification of unambiguous love" (43). The adjectival use of "unambiguous" in this sentence suggests that for most Christian theology everything about God's love has been regarded as absolutely clear and straightforward: there are no problems, questions, or doubts about its reality or its meaning. But this would be an incredible claim. The tradition is full of questioning and arguments about how God's love is to be understood in view of God's wrath and God's justice; about the difficulty or impossibility of reconciling claims about God's love with the many evils found in the world; about the extreme demands—including enormous suffering and humiliation, even death—laid upon those whom God is believed to love most of all. The divine love is far from unambiguous—that is, far from clear and intelligible—in Christian faith and reflection: it is, in fact, a profound, almost inconceivable, mystery. Was it Loomer's odd reified use of the term "ambiguous" that led him to formulate such an ambiguous(!) assertion?

Another example. Immediately following the above sentence Loomer turns to christology: "Jesus Christ," he says, "has . . . been conceived as unambiguous in His being, sinless and completely at one with the divine purity" (ibid.). Again, a very strange remark; if we were not already aware that Loomer is using a reified notion here (clearly apparent in this sentence), we might well wonder what could have led him to make such a comment. For what could be more ambiguous, more mysterious, more incredible—even self-contradictory, as Kierkegaard argued—than the idea of Jesus the God-man (a concept to which the sentence directly alludes)? The christological doctrines and formulas are shot through with ambiguity and obscurity, and have been the occasion for countless disagreements during the past 2,000 years. How did Loomer manage to overlook these well known problems and speak simply and straightforwardly as though Christians recognized no ambiguities in their christological

this he has concluded, that God, if God is to be concretely actual, must also possess this property. The argument appears to rest on a succession of errors, largely involving fallacies of misplaced concreteness.[16] Impressed by the complex balances that make life possible, by the dialectical interdependence of good and evil in finite selves, by tensions between needs for freedom and needs for institutionalization, and the like (SG, 45-48) Loomer concludes that all concrete reality is "ambiguous"; and the "notion of ambiguity becomes [for him] a metaphysical principle" (SG, 51). Therefore God—if God is "concrete"—must be "ambiguous" also.

The problems with this argument go beyond Loomer's fallacies of misplaced concreteness. Loomer apparently fails to note that all of the "concrete actualities" he mentions (as a basis for his generalization about ambiguity) are *finite*. To what extent is *God* to be conceived on the model of finite actualities? Does the criterion of "greatness" or "stature" imply *qualitative* distinctions between God and other realities or only quantitative ones? Loomer does not discuss this point directly, but he apparently adheres to the Whiteheadian dictum that God should never be made an exception to one's metaphysical principles but is rather their exemplification;[17] so God's "concrete actuality" must be in principle like that of every other event, entity, or society. It is not, however, as easy to take this position as Loomer may have supposed, for he wants to identify God with the world as a whole. But the world is surely a unique reality in important respects, since all other realities are included within it (SG, 41) in a way that it is not included within any of them. Does this not suggest, then, that there is a significant *qualitative* difference in "stature" between the world and other "concrete actualities"? And would this not mean—if God is to be identified with the world—that it is by no means clear that what obtains with respect to finite actualities (for example, "ambiguity") must necessarily obtain with God?

Without attempting to answer this important question, let us turn to some deeper problems with Loomer's proposal to identify God with the world. We need to ask: is Loomer's basic assumption, that the world is a "concrete actuality," in fact justifiable? Since much of the concreteness to be attributed to the world (what was actual in the past) has long since disappeared, and much of its remaining concreteness (the entire future) has not yet come into being, how are we to understand this assumption? The world is not a "concrete actuality" in any ordinary sense at all; our word "world" represents, rather, a heuristic idea of ours, a highly abstract and vague (but nonetheless indispensable) imaginative construct by means of which we order our experience and thinking.[18] "The world" is very far from possessing the kind of concreteness for which Loomer seems to be looking: precisely that aspect of "stature" in which Loomer is most interested ("concrete actuality") seems largely missing from the world. In his identification of God with the world Loomer has, thus, actually moved us deeply into "abstractionism."

---

contentions? How could he have written this sentence without noting that something quite peculiar was going on in his discussion of "ambiguity"?

[16]I have no idea why Loomer fell into this trap (perhaps this is just one more example of the dangers of an overconfident epistemological realism). He seems to have derived his notion of ambiguity from Reinhold Niebuhr (43-44), and it may be that Niebuhr was using the word in this reified way; I have not been able to check that out.

[17]Meland warns theologians against using this Whiteheadian principle in this way with respect to God (FFS 135-36).

[18]For further discussion, see my *Essay on Theological Method*, 24-25, 43ff.

As we have seen, however, this matter of abstractionism really does not have the sort of theological importance that Loomer gives it, for all conceptions of God are built up out of abstractions. A much weightier question to be put to Loomer's proposal is this: does the identification of God-as-the-world perform the essential *functions* of the symbol "God" more adequately than any other conception? (Here, in giving the functions of the symbol "God" primacy [instead of metaphysical claims about God] I am picking up on what we have seen to be one of Loomer's own moves; see 152-53, above.) I cannot take up this question in detail here, but in my opinion thinking of God-as-the-world is functionally quite problematic. The principal function which the symbol "God" performs (as we can see from Loomer's own fine characterization, quoted on 152, above), is to provide a focus for devotion, loyalty and worship in human life, a focus on value and meaning and reality. What is the purpose of this focus? Loomer does not address this question, but I suggest that it is to enable men and women to see more clearly at what they should aim in their living and thinking; it is a focus that is expected to help them develop guidelines and criteria for making judgments about how they ought to live, what they should value, a focus that should disclose to them who they are, what is their place in the world.

In my view, our conception or picture of the world-as-a-whole is not definite enough or specific enough to provide the sort of focus for attention, devotion, and indeed all of life, that is needed here. It is of little use, for example, with respect to our continuous necessity to make choices and to act. (Loomer seems to agree with this point [SG, 42], but he does not draw the conclusions from it which I do in what follows.) We need criteria and norms to which we can turn for guidance as we decide whether to move this way or that, to favor this alternative over another; the traditional notion of God's will (as righteous, holy and merciful, etc.) was thought to provide such guidance for specific situations and decisions, but there is no way that the world-as-a-whole can give this kind of specific help. Loomer fails to note that the symbol "God" has always performed important *practical* functions of this sort (which "world" cannot); and he fails to see, therefore, that this raises serious questions about his idea that God can be straightforwardly identified with the world[19]—or, to put this matter more in my own terms, he fails to see that the concept of God simply cannot be constructed out of components identical to those used in constructing the concept of the world. To facilitate the sort of practical orientation in life which the symbol "God" promises, a range of *abstracted* characteristics of things (for example, a range of *values*, like goodness, truth, harmony, contrast, meaning, right, justice, etc.) is needed. A picture or concept of everything-in-its-place-within-the-whole is of little help here (though it cannot be entirely dispensed with). Loomer's further suggestion that the vague concept of "stature" can be invoked for major choices (SG, 42) seems almost totally empty. Moreover, his stress that God is *ambiguous* in all respects would seem virtually to destroy this practical function of God-talk.

VIII

In the second half of this paper I have been trying to show that there are serious methodological problems with Loomer's theological proposals. Despite this, I want

---

[19]For further discussion of this distinction between "God" and "world," see ibid., esp. chap. 3; see also, *Theology for a Nuclear Age*, chap. 3.

to emphasize now, it would be a mistake to conclude that Loomer's work should be discarded or ignored. To draw that conclusion would be to misunderstand a principal point that I am attempting to make in this paper, namely, that theology is an ongoing conversation about the ultimate mysteries of existence—a conversation in which no one has final answers; it is a conversation, therefore, to which we must welcome every voice that undertakes to speak thoughtfully and honestly (and Loomer is certainly among those voices). The greatest danger to theology is dogmatism—whether grounded on revelationism, some form of epistemological realism, or whatever—that dogmatism which, on the one hand, produces in the theologian a less self-critical stance than is necessary for careful theological work, and, on the other hand, which all too often leads into arrogant and domineering campaigns against other participants in the discussion.

Despite all claims about God's concrete actuality, from the time of Second Isaiah and before down to Bernard Loomer, the idea of God with which the theologian has worked has always been an imaginative construct, created by the human mind and introduced into human discourse to help order and orient life by providing it with a focus of value and meaning and reality. For adequate theological work it is essential, in my opinion, to give close attention to this fundamentally practical and pragmatic need which has generated the symbol "God"; but it is also important to take up (as Loomer, for example, has done) the metaphysical and ontological questions to which this symbol gives rise. Such a move may lead us in any number of different directions: down Wieman's route investigating the "source of human good," or following out Mathews' interest in identifying the "personality producing powers" in the world, or exploring Tillich's conception of the "ground of being"; or we might move toward some more traditional notion of a cosmic agent or infinite person.[20] In my opinion, however—and here I am in agreement with Loomer—each of these familiar notions, in light of the ecological sensibilities to which we are now becoming increasingly attentive, tends to reinforce our anthropocentrizing proclivities too much: today we need orientation with respect to the world-as-a-whole as well as with respect to the particular values and meanings which have been generated in our historical experience. So our God will have to be conceived, at least in part, in terms of wide ecological and evolutionary metaphors as well as models that relate more directly to the historical dimensions of our existence. If we wish to develop the metaphysical side of theological reflection in a manner appropriate to our contemporary understanding of humanity-in-the-world, God will need to be thought of in "biohistorical" terms, as I like to put it.[21]

Whatever specific ontological or metaphysical views we may develop, however, it is essential that we recognize and acknowledge that our notion of God is an imaginative construct, put together (largely out of abstractions) to orient us in life. Loomer's and Meland's epistemological realism—like the many other realisms of the Christian tradition—has led them to take the primary significance of this symbol to be its (supposed) metaphysical or ontological reference rather than its orienting

---

[20]My own work with respect to this issue has been significantly influenced by Wieman's program (see *Theology for a Nuclear Age*, esp. 35-46; and also "Constructing the Concept of God" in *The Theological Imagination*, esp. 48-50, 54-55, for examples of this); but I am convinced now that we must move beyond the anthropocentrism implied in Wieman's focus on "human good."

[21]My own attempt to thoroughly reconceive God in these terms will be found in *In Face of Mystery*.

function. This is a long-standing theological error (in my opinion) that is founded largely on another mistake: the quest in the Christian tradition for absolute certainty, the desire for an ultimate security, an ultimate grounding, for life—something simply unavailable to finite historical women and men. Only quite recently have we (at least in the West) begun to extricate ourselves from this profound confusion in religion and theology inherited from our tradition. But today we are beginning to realize that all our symbols—and all our experiences as shaped by these symbols—are human creations; and, as such, they are always questionable and corrigible, never to be given our unqualified belief or trust, however indispensable they may be to our day-by-day living in the world.

In Meland's work—despite his professed epistemological realism—there are many signs of a theological sensibility closely in accord with this newer, more tentative (antirealist) consciousness; it would not be hard to wed his rich theological insights to a thoroughly constructivist theological methodology. In my opinion it would be much more difficult, however, to bring such a methodology into intimate connection with Loomer's more dogmatic, less self-critical procedure. But these methodological limitations of Loomer's work do not mean that he has nothing significant to offer contemporary theological reflection: his movement toward a functional approach to the question of God, his insistence that our thinking about God and about the world must be brought into much closer connection with each other than our theological traditions ever imagined, above all his powerful vision of reality as a "societal web of interrelatedness" (SG, 20), is surely correct for the ecological age into which we are just beginning to move. Constructivist approaches to theology, since they need not be constrained by the authority of theological tradition, are free to appropriate just such illuminating insights. A principal advantage of constructivism, in a time (such as our own) of massive new human problems, is precisely this openness to appropriating significant new insights wherever they appear, as we attempt to create a new theological vision appropriate to the new world into which we are so rapidly moving.

The World's Parliament of Religions Revisited

James A. Kirk

Celebration of the Anniversary of the World's Parliament

Among the celebrations of the four-hundredth anniversary of the arrival of Columbus in the Western Hemisphere, was an event called the World's Parliament of Religions, held in connection with the Colombian Exposition in Chicago in 1893. The forthcoming centennial of the Parliament will likely be celebrated extensively among diverse groups, some of whose claims and enthusiasms may be as grandiloquent as those of the Parliament leaders themselves.

There are several reasons for interest in this event. The World's Parliament was the first large-scale intercultural penetration of Asian religions and spokespersons into the American Christian hegemony. Within the Christian communities it was a controversial event, greeted with vigorous objection by numerous influential leaders. It may be doubted whether the Parliament "caused" much of profound substance or enduring influence beyond itself,[1] but it cannot be doubted that it had a stunning and welcome impact on those who were present.

For persons specifically concerned with the University of Chicago there are several additional reasons for interest. The World's Parliament was *not* predominantly a gathering of scholars, but contributions of scholars were important to its achievement. George S. Goodspeed, from Yale, who had just been appointed associate professor of Comparative Religion and Ancient History, in the faculty of Arts, Literature and Science, at the new University of Chicago for its opening year in the fall of 1892, was a delegate and read a paper.[2] Dr. Albion Small, head professor of Social Science and Anthropology at the University, also read a paper. Louis Henry Jordan, one of the major speakers at the Parliament, was later

---

[1]At least this appears to be the conclusion of Kenten Druyvesteyn, who, in March 1976, completed a dissertation at the University of Chicago Divinity School entitled "The World's Parliament of Religions."

[2]Richard J. Storr, *Harper's University: The Beginnings* (Chicago: University of Chicago Press, 1966) 75n.

appointed special lecturer in Comparative Religion at the University of Chicago. John Henry Barrows, chairman of the general committee, moderator of the Parliament sessions, and editor of the proceedings later became adjunct professor at the University of Chicago in addition to his role as senior minister of First Presbyterian Church of Chicago. He had just secured for the University an endowment for two lectureships, the Haskell Lectures, and the Barrows lectures (sponsored by the University of Chicago but delivered in India), and the gift of the Haskell Building and Oriental Museum to President William Rainey Harper. Most of the major Parliament meetings were held in the building, now the Art Institute of Chicago, which was constructed with funds provided both by the Exposition and by the directors of the Art Institute (an early example of "matching grants"). The Columbian Exposition itself was built on 700 (!) vacant acres a few miles south of the Parliament buildings and city center in an area now known as Jackson Park, and part of the campus of the University of Chicago, including the administration building of the School of Business, remains from the Exposition.

Character of the Parliament

The Parliament as a whole met three times daily for seventeen consecutive days, September 11-27. Separate meetings called the "Scientific Section" were held on seven of the seventeen days, for the particular concerns of the scholars and for analysis of ethnic cults and Christian sects. Although some of the more important scholarly contributions came in the scientific section, many were never published or described in the official publications. A number of denominational conferences were also held in conjunction with the Parliament, and an eight day missionary conference followed the Parliamentary adjournment. Dwight L. Moody was so distressed by the Parliament that, across the street, he conducted a sustained evangelical revival with prayers for the souls of the delegates throughout the days of the meetings. There were 400 official delegates to the entire conference and 3,000–4,000 individuals gathered in each of the two main rooms to hear the opening and closing ceremonies and the more eagerly anticipated addresses. Foreign delegates represented India, Japan, England, the Near East (Turkey and Lebanon), Europe, China, Ceylon, Siam, and Canada.

Symbolism of the World's Parliament

To look in some detail at a 19th century world's fair, held in the American midwest, presenting examples of technological and commercial achievement, and also offering addresses on religious and moral subjects, is to have the opportunity to see many of our changing sensibilities more clearly. A recent dissertation, done at Harvard by Richard H. Seager,[3] reflects on some of the ethnocentrism.

---

[3]Seager, Richard Hughes, "The World's Parliament of Religions, Chicago, Illinois, 1893: America's Religious Coming of Age," Ph.D. diss., Harvard University, 1987.

> The White City (Exposition grounds and buildings) portrayed the United States as standing at the summit of the many civilizations of the world. It represented an America that was both a particular nation and a universal ideal that enlightened the world. It suggested that America stood for "the best and the brightest," all the "barbaric," "inferior," "picturesque," and "ethnic" worlds of other people were portrayed as being ultimately assimilated to its ideals and measured by its goals and accomplishments.[4]

The Columbian Exposition itself was authorized by the United States Congress and supported rather handsomely with Federal money. The idea of the World's Parliament of Religions was conceived, promoted and first published in 1889, primarily by Charles C. Bonney, a lawyer and judge, and a Swedenborgian, who worked closely with Paul Carus, editor of the Open Court Press. It is generally conceded that it would have been utterly impossible to have had any successful ecumenical religious meeting had the planning been expected from ecclesiastical associations. In fact those ecclesiastical assemblies which considered participation in the Parliament most frequently denounced it and refused participation. Bonney and Barrows created a committee of Chicago area clergy, sent invitations worldwide to groups who might participate. In the final analysis, though advised by denominational committees, participation was the result of invitations and urging as described in the prospectus. At that point in American religious life not one denomination was willing to address invitations to others which might suggest a legitimacy in their institutional and ecclesiastical claims.

For many conservative, evangelical, or orthodox commentators the conference was seen from beginning to end as a disaster. The participation of a Roman Catholic delegation, headed by Cardinal Gibbons of Baltimore, Bishop John Keane of Catholic University and Archbishop Patrick A. Feehan of Chicago, and of an important Jewish delegation led by Isaac Wise and Emil G. Hirsch aggravated the controversy with the Protestant evangelicals. The addition of representatives of Hinduism, Buddhism, Islam, Shinto, Confucianism, and papers about other groups only poured gasoline on burning passions. Barrows and Bonney and their committees were heavily criticized for the "unrepresentative" character of the delegates. The official representative of Confucianism was a member of the diplomatic delegation to Washington, D.C. appointed by the Chinese Emperor, but most of the delegates were self-appointed, and were not considered to be authoritative spokespersons for their own traditions. In fact, however, it appears that none of the various traditions was substantially betrayed by the descriptions and assertions provided by their own representatives. Some of the descriptions of non-Christian religions, provided by Christian missionaries, would not have been acceptable to any articulate representative of the religion itself. The World's Parliament, as the first large scale religious meet-

---

[4]Seager, 21.

ing to invite global participation, helped to identify those segments of the Christian community which would be interested in pursuing further mutual conversations. The fact that the Parliament had to be conceived, planned and executed largely by self-appointed clergy and religious representatives, and undertaken in the face of determined opposition by ecclesiastical organizations is a further indication that the ecclesiastical organizations which have finally seized control of the ecumenical enterprise had to be dragged kicking and screaming into it.

Participation of Women

A second point of interest was the fact that the World's Parliament had substantial participation and leadership from some of the most influential women of the day. Frances Willard and Julia Ward Howe were delegates. Elizabeth Cady Stanton contributed a paper which was read by Susan B. Anthony. Mary Baker Eddy sent a paper. Rev. Ida C. Hultin, Lady Henry Somerset, Rev. Anna G. Spencer (Providence), Jeanne Sorabji (Bombay), Henrietta Szold, Rev. Olympia Brown, Alice C. Fletcher (Cambridge MA), and Fannie Barrier Williams (Chicago) Rev. Antoinette Brown Blackwell (Elizabeth, N.J.), Mrs. Celia Parker Wooley (Geneva, Ill.), Lydia Fuller Dickinson, Laura Ormiston Chant, Dr. Eliza P. Sunderland, Josephine Lazarus, Rev. Annis F. F. Eastman, Rev. Marian Murdock appeared upon the program. Although too late to be a precedent the World's Parliament gave public platform and serious and profitable attention to some of the prominent women of religion of the day.

Ground Rules of the Conference

The ground rules of the conference made some kinds of things very difficult—as, for example, sustained argument or response to points made in other papers, or coordinated inquiry on common topics, and at the same time made it clear that this was a Christian oriented conference in which other religions had been invited to participate. The objectives stated in the prospectus and first report include the following (as edited and summarized).

1. A conference of leading representatives of the historic religions of the world.
2. "To show to men, in the most impressive way, what and how many important truths the various religions hold and teach in common."
3. To promote brotherhood among men of diverse faiths, but not to foster indifferentism, not to achieve any formal or outward unity.
4. To set forth truths of each religion and by various branches of Christendom.
5. "To indicate the impregnable foundations of theism, and the reasons for man's faith in immortality, and thus unite and strengthen the forces adverse to a materialistic philosophy of the universe."
6. To discover the effects of religions upon other aspects of culture.
7. "To inquire what light each religion has afforded, or may afford to the other religions of the world."

8. To assess the outlook for religions.

9. To discover what light religion has to throw on the great problems of the present age: temperance, labor, education, wealth, and poverty.

10. "To bring the nations of the earth into a more friendly fellowship in the hope of securing permanent international peace."[5]

The ground rules stipulated that the presence of any individual or group on the program did not presume any recognition of others present as legitimate or competent representatives of true religion. Each was to keep to the presentation of his or her own views, avoid direct criticism of others. Forthrightness and courtesy were both encouraged. No resolutions could be presented and no votes would be taken. It was not intended that the Parliament would lead to any unity other than that essential to discussion. There all were equals, but as F. Max Muller pointed out in a letter to the committee,

> It is in the nature of things that no religion places itself on a level with any other religion. Every believer is convinced that his own religion is *sui generis*. People unacquainted with any religion but their own are apt to think that all other religions are false, mischievous, if not the work of the Evil Spirit. . . . If we are truly convinced of the truth of our own religion we desire no privileges for it. So much for the spirit in which religions should be compared, and, from what I know of your Meeting at Chicago, you do not intend more than that representatives of different religions should compare notes, and come to know each other and if possible to respect each other better than they do at present."[6]

Muller sent a paper to the Conference, on Greek contributions to Christian thought, but later regretted that he had not come to the Parliament which he regarded as the major religious event of his generation. When in the course of events vigorous criticism, mostly directed against Asians but in some instances by them against Christianity, did arise, and when there were occasional outbursts from the audience of "Shame, shame!" (as when a brief explanation of polygamy among Muslims was anticipated) Chairman Barrows endeavored to take little notice, either in presiding or in print. Considering the immense crowds and the powerful feelings aroused, the general decorum was amazing.

Criticism of the Parliament

Numerous critics of the Parliament refused to appear on a program with representatives of other religions on grounds that that would amount to a recognition

---

[5]Druyvesteyn, Chicago diss., 33-34.

[6]John Henry Barrows, *The World's Parliament of Religions: An Illustrated and Popular Story of the World's First Parliament of Religions, Held in Chicago in Connection with the Columbian Exposition of 1893*, 2 vols. (Chicago: Parliament Publishing Co., 1893) 1:800.

of their faiths as legitimate. The archbishop of Canterbury declined to endorse the conference with the statement that

> I do not understand how that religion can be regarded as a member of a Parliament of Religions without assuming the equality of the other intended members and the parity of their positions and claims. . . . A presentation of [one's] religion must go far beyond the question of evidences and must subject to public discussion that faith and devotion which are its characteristics, and which belong to a region too sacred for such treatment.

He also objected that the word "Catholic" was included only in the title of the Roman Catholic Church, and not as a designation for the Protestant Episcopal or Anglican Churches—an attitude he found "untenable." The Sultan of Turkey also vigorously declined to encourage Muslim participation in the conference. As indicated previously the Protestant evangelicals were generally in opposition as were many, but not all, missionary groups and pastors. Some complaints that the Parliament would be likely to vitiate the enthusiasm and direction of the missionary effort in foreign lands proved in certain respects to be valid.

One of the most aggravating issues, especially to the American evangelicals, was the decision that had already been reached with respect to the "White City" Exposition grounds and which was agreed to also by the Parliament that the program would continue on Sunday. Vigorous protests were mounted to oppose the Satanic inspiration for the Sunday operation of the fair. Opening the Parliament daily with prayers, hymns and discourse on religious themes, much of which is indistinguishable from sermonic material, did nothing to alleviate the objections. The Baptists and the Christian Endeavor withdrew denominational conferences which they had scheduled in Chicago because of the Sunday opening of the Fair and Parliament. This drove an even sharper wedge between more liberal and more evangelical Christians and kept many of the more conservative Christians from participating. Some of the Japanese groups expressed reservations as to whether they could expect to be received with courtesy and respect, based on their experience with Christians in their own land.

The net result of these various kinds of objections and withdrawals was a more clearcut division than had heretofore existed among evangelical opposition, orthodox (also conservative and traditional, but willing to participate in the Conference), and liberals who were most eager to hold the conference and to share discussion with representatives of other religions. Barrows himself (a Presbyterian) belonged to the group here called "orthodox." He insisted on Christ as the only divinely chosen mode of salvation. His denomination refused to participate officially but did not seek to prevent the participation of individual clergy and teachers. Therefore, the World's Parliament of Religions was an event primarily in the liberal religious tradition. The Congregationalists, Unitarians, and Universalists appear to have had the largest number of active participants (though the records for denominational affiliation are incomplete). Episcopalians, Methodists, Presbyterians, and some Baptists participated gladly, though their denominations did not.

Roman Catholic Participation

The Roman Catholic case was special. Martin Marty has made Catholic participation in the World's Parliament a prominent issue in the gradual Americanization of Catholicism.[7] Cardinal Gibbons made the decision to participate, as part of the Catholic utilization of American freedom and liberty. Seven Roman Catholic delegates were appointed, including Archbishop Patrick A. Feehan of Chicago. The pope sent his legate to provide independent reports on the behavior of the Church's representatives there. It remained controversial. Archbishop Gibbons participated resplendently in the opening procession, sat center stage with the orange robed Buddhists and Hindus, and delivered the opening prayer. Poor health prevented his regular participation in most sessions, and John Keane read his paper for him, but the Catholic presence throughout the Congress was carefully orchestrated. In his speech at the opening session Gibbons gave the tenor of the Catholic presentation—no surrender of claims to ultimate truth, welcome to others, willingness to listen to all, and concentration on matters of essential civility. He said:

> I should be wanting in my duty as a minister of the Catholic Church if I did not say that it is our desire to present the claims of the Catholic Church to the observation and, if possible, to the acceptance of every right-minded man that will listen to us. But we appeal only to the tribunal of conscience and of intellect. I feel that in possessing my faith I possess a treasure compared with which all the treasures of this world are but dross; and, instead of hiding those treasures in my own coverts, I would like to share them with others, especially as I am none the poorer in making others the richer. But though we do not agree in matters of faith, as the Most Reverend Archbishop of Chicago has said, thanks be to God there is one platform on which we all stand united. It is the platform of charity, of humanity, and of benevolence.[8]

At the conclusion of the meetings Cardinal Gibbons sent his report to the Vatican, (supplemented, of course, with the pope's private report), but the final word for Catholics on the Parliament of Religions came tersely from Pope Leo XIII: "No more promiscuous assemblies!"

---

[7]Cf. Martin E. Marty, *Pilgrims in Their Own Land: 500 Years of Religion in America* (New York: Penguin Books, 1984) 282-85.

[8]Barrows, 80.

The World's Parliament as a Christian Convention

The motto of the Parliament, as suggested by H. Adler, chief rabbi of the British Empire, was, "Have we not all one Father? Hath not one God created us?" (Malachi 2:10). The Congress was opened by the prayer of Cardinal Gibbons, and by hymns from the Psalter. Each day's assembly prayed the Christian Lord's Prayer, called there the "Universal Prayer," and it was also used as the final words to close the two volume report on the Parliament and sections. The definition of religion (provided by Charles C. Bonney) was, "Religion means the love and worship of God and the love and service of man."[9] This was followed by a text quoted often in the sessions, "Of a truth God is no respecter of persons, but in every nation he that feareth God and worketh righteousness is accepted of him." Despite protest of the Buddhist delegate, Dharmapala, and a careful attempt on the part of the Chinese delegate to differentiate more clearly between Jesus' rule of doing to others what you want done to yourself, and Confucius' principle of avoiding doing those things which you would not wish done to yourself, there is little evidence that the Christian delegates ever questioned the universality of these principles. The final comments of Chairman Barrows were: "I desire that the last word which I speak to the Parliament shall be the name of Him to whom I owe life and truth and hope and all things, who reconciles all contradictions, pacifies all antagonisms, and who from the throne of His heavenly kingdom directs the serene and unwearied omnipotence of redeeming love—Jesus Christ, the savior of the world."[10] It is, of course, fitting that, in the final moments at least, he should enjoy the freedom of personal confession which every other delegate had utilized throughout the meetings, but in the preparations and evaluations he makes it quite clear that the sentiments of this sentence always pervaded his work and his expectations concerning the Parliament. Despite his scrupulous fairness, calm demeanor, courtesy and respect for each speaker, he could not approve of their points of view or religious presuppositions. This gentlemanliness is what he had hoped for from every participant.

Dharmapala, the Buddhist teacher from Ceylon, Virchand A. Gandhi, a Jain, and Pung Kwang Yu, the Confucian delegate, tried to clarify that these criteria are not appropriate for a truly global sense of religion. In the more technical papers dealing with concepts of God, Milton Terry's paper on Taoism tried to show that God as author of creation is a mischievous notion, while D'vivedi, Vivekenanda and others tried to clarify Vedantic notions of God. A more dramatic moment was struck when Kinza Riuge M. Hirai took occasion to point out that Japan had no special difficulty in listening to Christianity, but found the immorality and injustice of

---

[9]Barrows, 68.

[10]Located in the proceedings but here quoted by Joseph Kitagawa, "The 1893 World's Parliament of Religions and Its Legacy," appendix to *The History of Religions: Understanding Human Experience* (Atlanta: Scholars Press, 1987) 364.

Christians in his country insufferable. Speaking to an audience, many of whom were missionaries, he pointed out that the early missions were convicted of trying to subvert the Japanese government on behalf of colonial powers and the later ones appealed only to advantages gained by entirely unequal treaties. He inserted the American declaration of independence into his speech as an appropriate expression of Japanese feeling against such exploitation. Vivekenanda, on the other hand, became famous for his irenic endeavor to show that Hinduism and other religions express the same basic concerns.

The evaluation of the Parliament depends entirely on the standpoint of the critic. A contemporary Buddhist critic[11] stands fairly near his contemporary liberal Christian colleague in asking for a comradeship in continued search of significant understanding.

Sequels to the Parliament

The story of what followed the Parliament is a curious one. Superlatives of self-congratulation radiated through the closing ceremonies. In the final chapter of Barrows's two-volume report he summarized his own judgment and that of his correspondents in a series of reflections. He believed that overall the Parliament was an "extraordinary success." He said:

Liberal Christians naturally looked upon it as one of their triumphs, but they could not have gained the cooperation of historic Christendom. Liberal-minded Jews saw in it the fulfillment of the prophecy that the knowledge of Jehovah should cover the earth, but Judaism alone could not have achieved a convention of Christians. The Brahmo-Somaj regarded the Parliament as fulfilling the ideas of the New Dispensation, but the Brahmo-Somaj would have been unable to draw together the representatives of the great faiths. No Christian missionary society could have achieved the Parliament, for fear of aggressive propagandism would have kept out the non-Christian world. No ecclesiastical body in Christendom, whether Catholic, Greek, Anglican, or Lutheran, could have assembled the Parliament. . . . But as a part of an international exposition, and controlled by a generous-minded and representative committee, under no ecclesiastical dictation, and appealing in the spirit of fraternity to high-minded individuals, the Parliament was possible, and was actualized.[12]

He concluded that the Parliament showed that humanity was drifting toward rather than away from religion, that it had widened religious fellowship, stimulated the study of comparative religion, enhanced confidence in the liberty of thought, clarified knowledge of the non-Christian religions and deepened Christian interest in their lands and traditions. He was grateful that no new universal or cosmic faiths

---

[11]Cf. Clay Lancaster, *The Incredible World's Parliament of Religions at the Chicago Colombian Exposition of 1893: A Comparative and Critical Study* (Sussex UK: Centaur Press, n.d.).

[12]Barrows, 1568.

were emerging from the conference, but that it had awakened a new world consciousness. He affirmed that orthodox Christianity had not been compromised and that it had made a favorable impression on those whom it had some desire and expectation of influencing. One might not be quite so sure of the drift of religion vis à vis the secularism which was on display in the rest of the Exposition, but most of the rest of the conclusions seem legitimate if not pushed too far beyond the events themselves. Mr. Seager, in his Harvard dissertation, describes some of the succeeding events and judgments.

The spirit of religious universalism was most conspicuous in Chicago where a number of delegates to the Parliament were declaring "the dawn of a new religious era." Almost immediately after the Parliament closed, a new movement of religious liberalism was inaugurated in Chicago with endorsements from Virchand Gandhi the Jain and B. B. Nagarkar of the Brahmo-Samaj, from representatives from the Ethical Culture Society and the Free Religious Association, and from Jenkin Lloyd Jones, Paul Carus, Emil Hirsch, and Merwin-Marie Snell. As reported in *Unity*, the magazine of the Chicago Unitarians, one goal of the movement was to form a bridge between liberals in ecclesiastical organizations and the numerous supporters of the liberal religious cause among the unchurched. In May of 1894, "The First American Congress of Liberal Religious Societies" was held in Emil Hirsch's Sinai Temple in Chicago. Hirsch, Jones, E.L. Rexford, Kinza Ruige M. Hirai and six hundred others signed the Congress's call that sought to promote "a nearer and more helpful fellowship in the social, educational, industrial, moral, and religious thought and work of the world."[13]

By 1895 Carus had announced the inauguration of the World's Parliament Extension to maintain the broad interests represented by the Parliament, but to be under the command of the liberal rather than of the orthodox sentiments. In the course of time this led to the International Association for the History of Religions, which continues to this day. Charles Little, of Garrett Theological Seminary, published an indictment of the Parliament which concluded that the old aims of liberty, equality and fraternity had been reinterpreted in the Parliamentary sessions to mean laxity, apathy, and compromise. It is often acknowledged that the Parliament had a substantial role to play in the acceptance of the Roman Catholic Church as a legitimate participant in the pluralistic religious picture in the United States.

It is curious that while many Christians believed the Parliament had been a kind of contest for supremacy and that they had won (after all they had made the rules), a hundred years later the Asians believe *they* won. Vivekenanda capitalized on his immense popularity at the Parliament, toured the United States for four years, and left a legacy of Vedanta Societies which continues to this day. D. T. Suzuki, who was a translator for Shaku Soyen's speeches at the Parliament, returned to be a

---

[13]Seager, 203-204.

translator, student, editor with Paul Carus at the Open Court and Monist press, with a legacy for Zen Buddhism which is well known. Even the ethnic churches, like the Tri-State Buddhist Church in Denver, had a burst of energy and development from the visits of their high-ranking leaders to Chicago. The yoga movement, which is among those planning to return to Chicago in 1993, dates its serious penetration of America with this event. It just may be that the Asians are right.

In the larger sense one of the results of the Parliament seems to have been a new kind of recognition of religious reality among many American intellectuals. All the religions have been born into a world of religious pluralism, but, on the whole they have ignored this fact. Each tradition maintains the idea of its own universality and sufficiency. Some teach a concept of development toward more inclusive, adequate, and enlightened religious forms—of which, of course, each tradition believes itself to be the noblest example. For many, the World's Parliament seems to have awakened an awareness of true pluralism. This moves relationships away from evangelization, whether genteel or aggressive, toward dialogue. This appears to be the stage we entered at about the beginning of the twentieth century and which will be bequeathed to the twenty-first.

Aftermath of the Parliament

The Parliament of Religions closed precisely on schedule with dramatic and satisfying closing ceremonies. The Exposition was scheduled to continue for about another month. The Chicago mayor, Carter E. Harrison, having formulated plans for an appeal to Congress for funding to continue the Exposition another year, attended a meeting of American mayors at the exhibition grounds. On the way home from the meeting he was assassinated by one of his young campaign workers. The closing ceremonies of the Exposition were much curtailed and dampened by the murder. When it had closed it was discovered that the Columbian Exposition had done much to shield Chicago from the recession which was depressing the rest of the country. Following the Exposition there were 200,000 unemployed workers in Chicago. With a depressed economy the hopes for commercial and civic use of the buildings of the White City were not immediately realized and the buildings were vacated. A group of transients took up residence in the Hall of Honor, and in the night of January 8 it was set afire. The fire destroyed many of the buildings and art of the "White City" and left a legacy of frustration and disappointment. By spring the Pullman boycott and strike were on and the Chicago economy was in shambles. Efforts to get Christians together in ecclesiastical assemblies simply displayed the deep fractures in Christian unity. The pope refused to permit further Roman Catholic participation in such open conferences. John Henry Barrows's thirteen-year-old son died while the father was editing the final pages of the proceedings. The immediate aftermath was gloomy.

However, in retrospect we can see that the World's Parliament of Religions both gave expression to and opened opportunity for a new kind of religious thinking. For many people it would no longer be possible to do theology without consideration of the insights and criticisms which other religions have to offer. Liberal Christianity has been a leading force in the engagement in this continuing dialogue.

How I Got That Way: My Intellectual Autobiography

Randolph Crump Miller

William James wrote that "a philosophy is the experience of a [person's] intimate character, and all definitions of the universe are but deliberately adopted reactions of human character upon it.[1]

"All theology is ultimately autobiography," said Frederick Buechner.

So how did I end up with an empirical, pragmatic, and pluralistic philosophy of religion? How did I manage to find solutions to life's problems that satisfied me? And how did I fit this in with membership and priesthood in the Protestant Episcopal Church?

My father was an Episcopal minister and I grew up in his parish. In 1917, he published a book entitled *Modernist Studies in the Life of Jesus*, and concluded with a description of a liberal faith.

> A liberal faith is a great faith; it constantly, like the chick, breaks the old shell, and walks into new life. But, mind you, it takes the essence of the old life with it, leaving only the shell. A truly liberal faith leaves nothing of value behind. . . . A man who calls himself a liberal and slinks back out of sight in the face of some crisis, is not a liberal; he is only a coward. A man who calls himself a liberal and lives an openly bad life, is not a liberal; he is only a libertine. If a man calls himself a liberal and you can only tell that he is by the number of things he does not believe, he is not a liberal; he is only a doubter. A liberal is one whose blood is growing warmer, whose charity is growing broader, whose vision is growing clearer; who, in the last analysis, is deeply in love with life.[2]

---

[1]William James, *A Pluralistic Universe* (New York: Longmans, Green & Co., 1909) 20; Randolph Crump Miller, *This We Can Believe* (New York: Hawthorn, 1976) 8.

[2]Ray Oakley Miller, *Modernist Studies in the Life of Jesus* (Boston: Sherman, French, 1917) 52.

This was the atmosphere of both our home and parish. At an early age I was grounded in a rich tradition and free to develop my own thoughts and attitudes, but I was greatly influenced by the religious outlook of my home and family.

I had given no thought to the possibility of becoming a minister until the summer of 1927, after graduation from secondary school. In a little town in the Santa Cruz mountains, Ben Lomond—a friend—and I went to church. The old preacher simply did not make sense in his sermon, and I became annoyed; and then it came to me, "Damn it, get out of that pulpit and let me preach!" Actually, all we did was take up the offering because no one else made a move, but this was my "call" to the ministry, and it has stayed with me for more than sixty years.

In the fall of 1927, I entered Pomona College. I enjoyed my courses and new friends. Some time along the way, I had a vague experience that I later identified as evidence of what William James called a "mystical germ," something unidentifiable and yet real. I could have dismissed it, but it stuck with me. In 1929, my mother came down with multiple sclerosis, and this was an immediate threat to my current religious outlook. How could a good God allow such things to happen? So it was a personal problem that I faced as I took a course in philosophy of religion that focused on Bergson, James, and Dewey. My old notes form 1930 simply mention that for James God was in a pluralistic world and had an environment and that evil was not part of God's purpose. I was immediately converted, for it solved my problem and also made sense to see the world as James saw it.

From then on, James has been one of my guiding lights. In my preliminary examinations for the Ph.D. at Yale, I chose James as the subject for the one examination on an individual philosopher. However, in both my dissertation and my first book, James is referred to only in passing, and I did not make full use of him again until I considered him as the primary model of radical empiricism, pragmatism, and pluralism in my *The American Spirit in Theology* in 1973.

From Pomona I went to Yale and immediately became involved in the teaching of Douglas Clyde Macintosh. It was the period when *Religious Realism* was published, with essays by the editor, Macintosh, Henry Nelson Wieman, Walter Marshall Horton, Robert Lowry Calhoun, James Bissett Pratt, H. Richard Niebuhr, and others who were more or less empirical and realistic. In a lengthy sentence, Macintosh introduced the volume as follows.

> Religious Realism . . . means centrally that a religious Object, such as may appropriately be called God, exists independently of our consciousness thereof, and is yet related to us in such a way that through reflection on experience in general and religious experience in particular, . . . it is possible for us to gain (as some would maintain) adequately verified knowledge or (as others would be content to affirm) a practically valuable and theoretically permissible faith not only that the religious Object exists but also, within

whatever limits, as to what its nature is.[3]

In Macintosh's chapter, the longest in the book, he established his version of an empirical approach to the existence of a divine value-producing factor, which he called God. It is an approach similar to that of Henry Nelson Wieman, except that Macintosh relied primarily on what he called "the right religious adjustment." He backed this with a theory of knowledge he called "critical monistic realism," which allows for the independent existence of the object. Through this argument, Macintosh established the existence of a "divine value-producing factor."

Macintosh was aware of Whitehead's philosophy of organism, and he examined it seriously. But he could not understand the relation between eternal objects and actual events. He pointed out Whitehead's "horror" of the "bifurcation of nature" which he shared, but he claimed that Whitehead was guilty of the bifurcation of God. There is so great a contrast and even contradiction between his "primordial nature of God" and his "consequent nature of God" that they are split into two "apparently irreconcilable notions of God." Important as Whitehead's thought is for modern philosophy of religion, "two half-gods do not make one whole God." Whitehead's philosophy may prove helpful, but in religion "he had deposited a cuckoo egg or two in the theological nest." Macintosh would like the primordial nature to be "conscious, fully actual, and creative," and then there would be a unitary conception.[4] Remember that Macintosh was responding, in 1930, to Whitehead's 1928 *Process and Reality*, and he was exploring what to him was a new and challenging metaphysical system to which he was largely sympathetic.

Macintosh was closely aligned with Henry Nelson Wieman. Both were empiricists, and they had a similar basis for their verified concept of God: Macintosh's divine value-producing factor and Wieman's "that something, however unknown, which would and which does bring human life to the largest fulfillment when proper adjustment is made to it."[5] But Macintosh disagreed with Wieman, accusing Wieman of "defining god in such a way that even the person who has freely denied the existence of God can now affirm it without changing in the slightest degree either his opinion or his life."[6]

This conflict makes understandable Macintosh's suggestion that I write my dissertation on Wieman and the Chicago School, which I did in 1935–1936, typing the final draft at the Episcopal Theological School, where I took courses that helped me understand the Protestant Episcopal Church. I began the dissertation with the question "Is Theism Essential to Religion?", a study of Gerald Birney Smith. From there

---

[3]*Religious Realism*, ed. Douglas Clyde Macintosh (New York: Macmillan, 1931) v.

[4]See *Religious Realism*, 389-92.

[5]Henry Nelson Wieman, *The Wrestle of Religion with Truth* (New York: Macmillan, 1929) 59.

[6]*Religious Pluralism*, 397.

I turned to the humanist reaction of J. H. Leuba, Paul Heyl, and Walter Lippmann. I quoted Lippmann's summary:

> Since nothing gnawed at his vitals, neither doubt nor ambition, nor frustration, nor fear, he would move easily through life. And so whether he saw the thing as *comedy*, or *high tragedy*, or *plain farce*, he would affirm that it is what it is, and that the wise man can enjoy it.[7]

If this is the ultimate of nontheistic humanism, I found it unacceptable.

This led directly into chapters on the Chicago School: the social idealism of Edward Scribner Ames, an analysis of John Dewey's *A Common Faith*, whose position influenced Wieman, and for whom I coined the term "semi-theist," Shailer Mathews's "conceptual theism," and on to the central portion of the dissertation, Henry Nelson Wieman. Most of what I wrote in 1935–1936 is summarized in the early chapters of *The American Spirit in Theology*.

Wieman was aware of Whitehead prior to 1927, when his *Wrestle of Religion with Truth* appeared. He provided a reasonably accurate summary of Whitehead's understanding of deity, and he claimed that this concept could be validated. Earlier, in *Religious Experience and Scientific Method*, Wieman had dealt with Whitehead's view of nature, which he continued to take seriously, but in 1946, in *The Source of Human Good*, Wieman rejected Whitehead's view of God in favor of his own developing concept of God as "the creative event."

By the time I had completed my dissertation in 1936 I had been deeply influenced by Wieman, favoring his position over that of Macintosh and Whitehead although today I lean toward James and Whitehead. William James wrote that few new ideas are gained after the age of twenty-five. I was twenty-five when I completed my dissertation, and I now think that the major direction of my thought was established.

Church Divinity School of the Pacific

Whitehead spoke of emerging novelty, which may be interpreted as chance, or a once-in-a-lifetime opportunity, or God saying, "Behold! I make all things new." The event may be ignored, or lost, or acted upon.

Just before I received my degree from Yale, my father wrote me about a small divinity school in Berkeley whose new dean was struggling to make ends meet on a $10,000 budget. Would I like to teach there? I immediately wrote to Dean Henry Shires. He replied offering me a job—for room and board; and I could make $10 a Sunday taking services. I accepted.

The dean and I had never met, and I had never seen the school, so we were both taking a chance. I stayed for sixteen years. My first course was philosophy of religion, and I had outlines and notes from my courses with Macintosh. My other

---

[7]Walter Lippmann, *A Preface to Morals* (New York: Macmillan, 1929) 330.

course the first quarter was Christian Ethics, and my background was H. Richard Niebuhr and Wilbur Urban. So I got off to a good start. The next term I had a course in Apologetics, sometimes called Christian Evidences, for which I used Macintosh's *Reasonableness of Christianity* as a text. These were my basic required courses, which left me free to offer some seminars. Among the electives I repeated most often were *The Normative Psychology of Religion* by Wieman and his wife and *Nature, Man, and God* by Archbishop William Temple. These courses were based on more study and although my basic viewpoint remained the same, I found myself greatly enriched. I began to write articles and book reviews and began thinking about writing a book.

In 1937, I was asked to become the chaplain to the Episcopalians at the University of California on a part-time basis. I had already been attending some of their meetings in order to meet contemporaries. As chaplain I would earn more than I was at the little mission I had been running. Among the girls I met was Muriel Hallett, and in a short time she became my primary date. On July 1, 1937, we became engaged to be married. The next fall, Muriel was a student at St. Margaret's House, a training center for women workers in the church, and she took my course in philosophy of religion. I considered this excellent background for marriage.

In June 1938, Muriel and I were married. I continued as chaplain and taught the same courses at CDSP. There was a theological discussion group for the Pacific Coast, sponsored by the Hazen Foundation, that drew the top theologians from the whole area, including John Bennett, James Muilenburg, both of the Pacific School of Religion, and Bernard Meland from Pomona College. Bennett was the chairperson until he left for Union Seminary in New York, and I was chairperson when we wrote the second volume of the Interseminary Series and until I left for Yale. It was a gathering of genuine scholars, and I gained much from my participation twice a year.

In 1940, a full-time chaplain came to the University of California and I asked the bishop to send me to St. Alban's, a storefront church in Albany, a suburb of Berkeley. This was a part of the practical testing of my theological position, for both with the college students and now with the average churchgoer I was translating my empirical theology into the language of the layperson and relating it to their experiences. I had been working on a book, which Scribner's published in 1941, *What We Can Believe*, which reflected what I had learned in Pomona, Yale, and by working with seminarians, university students, and laypeople.

But now there came a shifting of gears. Because I was low person on the faculty totem pole, I was asked by the dean to teach a course in religious education. I protested that I had no background in the subject. He suggested I borrow my wife Muriel's notes from a course she had taken at the Berkeley Baptist Divinity School. So I had the outline of Sandford Fleming's course as a basis for my attempt to teach a new subject. (Incidentally, Fleming's outline was so comprehensive that I used it for my introductory course throughout my career and as the basis for my textbook

Education for Christian Living—and he knew it.) I continued with my two courses each quarter in philosophy of religion, Christian ethics, and evidences, but taught a third course in religious education. I found that my theological training gave me an approach to education that differed from that of many professionals in the field.

By the end of 1941, we had two daughters, *What We Can Believe* had arrived, the Japanese had attacked Pearl Harbor, and my mother had died just before Christmas. From a theological perspective, plenty of empirical data were available, and I found that my theology withstood these critical events. There was a shift in the demand for my time as churches asked for lectures in the field of religious education, and in 1943 I published *A Guide for Church School Teachers*.

Because I was the only Episcopalian in the West teaching religious education, I was asked to be on the editorial committee to plan and guide the formation of the Seabury Series. Beginning in 1947, I flew east four times a year for five years. Those meetings were rich in educational and theological insights, especially in the existential thinking of Martin Buber as interpreted by Reuel Howe, and I found myself using their ideas as I formed a more substantial base for my educational philosophy. I wrote a paper for discussion on the theological base for education that subsequently became the opening chapter and the basic theme of my book *The Clue to Christian Education*.

In May 1948, when I returned from a Seabury meeting, my wife met me at the airport. But the next day she seemed ill with the flu. Within ten days she died of polio. We had just less than ten years together and had four daughters aged two, four, six, and eight. Here was another test for my theology, especially as found in William James. Nothing helped the grief, but at least I could not blame God for such a chance event when there had not been a polio case in the entire county for some time. I found that God was a present help in time of trouble but that God does not take our troubles from us. As the Letter of James says, God does not show partiality, does not play favorites. I had to preach to my congregation two weeks later, and my theme was "God is love." Love must be dependable and constant. God does not change natural law.

> When, according to natural law, the winds blow and the floods come, we must either meet the challenge with proper safeguards or take the consequences. When someone suffers or dies from the effects of natural law, I do *not* believe it is because God *wills* such results. I believe that God is dependable in his goodness and love, and, therefore, he will not reverse his laws or suspend their operation to help us escape suffering.[8]

---

[8]Randolph C. Miller, *Be Not Anxious* (Greenwich CT: Seabury, 1957) 186.

I continued with a discussion of God's power of persuasive love and human freedom, and ended with the hymn of St. Patrick: "I bind unto myself today / The strong Name of the Trinity."[9]

The next year at a meeting of the Seabury group, I was asked to give a lecture in Richmond, Virginia, after two others had been unable to accept an invitation. So I was a third choice. Again, chance or creative novelty was working and I accepted. After my first lecture, I was invited to speak at a local church, and after some arm twisting, I accepted. There I met a young widow. We spoke briefly at the dinner, but I was intrigued. However, all I knew was her name, and when I returned to California I thought about writing her. After wondering how to find her, I remembered that woman workers were listed in the clerical directory, and sure enough I found her name and church. So I wrote a letter to "Dear Mrs. Fowlkes" at St. Thomas Church, Richmond. She replied and we began writing regularly. To make a long story short, Elizabeth and I were married a year later in St. Thomas Church. Her two children and my four gave us six children before we were even married.

In the meantime, I had finished writing *The Clue to Christian Education*. It was my attempt to bring my two interests together, with theology as the "clue." There were fewer references to James and Macintosh, and Wieman and Whitehead did not appear in the index. I used more traditional language in this book, but I also sought to give educational applications at various age levels. It was still an application of radical empiricism to theology. It was this book, I think, that led to the next unexpected event.

On June 5, 1951, I received a phone call from Liston Pope, dean of Yale Divinity School, asking if I would accept an appointment in the field of religious education. Arrangements were made for me to fly from Nashville (where I would be teaching at Sewanee) to New York. I met with both Paul Vieth and Liston Pope and heard the proposition. I was assured that they wanted a theologically trained educator for a new chair named for Luther Weigle who had retired. This was the issue I took back home with me.

Yale

I had thought of myself as a philosopher of religion who taught religious education on the side and now I was asked to reverse that arrangement. Lib and our six children were happy in Berkeley and had expected to stay there. My father was all for accepting the Yale appointment, and I believe that Lib was excited about it, but there was no pressure from her or the children. It was up to me. I tried to consider all the angles, including the activities I shared in both areas. *The Clue to Christian Education* was obviously more in demand than my books *What We Can Believe* or

---

[9]Ibid., 187.

Religion Makes Sense, a book for laypeople. Finally, after six weeks of trying to decide about such a radical vocational change, I made the decision to go to Yale.

Working with Paul Vieth, we developed a balanced curriculum of courses that included graduate seminars. A few students concentrated on religious education, and we had outstanding Ph.D. students who today are leaders in the field. Hugh Hartshorne also offered courses related to religious education. A popular topic of the day was biblical theology, and I had worked on it in connection with the Seabury Series. I began lecturing and then writing on the drama of redemption, and published *Biblical Theology and Christian Education* in 1956. Along the way, however, I published a book of sermons based on my experience at St. Alban's, Albany, and then developed a textbook for college and seminary courses, *Education for Christian Living* (1956). Also from my pastoral experience I published *Be Not Anxious* in 1957.

After twenty-three years of teaching, we finally took a sabbatical, starting at the Ecumenical Institute at Bossey, Switzerland. We placed out six children in British schools. The lectures at Bossey were on the church and its ministry, which were the subjects of the first two chapters of a book I planned to write. We settled in at St. Deiniol's Library, Wales, after Christmas, and I wrote for eight hours a day, using the outlines of lectures I had given on the subject. The finished manuscript on *Christian Nurture and the Church* became the basis for ten lectures at St. Augustine's College, Canterbury, and the source of a study guide I was asked to write for the World Council of Christian Education. For the chapter on communication, I wrote of the language of relationships, based on insights I had gained from Reuel Howe, the language of words, with an interpretation based on Ian Ramsey's *Religious Language* and Francis Drinkwater's treatment of poetic simple and the language of things, a brief statement about symbols.

In 1958, I became editor of *Religious Education*, a journal for professionals published six times a year. This brought me into relationships with Catholics and Jews as well as other Protestants. I had control of what was being published, and with my interest in theology many articles were related to the relationship of theology and education. I remained the editor for twenty years.

In 1962, the World Council of Christian Education held its convention in Belfast. I had written the study guide for it and was the leader of the bible study each day. But for me the opportunity to meet with educators from all over the world was its primary value. This continued with sabbaticals in 1966–1967 and 1970 which took us around the world twice, teaching, consulting, and learning in many cultures. But I was doing little with my theological thinking.

However, my exposure to Ian Ramsey's theory of religious language, which I could apply to religious education, continued to attract me, and I spent time reading in the field of linguistic philosophy. This led to a summer course at the United Theological College in Vancouver and to a seminar at Yale. I went back to Horace Bushnell's "The Nature of Language, as Related to Thought and Spirit." In Beirut, in 1967, I wrote the first draft of what became *The Language Gap and God* and gave ten lectures on the topic at the Near East School of Theology. This book brought to bear on my thinking insights from Amos Wilder, Ludwig Wittgenstein, F. S. C. Northrop, Charles Hartshorne, Rudolf Bultmann, Schubert Ogden, Donald Evans, and others previously mentioned, and it led to a culminating chapter on a worldview.

God is in our midst. John Cobb says that God is

> everywhere, but he is not everything. The world does not exist outside God or apart from God, but it is not determined by him, and the world in its turn contributes novelty and richness to the divine experience.[10]

Because of my dual interest in theology and education, I ended each chapter with the educational implications of the various views of language. Because language of belief *in* God is distinct from one's view *about* God, I was impressed by Ramsey's and Dallas High's views on "I" language. The change in the creed to "We believe in" from "I believe in" seems to me to make the creed a committee report rather than a personal commitment based on discernment and relationship. I recall the long-drawn-out credo in Bach's mass as close to the truth. The creed is a pledge of allegiance and not a theological statement that can be doubted. The creed is not a literal statement but a poetic and mythological reconstruction of a person's faith.[11]

During the next three years, I wrote *Living with Anxiety*, a rewrite of *Be Not Anxious*, and *Live Until You Die*, about the art of dying and what happens afterwards, using some insights from Wieman and Hartshorne.

For thirty years I had wanted to make use of my doctoral research in a book. The material had been reworked entirely as a basis for my *What We Can Believe*, and I had rewritten the dissertation in an attempt to get it published. So for my sabbatical in 1973, we stayed at home, where I had access to all the books I needed, and I wrote a new book growing from my original research. The first half dealt with scholars I had used then, and for the second half I made use of additional thinkers to round out a process-oriented, radical-empirical theology in *The American Spirit in Theology*. It took me more than a month to write the chapter on Whitehead, but the ones on Hartshorne, Schubert Ogden, and Daniel Day Williams came more easily. Williams had read and approved of his chapter, and he was planning to meet my seminar to discuss it on the day he died, and I added his name to the dedication. Wieman lived long enough for his wife Laura to read to him my chapter on his position. The final chapter dealt more briefly with F. S. C. Northrop, John E. Smith, and Bernard Meland. Meland was closer to James than any of the others. He did pioneer work on the relation of religion to culture, and made creative use of Whitehead's metaphysics.

---

[10]*The Language Gap and God* (Philadelphia: Pilgrim Press, 1970) 146; John B. Cobb, Jr., *God and the World* (Philadelphia: Westminster, 1969) 80.

[11]*The Language Gap and God*, 159-60.

In 1976, we spent our last sabbatical in Claremont, the perfect place for anyone interested in process philosophy. I had graduated from Pomona College in 1931, so we enjoyed Claremont as the college town it still is. I was asked to give a seminar and took the obvious way of offering one on "Process Theology and Religious Education," which was a culmination of my two major interests. From then on, I offered this seminar at Yale until my retirement in 1981.

One way of deciding how my mind has changed or remained basically the same but enriched over the years is to compare my *What We Can Believe* (1941) with its revision in 1976 as *This We Can Believe*. In 1943, in *Christianity and the Contemporary Scene*, I wrote:

> Just as Thomas Aquinas christianized Aristotle, so modern theologians must come to terms with Whitehead. This perhaps is the great metaphysical task of modern theology.[12]

Whitehead appeared in the index in *What We Can Believe* just once in 1941 and eighteen times in 1976. Many new names appeared in the index: Ian Barbour, Delwin Brown, John B. Cobb, Jr., Ewart Cousins, Nils Dahl, Paulo Freier, David Griffin, Peter Hamilton, Bernard Lee, Norman Pittenger, Ian Ramsey, Harry Stack Sullivan, Teilhard de Chardin, and Daniel Day Williams. So it was not the same book, but was revised in terms of a more self-conscious Whiteheadian point of view. But the basic paradigm was the same as thirty-five years before. Perhaps I had *not* grown much after the age of twenty-five!

In 1980 in my last book, *The Theory of Christian Education Practice*, I attempted to provide a basis in process thinking for religious education. In the earlier chapters, I described process theology and made some applications to educational issues. I examined empirical method in theology, an approach to values, and ethical thinking. Horace Bushnell, William James, Bernard Meland, H. Richard Niebuhr, Harry Stack Sullivan, Whitehead, and Wieman appeared most often in the index. I even reprinted my 1952 address on "Christian Education as a Theological Discipline and Method." So my dual interests in theology and education stayed alive.

I concluded my book *The American Spirit in Theology* with these words:

> Today, again, some people find empirical process thinking the best way to get at a meaningful and religious truth, but there are those who are using their subcultures and ethnic groups as a way to escape from the pressures of our culture, and they have set up protective devices to keep religious thinking out of the clutches of empirical findings, partly because of their rejection of certain aspects of the culture. Because religion has the capacity to sit in judgment on culture as well as to benefit from it, this is to be expected. But

---

[12]Randolph C. Miller, *Christianity and the Contemporary Scene*, ed. Miller and Henry H. Shires (New York: Morehouse Gorham, 1943) 11.

there are those who agree with Erasmus that the new learning must not be identified with heresy, because that makes orthodoxy synonymous with ignorance.[13]

Books by Randolph Crump Miller

What We Can Believe. Scribner's, 1941.
A Guide for Church School Teachers. Cloister, 1943, 1947.
Religion Makes Sense. Seabury, 1950.
The Clue to Christian Education. Scribner's, 1950.
A Symphony of the Christian Year. Seabury, 1954. (Religious Book Club)
Education for Christian Living. Prentice-Hall, 1956, 1963.
Biblical Theology and Christian Education. Scribner's, 1956.
Be Not Anxious. Seabury, 1952.
I Remember Jesus. Seabury, 1958.
Christian Nurture and the Church. Scribner's, 1961. (RBC)
Your Child's Religion. Doubleday, 1962; Hawthorn, 1975.
Youth Considers Parents as People. Nelson, 1965.
The Language Gap and God. Pilgrim, 1970.
Living with Anxiety. Pilgrim, 1971.
Live Until You Die. Pilgrim, 1973.
The American Spirit in Theology. Pilgrim, 1974.
This We Can Believe. Hawthorn, Seabury, 1976.
The Theory of Christian Education and Practice. Religious Education Press, 1980.

Festschrift

Process and Relationship, ed. Iris Cully and Kendig Cully. Religious Education Press, 1978. See bibliography, 124-33.

Editor

The Church and Organized Movements. Harper, 1946.
What Is the Nature of Man? United Church Press, 1959.
Empirical Theology: A Handbook. Religious Education Press, 1992.

Coeditor

With Henry H. Shires, *Christianity and the Contemporary Scene.* Morehouse-Gorham, 1943.

---

[13]*The American Spirit in Theology* (Philadelphia: Pilgrim Press, 1974) 240. For a complete bibliography through 1976, see Iris V. Cully and Kendig Brubaker Cully, eds., *Process and Relationship* (Birmingham: Religious Education Press, 1978) 124-33; *Panorama* (Winter 1990): 10-19.

Selected Articles of Theological Import in Books

"Some Trends in American Theology," in *Christianity and the Contemporary Scene*, ed. Miller and Shires, 1-16. Morehouse-Gorham, 1943.

"Authority and Freedom in Doctrine," in *Episcopalians United*, ed. Theodore Ferris, 12-36. Morehouse-Gorham, 1946.

"Wieman's Theological Empiricism," in *The Empirical Theology of Henry Nelson Wieman*, ed. Robert W. Bretall, 21-39. Southern Illinois University Press, 1963.

"Relationship Theology," in *Westminster Dictionary of Religious Education*, ed. Kendig B. Cully, 563-65. Westminster, 1963.

"The Discipline of Theology—Seminary and University," in *Does the Church Know How to Teach?* ed. Kendig B. Cully, 289-313. Macmillan, 1970.

"Process Thought and Black Theology," in *Black Theology II*, ed. Calvin E. Bruce and William R. Jones, 107-20. Bucknell University Press, 1976.

Selected Articles of Theological Import in Journals

"Liberal Religious Thought Today: Professor Wieman's Position," *The Churchman* (15 April 1936): 14-15.

"Has Liberalism a Theology?" *The Churchman* (15 September 1936): 15-16.

"Religious Realism in America," *Modern Churchman* (December 1937): 495-506.

"Is Temple a Realist?" *Journal of Religion* (January 1939): 44-54.

"The New Naturalism and Christianity," *Anglican Theological Review* (January 1940): 25-35.

"Theology in Transition," *Journal of Religion* (April 1940): 160-68.

"Professor Macintosh and Empirical Theology," *The Personalist* (Winter 1940): 26-41.

"Empirical Method and Its Critics," *Anglican Theological Review* (January 1945): 27-34.

"Weaknesses and Resources of the Christian Church," *Journal of Religious Thought* (Autumn-Winter 1946): 16-33.

"God as Idea and as Living," *Christendom* (Winter 1946): 57-64.

"Authority, Scripture, and Tradition," *Religion in Life* (Autumn 1952): 551-62.

"Revelation, Relevance, and Relationships," *Religion in Life* (Winter 1957): 132-43.

"The Holy Spirit and Christian Education," *Religious Education* (May-June 1962): 178-84; *Biblical Theology* (Belfast, October 1962): 49-63.

"The Easter Event and Linguistic Analysis," *The Near East School of Theology Quarterly* (April and July 1967): 6-21.

"Linguistic Philosophy and Religious Education," *Religious Education* (July-August 1970): 309-17.

"Process Theology and Religious Education," *St. Luke's Journal of Theology* (March 1973): 3-10.

"Whitehead and Religious Education," *Religious Education* (May-June 1973): 315-22.

"Process Thinking and Religious Education," *Anglican Theological Review* (July 1975): 271-88.

"Empiricism and Process Theology: God Is What God Does," *The Christian Century* (14 March 1976): 284-87.

"Process, Evil, and God," *American Journal of Theology & Philosophy* 2 (May 1980): 60-70.

"Meland: Worship and His Recent Thought," *American Journal of Theology & Philosophy* 5 (May and September 1984): 96-106.

"Dewey, Whitehead, and Christian Education," *The Living Light* 22/1 (October 1985): 35-44.

"The Problem of Evil and Religious Education," *Religious Education* (Winter 1989): 5-15.

"Rethinking Empiricism in Theology," *The American Journal of Theology & Philosophy* 10 (September 1989): 159-70.

"The Educational Philosophy of William James," *Religious Education* (Fall 1991): 619-34.

John H. Dietrich: On "Ethics without God"

Mason Olds

John H. Dietrich (1878–1957) was an autonomous thinker in both religion and ethics.[1] In theology, he was one of the first if not the first in the United States to rethink traditional religious doctrines from the perspective of naturalistic humanism. Specifically, he advocated a "religion without God." Though his interpretation of ethics was not as novel as his theology, he promoted an "ethic without God."

Like so many ethical thinkers, Dietrich did not draw a firm line between ethics and morality. However, occasionally he spoke of ethics as having established principles, whereas morality tended to be more flexible and even changed. This suggests that ethics deals with a higher and more theoretical level than does morality. Morality addresses the immediacy of right and wrong actions, whereas ethics provides the basic principle for determining actions. In other words, how do you validate the statement that a particular action is wrong? You appeal to a basic ethical principle. Of course, you may go on to ask: how do you vindicate the use of that particular ethical principle? This is even a higher level question. The purpose of ethics is to examine these kinds of questions. My intent then is to discuss Dietrich's "ethics without God" with respect to such questions as validation and vindication.

At the outset let me caution that I do not wish to be misleading about Dietrich's theory of ethics. Obviously, he was not aware of the more recent terminology employed in ethical discourse. However, it is possible to interpret Dietrich's theory in terms of contemporary discourse. In other words, though my presentation is an interpretation, I believe the primary sources will support it.

---

[1]Sources most readily available for understanding Dietrich's life and thought are Mason Olds, *John H. Dietrich: The Father of Religious Humanism* (Yellow Springs OH: Fellowship of Religious Humanists, n.d.); "John H. Dietrich: A Pilgrim's Progress," *Religious Humanism* 18 (1984): 156-67, and 19 (1985): 2-10; and John H. Dietrich, *What If the World Went Humanist?*, ed. Mason Olds (Yellow Springs OH: Fellowship of Religious Humanists, 1989).

I

Although ethics was the primary concern in his theology, Dietrich's theory of ethics was not the most lucid part of his thought. In fact, his theory involves the balancing of a number of components gleaned from several traditional theories of ethics. If one of the components is omitted, then one gains a distorted understanding of his theory. In other words, there is a kind of reciprocal interplay between the various components which provide a principle for making responsible moral decisions.

At the center of Dietrich's religious and ethical thought is the evolutionary model. Though he had heard of Darwin prior to his entering college in 1896, it was during his undergraduate years that he came to understand the theory of evolution, mostly from his private reading in the college library. It also may be noted that he did not come to his knowldge of evolution so much from the works of Darwin but from those of Alfred Russell Wallace (1823–1913).[2] Of course, Wallace was the scientist who discovered the theory of evolution independently of Darwin and even sent Darwin a copy of the paper containing the theory. As Darwin had been sitting on the theory for sixteen years while collecting evidence supporting the theory of natural selection, Wallace's work forced Darwin to come out of the evolutionary closet. Through the years, Dietrich read a number of Wallace's books, specifically mentioning *Darwinism* (1907), *World of Life* (1910), *Social Environment and Moral Progress* (1913), and *The Revolt of Democracy* (1913).

As several of the titles suggest, Wallace was not only a scientist, but also a critic and social reformer, with much of his motivation derived from the theory of evolution. Although Wallace had some questionable views, such as being opposed to vaccinations, he captured Dietrich's attention with his philosophy of social reform. It also should be noticed that Wallace was a theist, who thought "some spiritual influx was needed" to account for "the special mental and spiritual nature" of humans. Of course, he postulated that God had provided it. In addition, he saw God at work in the evolutionary process somewhat along the lines of a modified version of the argument from design.

Dietrich accepted the theory of evolution, but did not feel compelled to accept Wallace's theory of God. He tended to side more with the late Darwin, thinking that natural selection provided sufficient grounds for explaining how evolution had taken place. The key idea which he adapted to his ethical theory was the notion that in humans the evolutionary process took on consciousness. This eventually enabled humans to realize that they were simply not victims of their natures, but could even change their environments and so modify their natures. For example, Dietrich says:

---

[2]John H. Dietrich, *The Fathers of Evolution* (Minneapolis: First Unitarian Society, 1926) 50-72.

> He (humankind) possessed a new force—an intellect—and with this he could transform nature, and make her serve his own particular needs.[3]

He then goes on to say: "upon this thought rests our whole theory of social reform."[4] Thus it was his reading of the works of Wallace which provided him with his "first logical reason" for social ethics.

Having accepted the evolutionary model, Dietrich applied it in another way to his theory of ethics. He felt that even morality had evolved out of the evolutionary process. In the struggle for existence, it was advantageous to develop rules for governing the relationships between people. Those groups which developed moral action guides lived better than those who did not, so morality was "wrought out of human experience in man's struggle for existence."[5]This implies that morality was a matter of convention and thus had a kind of relativity about it. For example, in ancient Greece it was thought that slavery could be justified, but today Dietrich thought it impossible to justify. Thus, it is the evolutionary process enhanced by consciousness, human experience, and the ability to reason which sifts through moral practices, retaining those which appear useful and discarding others.

II

Now let us shift our focus from the evolutionary component in Dietrich's theory to that of the individual. It was obvious to him that humans possessed different endowments and potentials. But regardless of the endowments an individual is born with, every person should be encouraged to develop them as far as possible. He believed there was a drive within the individual similar to what Abraham Maslow called the need for self-actualization. Obviously heredity has an influence as well as environment; but beyond both, an individual can set goals and then strive to attain them. One can channel the basic drive and employ it to realize one's potential. Frequently Dietrich referred to the distant goal as the "good" or "abundant life." It was the byproduct of developing one's talents and maximizing one's potential. Often self-actualization was accompanied by happiness.

So, if Woody Allen should ask: what is the meaning of life? Dietrich would reply: "the purpose of life is to live, and therefore the supreme thing to be attained is the full, free, complete, abundant life."[6]

When Dietrich took his notion of the "abundant life" and related it to the institutions in society, he contended that institutions are created by humans to serve them. Thus, every institution—the family, church, school, business, and the state—was

---

[3]Ibid., 68.

[4]Ibid., 68-69.

[5]"Do We Need a New Morality?" *Humanist Pulpit II* (Minneapolis: First Unitarian Society, 1928) 85.

[6]"The Advance of Humanism," *Humanist Pulpit II*, 43.

created for the purpose of enabling people to live the abundant life. Social issues such as feminism, civil rights, and civil liberties are advanced and should be promoted in order to free the offended so that they might have the opportunity to realize their potential. Therefore, institutions and social action "stand or fall according to their contributions to human life." Dietrich asked: "do they foster, enlarge, liberate and ennoble the lives of people? Then they stand justified and call for protection and support. Do they weaken, enslave, impoverish, and degrade human life. Then they stand condemned and should be eliminated."[7]

Dietrich was quite critical of his contemporaries who advocated divine command theories of ethics. Of his many criticisms, he thought they focused too narrowly on individual actions. They tended to do this because they had not sufficiently taken into account the developments which were ushered in by the industrial revolution, e.g., such things as people moving from farms to cities, from cottages to innercity tenements, from the small craft shop to the factory operated by a large corporation, etc. The old ethic, according to Dietrich, was tailored to the pre-industrial situation and thus was no longer viable in a society composed of a modern industrial complex. For example, the old moralists condemned the prostitute for acting immoral, but they had little to say about the social conditions which drove her into the streets. Often they condemned the parent who beat a child to death, while honoring the factory owner who brought premature deaths to dozens of children who were forced by economic necessity to sweat long hours in their shops. So Dietrich's point was that institutions can and do operate from structures which are immoral though they do not commit individual acts of prostitution and murder. However, if the institutions frustrate rather than enhance the living of the abundant life for the people affected by them, they are immoral and must be restructured.

At the same time that Dietrich perceived the dangers of reducing morality to individual acts, he also saw the threat posed by mass society to the development of individuals with strong character who would stand up and criticize the status quo. He often referred to mass produced funiture, clothes, and city apartments which looked exactly alike. He thought the major radio stations and newspapers by carrying the same national commentators and columnists were molding a unified public opinion. Thus there were strong forces in all areas of society which encouraged conformity with an attendant mediocrity. These pressures for conformity frustrated the need of individuals to develop their uniqueness and to realize their potential, so he judged such developments to be harmful.

That Dietrich saw an interaction between the individual and mass society is quite evident. Whether an individual act or the operation of an institution be considered, both could be judged moral or immoral. He affirmed: "right action is that action which tends to the preservation and enrichment of both individual and social

---

[7]Ibid., 45.

life, wrong action is that which tends to the destruction and impoverishment of life."[8]

III

Dietrich had read John Stuart Mill's *Liberty* and *Utilitarianism* and had found Mill's argument for freedom of speech compatible with the Unitarian doctrine of freedom of belief and expression. Though Unitarianism was a noncreedal faith, its members had always assumed that a member would remain comfortably within the bounds of liberal Christian theism. Of course, with the passing of time, Dietrich, along with others sympathetic to his views about religious humanism, radically tested the doctrine to determine whether Unitarians did believe in the freedom of thought and expression, not only for the laity in the pews, but for the minister in the pulpit. His naturalistic views precipitated the so-called humanist-theist controversy in the American Unitarian Association. The controversy raged from about 1920 to 1938, the year Dietrich retired as minister of the First Unitarian Society of Minneapolis. The final outcome of the controversy was probably a bit of a surprise to both factions, for Unitarians not only affirmed the doctrine of freedom of belief but actually practiced it.[9]

With the evolutionary component in his ethics and the belief the purpose of life was to live it abundantly, Dietrich thought freedom of thought and expression followed naturally from them. The person who had ideas which ran contrary to the conventional wisdom must be protected. For, if the nonconformist has the whole or perhaps only a part of the truth, but is silenced, the majority is depriving itself of the truth which the nonconformist has. Of course, if the nonconformist is in total error, the majority should be able to demonstrate it with solid evidence and valid argument. In so doing the majority is justifying the truth which it possesses. Dietrich was convinced that if freedom of expression were permitted in the various institutions and groups in society, eventually basic ethical principles would assert themselves.

It seems the kind of ethical theory which Dietrich thought would eventually evolve was teleological in nature. In other words, the basic prescriptive norm would focus on the consequences of the action. For instance, some actions enable the individual to take a step forward toward the goal of self-actualization, and other actions frustrate that goal. Some actions contribute to the common good or "social life" whereas others hinder its attainment. In these cases, it is the consequences of the action which determine the morality of the action. On this, Dietrich said: "that things are right or wrong, according to whether the results are good or bad."[10]

---

[8]"Do We Need a New Morality?" *Humanist Pulpit II*, 85.

[9]Mason Olds, *Religious Humanism in America* (Washington DC: University Press of America, 1977) 30-52.

[10]"The Ethics of Birth Control," *Humanist Pulpit IV*, 165.

Obviously, Dietrich's ethic raises the problem of priority, namely, when there is a conflict, does the consequence or result on the individual take precedence over the consequence or result on the group? So far as I have been able to determine, Dietrich was not sensitive to this as a problem. But today we certainly know that if we give the priority to the individual, this can lead to a crude "egoism". As we have seen, Dietrich was concerned with the self-actualization of all individuals and argued for the freedom of the nonconformist. However, he was also concerned about the result of the action on the group. When we recall that he had read John Stuart Mill who advocated the importance of the group, and that Dietrich was likewise concerned about the future evolution of humanity, it seems safe to infer that he would give priority to the consequences on the group. Though he did not employ this term, there was a "universal" component in his kind of teleological ethical theory.

IV

That Dietrich was working within the perspective of utilitarianism is evident, but there are certain restraints placed on the theory. As we have noted, there is the constraint with respect to the consequences of a present action on the future evolution of humans. In addition to this, he places a further constraint which is the inherent value of a person. At this juncture a deontological component arises in his theory. Often he stated this component in a manner similar to one of the formulations of Kant's categorical imperative. Dietrich had read the works of Felix Adler, the founder of the Ethical Culture movement, and Adler was a Kantian idealistic transcendentalist who accepted Kant's ethic with a few modifications. So, it is not clear whether Dietrich was influenced directly by the works of Kant or indirectly by the works of Adler.

Dietrich expressed the deontological component in this fashion: "Humanism believes in the supreme worth of human life, and that man (humans) therefore must be treated as an end, not as a means to some other end."[11] He construed this value or worth to be intrinsic to human nature. In fact, one of his criticisms of theism was that it viewed humans as a "means" to the glorification of the supreme being. Also, we might note that Dietrich overstates Kant's maxim. Kant said something to the effect: "Treat all humans as ends in themselves and not as means only." Presumably Kant would allow a shop owner to hire a clerk for the purpose of selling goods and thus maximize his profits, but the owner must treat the clerk with respect and dignity. In other words, Kant allowed for the clerk as a means (maximizing of profit) so long as the owner treated him as an end in himself (a person with value and dignity). So it appears that Dietrich overstated Kant's maxim. If one never treated a person as a means to some end, one most likely would be forced to become a hermit. Even between two lovers, each is the means to the others joy.

---

[11]"The Advance of Humanism," *Humanist Pulpit III*, 44.

Although Dietrich overstated the maxim, he clearly sought to make the point that a human being has inherent value. This means a person has thoughts, feelings, and desires, and they should be taken into respectful account in dealing with that person. When the maxim is related to the utilitarian principle about the common good, its importance becomes obvious. Dietrich is placing a significant constraint on the utilitarian principle. Had he spelled it out, it would be something like this: one ought to act in such a way that the consequences of that act will contribute to the common good, provided the act does not violate the inherent value of the people involved in the action. One of the frequent criticisms levelled against the utilitarian theory is that you can justify using a person "as a means only" if the overall utility of the action will increase the utility of the group. Although Dietrich may not have seen clearly the importance of his constraint, it is an important modification which undercuts some criticism. In following the utility principle, one must not violate the qualifying principle of "the intrinsic worth" of the person.

V

Moreover, Dietrich thought that an understanding of the nature of "moral law" was an important ingredient for an ethical theory.[12] He noted that the universe operated in a consistent manner. This consistency was inherent in the universe, not built into by some intelligent cosmic designer. However, humans, using experience and reason based on that experience, observed causal relations operating in nature. Hence scientific laws were established from observing, suggesting hypotheses, testing them, and eventually confirming some and refuting others. In a similar way, if one promoted a goal such as the common good, some actions would lead in that direction, whereas others would make a detour. Dietrich referred to the moral law as the rules, discovered by the empirical method, which contributed to the common good. Of course, similar rules could promote the "self-development" of a person. For instance, if a person wished to be healthy, then she must do those things which promote health and avoid those things which do not. He thought, in principle, with the use of the scientific method, we could discover those factors which contribute to both self-development and the common good. He maintained that it was contradictory for people who claim they seek either self-development or the common good to act in ways that hinder them from reaching their goals. Thus the moral law consisted of discoverable ways for living which enable individuals and groups to move toward their ethical goals. For instance, Dietrich said: "The moral laws, as we know them, are simply statements of the fact that if we would live peacefully and happily together, we must live in a certain way."[13]

There are two points which Dietrich sought to make by interjecting the moral law component into his ethical theory. The first is: moral law is a creation of hu-

---

[12]"Is There a Moral Law?" *Humanist Pulpit II*, 96-112.

[13]Ibid., 103.

mans. When consciousness developed in humans and they developed their cognitive skills, they were able to discern pattterns of cause and effect. They inferred that some things were injurious to the human enterprise, whereas other things were helpful. The former they designated bad and thus wrong; the latter were called good and thus right. The second point is: causal connections exist which have important implications for morality independent of people's changing opinions about them. For example, regardless of what people think about the morality of artificial means of birth control, our planet has the natural resources to adequately support only a finite number of organic beings. Once that number is reached, regardless of how efficient the resources are distributed, the quality of life will diminish. Although it might be impossible to determine exactly where that disastrous point is, it is there and the scientific method is the best way to determine its location. To ignore the issue will hasten the day of reckoning, while acting in certain ways might prolong or even prevent the day of impending disaster. Moral law then will express the course of action needed for survival.

VI

As we have thus far seen, the basic components of Dietrich's theory of ethics are: evolutionary theory, self-actualization, the common good, the inherent value of the human being, and the moral law. But before we pull these various ingredients together into a definite prescriptive principle, we must consider a term which he employed to relate his ethics to his religion, and that term is the "commonwealth of man."[14]Today this term appears gender exclusive, but he certainly did not construe it that way. In dealing with so many of the social issues of his time, he also was in the forefront of the feminist movement. Because of this, there is no reason to think he would object to a modfication of his term. Perhaps we could change it to the more inclusive term "the commonwealth of humanity."

At any rate Dietrich advocated the commonwealth concept in contrast to the traditional Christian term "the kingdom of God." By promoting the commonwealth concept, there is an implied criticism of the Christian doctrine. The kingdom of God focuses on the supernatural world and contends that an "outside help" will usher it in. In contrast, the commonwealth doctrine places emphasis on creating the "ideal world" right here on earth. And, if the commonwealth is to be built, it must come about by the joint efforts of human beings. With this term, he also sought to emphasize the essential unity of all humanity. Dietrich explained:

> We would realize there flows through the whole human race, from the lowest to the highest, one life and one blood, that we have a common life and a common interest, and we would march on toward our common purpose and ideal, realizing what hurts one hurts all. This would mean the elimina-

[14]*What If the World Went Humanist?*, 110.

> tion of all racial antagonisms, national jealousies, class struggles, religious prejudices, and individual hatreds. All these would dissolve in realization of human solidarity, in which each person considers himself a cooperative part of the whole.[15]

These essential components of Dietrich's theory of ethics pose the problem of expressing them in a basic prescriptive principle which is a fundamental ingredient of any ethical theory. It is by means of such a principle that a particular ethical judgement is validated. For instance, Kant promoted the categorical imperative, and John Stuart Mill advocated the greatest happiness principle. Many traditional Christians accept a "divine command" principle. So what basic ethical principle does Dietrich offer? This is one formulation of it:

> Morality . . . is simply the accepted rule of social conduct—the measure of right conduct between individuals in their social relations. All actions which promote the well-being and happiness of society, or individuals, which are the units of society, are moral. . . . Every act is immoral which needlessly injures any fellow creature or which tends to the degeneration of our social life. . . . Moral standards are evolutionary, and change from time to time.[16]

Although this statement provides the thrust of Dietrich's basic ethical principle, it conceals a great deal. Both the utilitarian and evolutionary components are present, but the inherent value and the moral law components are either totally missing or at best vaguely implied. The point is that even Dietrich himself did not adequately formulate his prescriptive principle so that it included all the essential ingredients of his ethical theory. Due to this shortcoming, I shall attempt a reformulation, encompassing all essential components.

The reformulation is: in order for an action to be moral, it must promote the commonwealth of humanity, which means (1) at the social level, it must contribute to the common good without (a) violating the intrinsic value of the people affected by the action, without (b) adversely affecting the future evolution of the human species, and without (c) violating any known moral law, and which means (2) at the individual level promotes the self-actualization of persons without violating any of the constraints imposed by a, b, and c.

It seems to me that the reformulation captures all of the essential ingredients of Dietrich's ethical theory. In order to abbreviate the principle, we may simply refer to it as "the commonwealth principle" somewhat analogous to Mill's "the greatest happiness principle."

Two points of clarification are in order. The first is that the commonwealth principle is an ideal principle. It certainly would be difficult when faced with a

---

[15]Ibid., 110.

[16]"The Ethics of Birth Control," 162.

rather simple moral dilemma to check it against every component of the principle, especially the concern about present actions on the future evolution of the species. Yet, taking into account the well-being of future generations is without doubt an important consideration in any contemporary ethical theory. In the concrete situation, the course of action which embraces the largest number of components in his theory will most likely be the right thing to do. The second clarification is that Dietrich realized that humans were less than perfect so their application of the prescriptive norm must be made in a specific context and at a definite time. In other words, they make their decisions with the knowledge at hand, but when more complete knowledge becomes available, it might be that the earlier action was not the most moral though it appeared so at the time. Hence, he was aware of the relativity and the possibility of error involved in dealing with almost any moral dilemma.

Although these clarifications have a cautionary tone, Dietrich thought that humans have much more knowledge than they employ in making ethical decisions. He said, for instance, "the all-important problem in life is to make men (humans) moral, to inject into their minds a principle that will lead them by the force of their own feelings to do what is right."[17]

VII

We turn now to the problem of ethical vindication. If one steps within Dietrich's ethical theory, one finds a basic prescriptive norm, which is the commonwealth principle. This principle has a place of legitimacy and superiority within his theory. With it, one can determine a course for moral action, and/or find support for a lower level moral action guide. One can move from a situation containing a moral dilemma to the commonwealth principle which provides the basis for resolving it. In other words, the commonwealth principle provides the norm for validating a moral course of action.

Yet, one might well ask: why should I accept the commonwealth principle for determining right from wrong? In other words, with this question, the person is outside the theory making inquiry as to why she should accept it. Since there are other competing theories, such as the divine command theory, why opt for Dietrich's theory? These questions call for a vindication of the theory.

There are roughly three responses which Dietrich provides to this kind of inquiry. The first relates to his world view. He construes that the universe is composed of matter which is eternal. This means, that though the universe is constantly changing, it has always existed and always will. The natural world is the real world, and there is no supernatural world. The inference drawn from this is that the universe is a self-contained system, without need of a cosmic creator. On earth, human beings have evolved through evolution by means of natural selection. Through his-

---

[17]"The Relation of Religion to Morality" (sermon given in Minneapolis, 9 Jan 1921) 3.

torical development, humans have created institutions and rules for guiding their behavior. Humans have created their own theories for morality, even their divine command theories, so Dietrich, as a part of humanity, proposes as the goal for social life the creation of "the commonwealth of humanity" by following the guidelines of the various components of his ethical theory.[18]

Obviously, there is much more to Dietrich's world view than these few doctrines, but they at least suggest the perspective from which he derives his theory of ethics. His second response involves a rational and critical aspect for vindicating his theory. Since he was primarily a religious thinker, his criticisms were levelled mostly against other religious theories of ethics. Traditionally, in the West, religion has been predicated on the existence of God, and morality derived from the will of God. Various thinkers found God's will revealed in different places. For example, some found God's will in the Bible, church, human conscience, mystical experience, or embedded in nature. In such views, something is moral because it expresses the will of God. So presumably if there were no God to express his will, people would not have a guide for determining right from wrong. Of course, Dietrich thought this line of reasoning nonsense. He maintained that it was humans, not God, who created the norms for morality.

He also raised the problem of the relationship of religion to morality. Throughout history, people have had various objects of worship. Some primitives worshipped a stone, later people worshipped the Virgin Mary, others Jesus, and others God the Father. Dietrich was not opposed to worship, but he disagreed about the proper object of worship. He thought that moral living should be the object of ultimate concern. He said: "morality may be the very ideal which a man (human) may seek all his (her) life to follow—it may be the supreme passion."[19]This aspiration to live morally is a legitimate focus of worship and can take the place of God in traditional religion. In fact, he thought the ideals of morality were the only objects fit for worship, and they too have a saving power. If one follows them, they can change a person.

Dietrich cautioned people about following the will of the gods, for they have asked people to do some rather immoral things. In fact, even in the West, "the God of the early Hebrews, instead of being a moral being, was guilty of demanding practically every immorality of his people—dishonesty, theft, murder, rape—all commanded by Jehovah, or turn to the history of Christianity, and how licentiousness and bribery and unblushing murder were associated with its very head, the pope; and how, when Christianity was at its highest, the moral life of Europe was at its lowest."[20]

---

[18]*The Fathers of Evolution,* 9-12.
[19]*What If the World Went Humanist?,* 78.
[20]Ibid., 72.

Also, Dietrich thought it a mistake to think something wrong because it was forbidden, rather it was forbidden because it was thought wrong. Thus he maintained it a harmful and pernicious doctrine to claim that morality rests upon religion for its foundation. In fact, the process should be reversed , and religions should be judged by moral norms. If religions do not measure up to the highest moral standards, they should be modified or discarded.

Moreover, Dietrich held that our social ills are created by humans; and, if they are to be eliminated, then humans must do it. Even the most ardent theist has learned: "If we leave our social ills to be cured by providence, they will never be cured. Experience has taught us that much."[21]Thus he felt that it was not faith in the gods that people need today, but faith in themselves to accomplish the things needed to create the commonwealth of humanity.

This brings us next to Dietrich's third response. If you generally accept his worldview and his criticisms of other religious moral alternatives, he thought his ethical theory provided the most rational theory consistent with his world view. He thought that if a person were rational, she would see that accepting his theory was the rational thing to do. So obviously, if a person is persuaded by these three responses and opts for Dietrich's theory of ethics, the theory has been vindicated.

In summary, the question of the relationship of religion to morality is an important issue, and Dietrich argued for the priority of ethics over religion. As such, he promoted an ethic without God. For him, the supernatural realm with its gods had disappeared, and with their disappearance, the door had opened for a new morality created by humans for living well in the natural world. Neither Kant's categorical imperative nor Mill's greatest happiness principle require God for their justification. So they refute the contention that one cannot be moral without belief in God. Dietrich makes the point further with his own ethical theory, and rationally justifies it within the context of his world view.

As Dietrich, though long dead, has been the object of this study, I shall allow him to have the final word. He said:

> We are alone in a terrifying and uncaring universe; it is for us to create and sustain whatever can make human life worth while. Our lives are very insecure upon this little planet as it swings through space, and upon us rests the hard and glorious task of deepening and enriching them. In spite of an indifferent universe, we ourselves must keep alive all the good the past hath had, and add to it such good as we can create.[22]

---

[21]Ibid., 75.

[22]"The Advance of Humanism," 47.

Pragmatically Defining the God Concepts of Henry Nelson Wieman and Gordon Kaufman

Karl E. Peters

This essay will explore how one can use Charles Sanders Peirce's understanding of meaning, formulated in his definition of pragmatism, in developing concepts of God. In doing this I will draw on some ideas of Henry Nelson Wieman and Gordon Kaufman.[1] First, I will make some comments on the pragmatic understanding of meaning advocated by Peirce in relation to some of Kaufman's ideas on theological construction. Then following the thinking of Henry Nelson Wieman, amplified in light of that of Ralph Wendell Burhoe and Holmes Rolston III, I will use Peirce's pragmatic maxim to construct a concept of God as an immanent creative process that is coextensive with but conceptually distinguishable from the world. Finally, I will compare this view of God with that of Kaufman's, which I also will express in terms of Peirce's pragmatism.

1. Pragmatism and Theological Construction

What I am doing is the beginning of a task in theological construction. With Kaufman I recognize that theology is a human enterprise; concepts such as God, Christ, creation, sin, and salvation are human formulations. Such concepts can take us far away from concrete, everyday experiences and thus make sense only as one elaborates an entire conceptual scheme or worldview.[2] Such a notion of theology is

---

[1]I first became acquainted with Wieman's work more than twenty years ago, when I wrote my Ph.D. diss. "The Concept of God and the Method of Science" to show how his empirical theology could become more scientific. Although I have just recently become acquainted with a small portion of Kaufman's theological work, like many others I think it is filled with insight and with possibilities for constructing a contemporary theology.

[2]See Gordon Kaufman, "Constructing the Concept of God" in *Is God GOD?* ed. Axel D. Steuer and James W. McClendon (Nashville: Abingdon, 1981) 108-43; and "Towards the Reconception of Theology" in *Theology for a Nuclear Age* (Philadelphia: Westminster, 1985) 16-29.

quite compatible with some contemporary understandings of science as a human enterprise; science also involves imaginative construction in which specific ideas often only make sense in terms of a wider conceptual scheme.

Peirce's own formulations of the pragmatic maxim seem to recognize this. In his essay "The Fixation of Belief," even though the "whole function of thought is to produce habits of actions"[3] and even though these habits give rise to sensible results, when Peirce formulates his rule for attaining the "third grade of clearness" for an idea, he says: "*Consider* what effects that might *conceivably* have practical bearings, we *conceive* the object of our conception to have. Then, *our conception* of these effects is the whole of *our conception* of the object."[4] When one looks carefully at this maxim, one realizes that it tells us to make something like a thought experiment: the whole enterprise remains in the realm of human conception; even the practical effects are those conceptualized, we might say constructed, by the human mind. When we apply this maxim to the idea of God, we will want to remember that we are conducting a thought experiment as a part of the task of theological construction.

Furthermore, I think one also must recognize that this maxim to determine the meaning of abstract ideas suggests a wider conceptual scheme or worldview, which can be called naturalism. If we apply Peirce's way of defining meaning in terms of habits of actions and sensible results to theology, we will be led to speak of an immanent God. Of course, God might still be transcendent in terms of our knowledge of God; our definition of the concept of *God* pragmatically may not exhaust all there is to God. However, the pragmatic way of defining *God* does rule out an ontologically transcendent or supernatural God. Pragmatism opposes ontological dualism and affirms naturalism by arguing that meaningful discourse is possible only in terms of a universe open to human action and experience.

Because Kaufman also opposes ontological dualism and affirms naturalism, I think a pragmatic approach to conceptualizing God might help him. In correctly stressing the constructive nature of all theology, Kaufman needlessly seems to shy away from tying theological concepts down to experience. On the one hand, he conceptualizes God naturalistically: "God should today be conceived in terms of the complex of physical, biological and historicocultural conditions which has made human existence possible, which continue to sustain it, and which may draw it out to a fuller humanity and humaneness."[5] On the other hand, he seems so concerned about problems of what some call naive realism—of assuming a one-to-one correspondence between human ideas and reality—that he does not clearly relate his own

---

[3]Charles Sanders Peirce, *Collected Papers* (Cambridge MA: Harvard University Press, 1965) 5.400. The numeration in the footnotes on Peirce refers to the volume and section number in this edition of Peirce's works.

[4]Peirce, *Collected Works*, 5.402 (italics mine).

[5]Kaufman, *Theology for a Nuclear Age*, 42.

theological constructs to experience as a way of justifying them. Instead, he seems to justify his concepts in terms of their coherence in an overarching worldview as well as in terms of the "capacity to provide insight and guidance in our situation today. . . ."[6] In addition to these criteria, later I will suggest a way that Kaufman's concept of God also can be partly defined and justified in terms of Peirce's pragmatism.

A part of the worldview associated with pragmatism is that it proposes we define abstract ideas in terms of actions and their resulting experiences. At times such an approach can be criticized for assuming, as Peirce states, that "our conception of these effects [the practical effects we conceive the object of our conception to have] is the whole of our conception of the object."[7] Kaufman would certainly want to point out that in theology our concepts cannot exhaust what the concept *God* means, for *God* must at least in part be conceived as mystery. Nonetheless, the pragmatism of Peirce suggests that we can go much further than Kaufman goes in not only defining abstract ideas in terms of experience but also, at least in part, showing how those ideas can be confirmed as true through experience. Pragmatism allows us not only to recognize the imaginative, constructive side of such human enterprises as science and theology; it also highlights the importance of confirmation in science through controlled observations, even if observations are theory laden insofar as they are directed by a proposed, constructed theory. Following pragmatism will also allow us to develop a stronger notion of experiential confirmation for theological constructs than Kaufman seems to allow. This is part of what I will attempt to show in the remainder of this essay.

2. Pragmatism, the World, and God

Since I have suggested that *God* defined pragmatically will be an immanent God, I want to begin by differentiating the concept of God from the concept of world. If this is not done, then from a pragmatic perspective the two terms will be equivalent, and one could argue that we do not need to talk about God at all. In the distinction that follows I am developing a distinction made by Henry Nelson Wieman between *created good* and *creative good*, expanded to the biological and cosmic spheres of existence in light of the evolutionary theology of Ralph Wendell

---

[6]Kaufman, *Theology for a Nuclear Age*, 28. This latter criterion that offers a functional approach to theological justification may be compatible with the pragmatism of William James.

[7]Peirce, *Collected Papers*, 5.2.

Burhoe.[8] I also will be making use of Holmes Rolston's analysis of values in the natural world.[9]

Both *God* and *world* are abstract nouns designating things that cannot be fully comprehended in human experience. Insofar as *world* refers to the totality of existence, and insofar as *God* refers to that which is the source of all existence or the creator, neither world nor God can be fully experienced. What is specified by these nouns extends beyond the experiences of a particular individual and even beyond the combined experiences of the entire human species. However, this does not imply that what we do experience is not some aspect of the world or some manifestation of God. For if *world* and *God* are concepts that designate the completeness of something, what we do experience is always a part of that totality; hence we can always experience the world and God.

What kinds of things can we then experience, and how do we differentiate between what is specified by these two comprehensive terms? Following Wieman, I think we can begin to make a distinction by suggesting that the term *God* refers to the activity or event of creation and the term *world* refers to the product or result of that activity—that which is created. In a naturalistic theology these often turn out to be two ways of looking at the same thing. Yet, in terms of pragmatism *God* and *world* can be differentiated by different sets of attitudes and actions on the part of humans and different resulting experiences. Let me illustrate.

In *Environmental Ethics* Rolston outlines different values "carried by nature" or the world in such a way that they shed insight for the pragmatist on how we can define the word *world* as created good, as instrumentally and intrinsically valuable. Rolston suggests that, instrumentally, nature has life-support value providing the sustenance for all forms of life but that for humans the world also carries economic value, recreational value, scientific value, historical value, and even symbolic value, the latter exemplified by such things as the bald eagle being a symbol of America. In other words, *world* is defined by the human activity of seeking support for human biological life and human culture, and the resulting experience is of a set of condi-

---

[8]Henry Nelson Wieman, *Source of Human Good* (Carbondale IL: Southern Illinois University Press, 1964) 54-83. Ralph Wendell Burhoe, *Toward a Scientific Theology* (Belfast: Christian Journals Ltd., 1981). A useful extension of Wieman's concept of God to the biological realm is found in Charles Birch and John Cobb, Jr., *The Liberation of Life* (Cambridge: Cambridge University Press, 1981) 176-202.

As will become clear below, Burhoe does not distinguish created and creative good as sharply as Wieman does. From Burhoe's evolutionary perspective products of the creative process, as they are formed, immediately become a part of the creative process. Hence, Wieman's two kinds of good are the result of human analysis that makes conceptual distinctions. I attempt to show, however, that these conceptual distinctions are pragmatically meaningful.

[9]Holmes Rolston III, *Environmental Ethics: Duties to and Values in the Natural World* (Philadelphia: Temple University Press, 1988) 3-27.

tions that responds to such activity. Rolston further suggests that, intrinsically, *world* is partly defined by life in all its diversity. Life is the value for which support is sought; each microorganism, plant, and animal values its own life intrinsically (though not necessarily consciously) insofar as it seeks to support and continue its own existence. Thus pragmatically *world* is defined as life, including human life, as the set of conditions that supports all life, and as the particular set of conditions that supports human life with human culture.

The conditions that support biological life include the sun, weather systems, water, minerals, and for animals the plants and other animals that make up "food chains" in predator-prey systems. These are integrated into local and regional ecosystems, which in turn are integrated in the total Earth-Sun system. The Earth-Sun system has historical ties to other stars, galaxies, and ultimately to the origin of the universe in the initial inflation, metaphorically called the "big bang."[10] The conditions that support human culture include all aspects of the planet Earth that are the conditions for the material substrate of culture, making possible such things as the exchange of goods and services, the technology of inquiry, and recreation. The world also includes the human brain with its capacities for feeling and perceiving, and for developing and using symbols. And it also includes those cultural developments such as language and mathematics that support scientific, historical, philosophical, and religious inquiry as well as the expressive arts. All these are the conditions that support the birth, development, and maintenance of human biocultural organisms.

Following Wieman's concept of created good and applying this to our discussion of the world, what the term *world* does not include is the set of activities, events, or processes that creates life and its conditions.[11] In keeping with the outlook of Western religion, that which creates life and its conditions is designated by the

---

[10]For an insightful discussion of how each individual organism is defined as an instance of the total Earth-Sun system, see Hwe Ik Zhang, "Humanity in the World of Life," *Zygon: Journal of Religion and Science* 24 (December 1989): 447-56. As a physicist, Zhang offers a view of life and earth comparable to the *Gaia* hypothesis.

[11]On this point there seems to be an important divergence between the thinking of Wieman and Burhoe. Following Wieman I am developing a conceptual distinction between world and God. However, Burhoe points out (personal communication) that from an evolutionary perspective a product of the creative process, e.g., a new species, even as it is emerging is already part of the creative matrix. In the continuous interaction of the biological world and human culture, new variations are not only selected for or against by their environment; they are also part of the environment that is exerting selection pressure on other already established species of organism or modes of human thought and behavior. If this is so, and I agree with Burhoe at this point, then God and world are the same thing, as I suggest below; however, I also show how conceptually differentiating this same "thing" leads to different attitudes and behaviors, and their resulting experiences. It may be that seeing the unity of world and God will also have still another set of pragmatic consequences.

term *God*. Of course, focusing on the immanence of God, which a pragmatic concept of meaning demands, we cannot distinguish God from the world by conceiving the creator to be a being that is ontologically distinct from the world. However, we can pragmatically define *God* as a kind of event or process, the kind of event that brings about transformations in the universe that go beyond the birth, growth, and maintenance of existing systems to create something new. The new may be new kinds of atomic arrangements called molecules, new DNA codes that give rise to new species or organisms, new human societies, new scientific theories, new religious movements. Traditionally, in Western religion human transformations have been specified by terms (in addition to the term *creation*) such as *salvation*, *liberation*, and *redemption*. While such terms have sometimes meant a rescue from sin and a recovery of an original way of being, they also have been used to specify the creation of a "new being." This latter usage fits with an evolutionary perspective aligned with pragmatism. In this perspective such terms can signify new instances of creation—the activity of the creative event or "God as continuing creator."

From my own work over twenty years attempting to specify more concretely the nature of the creative-type event, I have come to the tentative conclusion that it consists of two subevents, each independent of the other. The first generates new alternatives, differences from an existing state of affairs. The second determines which of the new alternatives will persist over time as stable physical, biological, or cultural entities. At the physical level of existence, an example of the first subevent is the subatomic interactions of positive and negative charges of energy that give rise to a new, possibly stable, atomic structure. An example of the second subevent is the strong and weak forces of the atom that at certain temperatures and densities bind the emerging new structure into a stable configuration such as a hydrogen or helium atom. At the biological level the first subevent is exemplified by the interactions between the DNA code of living organisms and the environment that give rise to new genetic variations, such as the interaction between the DNA of an individual organism and the radiation that displaces one of the nucleotide bases. This alters the DNA sequence and gives rise to a new genetic variation and a new resulting offspring. The second occurs when interactions between the genetically altered offspring and its surrounding environment determine whether the new offspring can feed and defend itself long enough to reproduce the new genetic variation. At the cultural level, the first subevent is illustrated by the interaction between ideas and experiences that leads to a new hypothesis in science or a new way of thinking about God in religion (what Peirce calls *abduction*). The second subevent (what Peirce calls *deduction* and *induction*) involves further interaction as the implications of the new idea are drawn out to see how effectively it solves unsolved problems while remaining coherent with ideas established as valid, how well it explains or interprets experiences considered significant in the existing system of thought, and how fruitful it is in leading to the uncovering of new experiences not anticipated by older ideas. As a variation in thought meets these conditions, it continues to be replicated from mind to mind and becomes a new creation. Further, during the course of the history of the universe, as new levels of existence such as life arise out of the matter and the human brain/mind and culture out of life, the processes of variation and selection operate across levels. For example, cultural variations in a particular society that give rise to new technologies for growing or processing food not only face selection pressures from existing cultural traditions but are also selected according to how well they meet the biological and physical-chemical conditions of the ecosystems in which that society exits.

In general terms, sometimes the first subevent is characterized as chance, the second as necessity or laws of nature; the first as random variation, the second as natural selection; the first as the generation of ideas, the second as their verification. I would argue that these all represent instances of the same basic pattern of the creative event, even though the causal mechanisms for the interactions vary at different levels of existence and between levels. From a theological perspective, in a recent essay attempting to show parallels between thermodynamic and Biblical concepts of creative activity, I suggested that the pattern specified by the two subevents could be conceptualized as Spirit and Word—two aspects of the immanent, divine creative activity.[12]

I have been trying to distinguish between what is specified by the words *world* and *God* as two ways in which humans can act toward and experience what is often the same "thing." From the pragmatic approach of Peirce, the difference between world and God can be conceived in terms of how humanity relates to—acts on and experiences—this same thing.[13] Let me illustrate. If one considers a local ecosystem as among the things specified by the word *world*, one would likely approach it in a utilitarian and aesthetic manner. In John Dewey's terms one would see it as something for human use and enjoyment. However, if one considers a local ecosystem as an instance of what is designated by the word *God*, defined as the creative event, one would be apt to seek the possibilities it might contain for new being. This has important implications for those interested in the environment. Many cogently argue that we should preserve the environment for future generations. But they view the environment as a created good, something to be utilized by humans. There may be nothing wrong with this. However, preservationist and conservationist movements could also argue that by preserving ecosystems, especially wilderness areas in which biological evolution can continue to occur, we are facilitating the work of God, the divine creativity in our midst.

---

[12]Karl E. Peters, "Toward a Physics, Metaphysics, and Theology of Creation: A Trinitarian View", in *Science and Public Policy*, ed. Frank Birtel (New York: Crossroads, 1987) 96-112.

[13]I use the word *thing* rather than *nature* or *reality* as a way of keeping the object of human action and experience as unspecified as possible.

Let us take another example of the difference between world and God, this time from human culture. We can look at contemporary science as a recent development of human culture and as part of what we mean pragmatically by *world*. As world, science becomes a system of ideas for humans to learn in order to increase our understanding and predict some course of events so we can respond appropriately in terms of human interests. As world, science also becomes the basis for technology that is used to fulfill existing human purposes. There may be nothing wrong with this, depending on the purposes for which science is used. However, I do not think we capture the excitement of many scientists for whom to do science is to participate in the creation of new solutions to problems and even new problems, thus transforming human understanding. The same term, *science*, can refer either to something that is created or to the creative process itself. I suggest that, as the creative process, science can be understood as one instance of the kind of creative event that theologians might call God.[14]

Finally, let me give an example from religion of the distinction between what is specified by *world* and what is specified by *God* as the creative event. In the history of Christianity there have been many ways of looking at Jesus as the Christ. I want to focus on two. The first sees Jesus as "lawgiver": his life and teachings formulate a code of conduct as well as an inner set of attitudes to be expressed in that conduct. In one sense there is nothing wrong with this. Yet, it can miss the dynamic interaction between Jesus and his cultural environment that produced this new way of living. It takes Christ as a cultural product and tries to replicate that product, but it may miss the Christ event that may continue to operate in history in new instances of religious creativity.

Insofar as the creative activity of Christ was in relation to the cultural and natural environments of the Middle East two thousand years ago, the results of that creativity reflect the historical circumstances of that time and place. It cannot be otherwise. However, today's historical circumstances are somewhat different. As Kaufman has put it, we live in a "nuclear age." As Sallie MacFague has put it, we live in an "ecological, nuclear age."[15] To simply replicate the results of the Christ event two thousand years ago may reinforce for some a human-centered lifestyle and ethics. Because of the increased power humans have, largely the result of the creative event working in the arena of science, what is needed in our time is a focus on the continued creative working of the Christ event to give rise, among other

---

[14]From the perspective of pragmatism, I often have wondered whether the success of science over the past few centuries might be theologically understood as scientists being in touch with God conceived as the creative event—maybe even better in touch than some people who call themselves religious.

[15]Sallie McFague, *Models of God: Theology for a Nuclear, Ecological Age* (Philadelphia: Fortress, 1987).

things, to an earth-centered lifestyle and ethic—which, pragmatically, is a new way of looking at a God-centered lifestyle and ethic.

Based on what I have said above about science, we humans have, largely without realizing it, cooperated with the work of God in one area, that of science, while we have not cooperated with it as completely in the area of religion. I think this is partly because we have seen Christ as product and not as process, as what I have been calling *world* and not as *God* conceived as creative activity. If we take Christ as a primary, historical example of the creative event, we will act differently in our present situation and expect different results from what we would expect if we take Christ as a cultural product. We will search out those mechanisms that can bring (perhaps are bringing) about a lifestyle that some have characterized as leading to a just, participatory, and sustainable world. We will support the creation of a way of life that both affirms the best humanistic values of Western religion as exemplified two thousand years ago by Jesus as the Christ and respects the physical-chemical-biological earth also as the locus of divinely created life and culture, and ongoing divine creative activity.

3. A Comparison with Kaufman's Concept of God

From a pragmatic perspective Kaufman's concept of God is of the same genre as the one suggested above. For him, "God should be conceived in terms of the complex physical, biological and historical-cultural conditions which have made human existence possible, which continue to sustain it, and which may draw it out to a fuller humanity and humaneness. Devotion to God conceived in terms other than these will not be devotion to *God*, that is, to that reality which has (to our best understanding) in fact created us, and a living connection with which is in fact needed if our lives are to be sustained and nourished."[16] Such a definition does begin to specify naturalistically and pragmatically that which we can conceive in terms of human actions to be performed and experiences to be expected. For if we focus our attention on the activities or processes in nature that Kaufman's functional definition of God implies and respond to them with appropriate devotion, we can expect experiences of continuing creation, sustenance, and richer human life.

There is much I like about Kaufman's definition as an alternative to the one I have developed above. For example, Kaufman's concept of God allows one to place a high value on nature and history as the past which has brought us to where we are today. At the same time, it expresses that more is to be done; it has a future goal of "fuller humanity and humaneness." Further, it does not consider all nature and history as divine. Of course, from the point of view of the Wiemanian concept of God developed above, one might point out that Kaufman's definition seems to confuse God and the world, because the conditions may be those for new creation or

---

[16]Kaufman, *Theology for a Nuclear Age*, 42.

those for maintaining systems already created. However, Kaufman's definition does contain an implied criterion—that of human existence and fuller humanity and humaneness—as a means of selecting from nature and history that which is specifically divine. In his 1981 essay "Constructing a Concept of God" he has written that "speaking of God would signify not only the fact that our humanity is cosmically grounded and sustained, but God would symbolize a fundamental *telos* in the universe toward the humane."[17]

The notion of a direction or telos in the universe toward the humane might at first glance seem difficult to pin down pragmatically. However, recent developments in the sciences, expressed in terms of the controversial "anthropic principle" that can be stated in many ways, suggest a possible Peircian pragmatic definition. In terms of the least controversial "weak anthropic principle," one might define *telos* by conceiving that one could discover at every major development in the history of the universe a narrow set of constraints that if not met would not have created atoms, galaxies, stars, a planet with life, a form of life capable of language and therefore culture and history, and a form of culture rooted in justice and love. God, teleologically conceived, would then be the total system of constraints that has evolved human existence and that makes possible fuller humane, human development.

I think a critical point of comparison between Kaufman's conception of God and my own concept (both of which I have attempted to formulate in terms of Peirce's pragmatism) is how each distinguishes its immanent God from the world. Kaufman seems to make this distinction teleologically in terms of the criterion of humane, human existence. Following Wieman, I make the distinction on the basis of creative and created value. Even though this distinction involves two ways of looking at a single "God-world" system (as Burhoe points out), it allows us to formulate pragmatically different sets of attitudes, behaviors and expected experiential results. Kaufman has worked with Wieman's thinking and finds it helpful, but he also finds it too anthropocentric.[18] Ironically, for some, Kaufman's view of God might also seem too focused on the human if I am correct in my observation that telos toward the humane is Kaufman's implicit criterion for distinguishing God from the world. Kaufman could avoid this, however, if he expanded his concept of God to that which creates, sustains, and supports the fuller humane, human development in harmony with the fuller development of all living creatures and the inanimate world. That could lead him teleologically to a notion of the peaceable kingdom, a harmony of all life on planet Earth.

Following Burhoe and others, I have responded to the problem of Wieman's anthropocentrism by expanding the notion of the creative process toward a pattern

---

[17]Kaufman, "Constructing a Concept of God," 138.

[18]Kaufman, "Empirical Realism in Theology: An Examination of Some Themes in Meland and Loomer," paper presented at the 1990 conference of the Highlands Institute for American Religious Thought, above, 159n.20.

of creativity that I think can be found operating throughout the universe. However, the idea of God as the creative event so conceived does not necessarily guarantee a direction in the universe culminating in the present state of humanity. That would be an additional claim. In not specifying the divine creativity in a teleological manner, I am in keeping with Wieman's contention that, from an empirical perspective, we cannot know whether the "source of human good" will continue to work toward a fuller humane humanity. If there is any "telos" to the creative event, it is simply that of continuing to create living and cultural systems in harmony with one another at particular places and times. Whether such continuing creation leads to a fuller humane, humanity will largely depend on how we humans respond to the creative process in our midst. If we do not respond appropriately, it is possible that the creative-type event will produce something that replaces humanity as the dominant species. Such a replacement would in effect be better than humanity in that through variation and selection God as creative activity always produces better forms in terms of their fitness in the current environmental situation. The greater good for Earth—defined as greater harmony among all living and nonliving systems—may be in terms of a diminished role for Homo sapiens. Of course, a diminished role with a diminished impact on the planet may be partly what could make us more humane.

One way of understanding the difference between Kaufman's view of God and the one I have presented is in terms of two concepts of evolution. According to psychologist Donald Campbell, who has written extensively on the evolution of human culture and on evolutionary epistemology, there are two views of creativity conceived in evolutionary terms. One is the extrapolatory view that thinks of evolution in terms of progressive development "toward ever greater adaptedness, ever higher levels of integration and organization."[19] Such a view of evolution was present in the thinking of Herbert Spencer; it may also be expressed by scientists advocating some form of the anthropic principle, and by Kaufman. The other view is mechanistic; it does not focus on the overall direction of evolution but on the pattern and mechanisms according to which evolution takes place. This was Charles Darwin's contribution to evolutionary thinking, and my view of God is consistent with this focus on pattern and mechanisms. Such a view does not preclude fuller human development but considers it possible only in terms of the mechanisms that constitute the ever-changing contemporary system of cultural, biological, chemical, and physical constraints or selection pressures on human biocultural organisms. Such a system of constraints constitutes an instance of the second subevent of the divine creativity, what Burhoe calls God as natural selection and what traditionally has been referred to as divine judgement.

---

[19]Donald T. Campbell, "The Conflict Between Social and Biological Evolution and the Concept of Original Sin," *Zygon: Journal of Religion and Science* 10 (September 1975): 236.

In brief conclusion, I suggest that Peirce's pragmatic conception of meaning can be used to help construct two concepts of God as immanent divine creativity. Included in the constructions are suggestions as to how one can empirically support each concept. Kaufman's concept of God seems to be more extrapolatory, teleological, and possibly anthropocentric. Mine is more mechanistic and universal. I think both make important contributions to a naturalistic, empirical theology. Possibly, if they could be integrated with each other, they might form the basis for an even fuller and richer concept of divine immanence.

Peircean Semiotics, Religion, and Theological Realism

William L. Power

In the first major study of Charles Sanders Peirce's philosophy of religion, Michael L. Raposa has noted that Peirce's religious thought has received relatively little attention and that his writings have had only a slight influence on scholars working in the diverse fields of religious studies.[1] There are various reasons for this neglect, not the least of which is his style of writing and strange terminology. Nevertheless, such a neglect is to be lamented, for scattered throughout his writings is a wealth of material that is significant for those interested in the study of religion in general and philosophy of religion and theology in particular.

In this paper, I want to focus on Peirce's semiotics, which is an expression of and the logical foundation for his commonsense realism and his "critical common-sensism" or his critical realism, and show its relevance for understanding religion and theology. In Section I of the paper, I will discuss Peircean semiotics as it has developed over the years with special attention to the syntax, semantics, and pragmatics of informative or descriptive discourse. In sections II and III, I will apply my discussion to an analysis of religion and theological realism. In so doing, I will be suggesting how religious communities, primarily theistic ones, assume and should assume commonsense realism and critical realism both in their use of language and in their lives.

I

Among historians of philosophy and logic, there is general agreement that Peirce is not only the first and perhaps the greatest of the American pragmatists, but he is also one of the creative pioneers in semiotics or the general theory of signs and the philosophy of language. Peirce's work in logic is continuous with the Ancients and the Medievalists, to whom he acknowledges his debt, and his studies in semiotics and the philosophy of language parallels the contributions of other giants of modern logic, such as Boole, De Morgan, Cantor, Frege, Russell, White-

---

[1]Michael L. Raposa, *Peirce's Philosophy of Religion* (Bloomington: Indiana University Press, 1989) 4.

head, Godel, and Tarski. Following the lead of the Stoics and Locke, Peirce can even claim that "logic, in its general sense, is . . . only another name for *semiotic*, the quasi-necessary, or formal, doctrine of signs" (2.227)* or the "doctrine of the essential nature and fundamental varieties of possible semiosis" (5.488).

Although Peirce explicated in detail only a small part of the general theory of signs that he envisioned, others have developed Peirce's insights and foundational work into what can be viewed as a "rational reconstruction" of his original doctrines or as a revised Peircean or pragmatic semiotics.[2] Thus, Peirce's semiotics has been nurtured and allowed to mature into a sophisticated theory with a wide range of applicability. In short, a well-developed logic and metalogic has been developed which can "meddle with all subjects," to use that delightful phrase of Peirce.[3]

Fundamental to a Peircean or pragmatic semiotics, is the recognition that human beings are the dominant sign-using, sign-interpreting, and sign-making animals. Indeed, the cognitive, conative, and affective capacities of the biocultural organism named *homo sapiens* are inseparable from the functioning of signs, the most important of which are linguistic, as Peirce noted more than once (5.420). This observation is not surprising, for it is by means of the use, interpretation and fabrication of linguistic and nonlinguistic signs that human beings practice the art of communication in order to live, live well, and live better in their common and all encompassing environment. In short, we desire to understand our environment and map our environment in order to find our way as *homo viator*. This is not to suggest that the sole use of linguistic and nonlinguistic signs is to represent reality in its various modalities and mixtures of good and evil, but it is to recognize that most, if not all, sign use and sign interpretation presupposes the representational or informative function of signs. Thus, Peirce is not wrong to view a sign as something that stands for some object for some interpreter by producing in that interpreter some logical, energetic, or emotional interpretant (5.470-90).

In Peirce's words:

> A sign, or *representamen*, is something which stands to somebody for something in some respect or capacity. It addresses somebody, that is, it creates in the mind of that person an equivalent sign, or perhaps a more developed sign. That sign which it creates I call the *interpretant* of the first sign. The sign stands for something, its ***object***. It stands for that object, not in all re-

---

**Collected Papers of Charles Sanders Peirce*, ed. C. Hartshorne, P. Weiss, and A. Burks (Cambridge MA: Harvard University Press, 1935, 1958). References are by volume and paragraph number: read 2.227 as vol. 2, para. 227.

[2]Charles Morris, *The Pragmatic Movement in American Philosophy* (New York: George Braziller, 1970) 16-47.

[3]As cited by Richard M. Martin, *Belief, Existence, and Meaning* (New York: New York University Press, 1969) 5.

> spects, but in reference to a sort of idea, which I have sometimes call the *ground* of the representamen. (2.228)

Again, Peirce writes:

> A *Representamen* is the First Correlate of a triadic relation, the Second Correlate being termed its *Object*, and the possible Third Correlate being termed its *Interpretant*, by which triadic relation the possible Interpretant is determined to be the First Correlate of the same triadic relation to the same Object, and for some possible Interpretant. (2.242)

Passages like these abound in Peirce's discussion of signs, and in every case, three terms of a triadic relation come into play—a sign, an object, and an interpretant or interpreter. One can, of course, expand these semiotic notions to encompass an entire system of signs, in which case, one would have to take into account multiple signs, multiple objects, and multiple interpretants or interpreters. Needless to say, the varieties of possible semiosis will increase in quantity and richness the more comprehensive the system.

Similar to the Medieval trivium, Peirce distinguishes three branches of semiotics: (1) pure grammar; (2) logic proper; and (3) pure rhetoric (2.229). The first branch studies signs and their interrelations; the second branch studies signs and their relations to the objects they represent, and the third branch studies the signs and their relations to the users or interpreters of the signs. These three branches, since the time of Morris and Carnap, have come to be commonly known as syntax, semantics, and pragmatics.[4]

Peirce developed his semiotics into a rich, elaborate, and complex classification and division of signs. In his most comprehensive vision, he identified sixty-six fundamental classes of signs, although, in his major discussion of signs, he concentrated on ten main classes. Peirce thought, however, that the division of signs into icons, indexes, and symbols (2.247) is the most important one, and of the three sorts of signs, symbols stand out as the most perfect of signs. For Peirce, the creation, use, and interpretation of symbols—primarily linguistic ones—distinguishes human beings from other animal species, and it is primarily through symbols that science and other forms of human culture become possible.

Peirce's discussion of icons, indexes, and symbols is the heart of his semantic theory which pertains to the way signs can stand for, signify, or represent their objects. An icon is a sign that signifies or represents an object by virtue of some qualitative or structural likeness which holds between a sign and an object, such as an ideograph, a photograph, or a scale model. An index is a sign which signifies or represents an object by virtue of its being dynamically affected by that object, such

---

[4]Rudolph Carnap, *Foundations of Logic and Mathematics*, in *International Encyclopedia of Unified Science*, vol. 1, no. 3 (Chicago: University of Chicago Press, 1939) 3.

as a weather vane, a barometer, a wound, or a state of wonder or awe. A symbol is a sign that signifies or represents an object by virtue of some implicit or explicit rule or convention which governs it use, such as the terms, phrases, and sentences of a language, a red light, a fraternity pin, and a flag. In speaking this way, however, one should not forget that no sign can function as a sign until it is interpreted, otherwise one will reduce the signification situation to a dyadic relation between a sign and an object, rather than a triadic relation between a sign, an object and an interpreter.

While there is much more that could be said concerning natural and artificial signs or signs fabricated by human beings, let me turn to the topic of linguistic symbols, for it is in the semiotics of language and informative discourse that a Peircean or a pragmatic semiotics has undergone the greatest development. As in the general theory of signs, the study of a language or a language system can be divided into syntax, semantics, and pragmatics. In syntax one is interested in the signs or expressions of a language and their interrelations. In semantics, which presupposes syntax and includes it as a part, one is concerned not only with expressions and their interrelations but also with the objects which the signs denote or designate or stand for in one way or another. In pragmatics there is reference not only to the signs and what they denote and designate or stand for but also to the users and interpreters of a language.[5] While one can focus on syntax alone, or syntax and semantics, a complete semiotics will include all three branches. In the final analysis, the three branches are distinguishable but not separable.

In Peirce's characterization of a sign or representamen as something that stands to somebody for something in some respect or capacity, we have seen that the notion of a sign is so broad that almost anything can function as a sign. If we restrict our attention to linguistic signs, however, the range of our discussion can be narrowed and the notion of standing for something in some respect or capacity can perhaps be made clearer.

In his discussion of terms, Peirce adopts Sir William Hamilton's expressions "breadth" and "depth" for the extension and comprehension or intention of a term, later applying the expressions to propositions and even arguments (2.407 and footnote). Interestingly enough, Peirce's views are very close to those of Frege who distinguished between the reference and sense of expressions.[6] While the debate still rages as to whether names or singular terms can have senses, and whether sentences or statements or propositions can have both senses and references, most logicians readily endorse the semantic notion that general terms or predicates, encompassing

---

[5]Richard M. Martin, *Toward a Systematic Pragmatics* (repr. West Port CT: Greenwood Press, 1974; 1959) xi. My wording is indebted to Martin.

[6]"On Sense and Reference," in *Philosophical Writings of Gottlob Frege*, ed. Peter Geach and Max Black (Oxford: Basil Blackwell, 1970) 56-78.

both class terms or one-place predicates and relational predicates, can have both references and senses or meanings.

For Peirce, barring some of his sharper distinctions, the "breadth" of a class term consists of "all the real things of which it is predicable," and the "depth" of a class term consists of "all of the real characters . . . which can be predicated of . . . whatever it is applicable to" (2.408-409 with footnote). For example, the class term or predicate "human being" denotes all members of the class of human beings and designates all of the known and unknown properties or attributes which human beings actually manifest or might manifest.

If I am correctly interpreting Peirce's meaning of the breadth of the predicate "human being," then it is obvious that as finite and fallible human beings we can never comprehend the comprehension of the term. We can only comprehend human beings in some respects or capacities. For example, we comprehend human beings in respect of being a sign-using, sign-interpreting animal, a language using, language interpreting animal, a rational animal, a political animal, a fabricating animal, a playing animal, a journeying animal, and a religious animal—to mention some of the major ways of being human.

Yet, there are many other respects in which the human animal can manifest his or her humanity. And in this respect, human animals are like other objects which our linguistic signs signify in some respect or capacity. As Peirce so well recognized, we humans can never comprehend all the respects in which something can be what it is. Thus, our signifying activity and our learning from signs potentially can go on ad infinitum (2.92,303).

Peirce's understanding of the meaning of a general term or predicate is very closely related to his pragmatic maxim. In one of his formulations, he writes:

> In order to ascertain the meaning of an intellectual conception one should consider what practical consequences might conceivably result by necessity from the truth of that conception, and the sum of these consequences will constitute the entire meaning of the conception. (5.9)

While this maxim may seem unclear, the basic notion is that the meaning of a concept or general term involves a fundamental connection between action and experience such that if certain sorts of actions were to be performed, then certain sorts of experiential results would necessarily be obtained.[7] In short, if one wants to know the nature of anything, then one has in principle the endless task of finding out all the ways something can act and be acted upon. This is the basic message in the pragmatic theory of meaning. It is also the basic message in Peirce's logic of relations, which he created, along with Augustus De Morgan.

By means of a logic of relations, one is able to make explicit not only the process of semiosis and the semantic notion of meaning, but also the very nature of the

---

[7]Morris, 22.

environment wherein all things and events are interrelated in a vast interconnected web. Indeed, Peirce's realism is one in which universals are recognized not primarily as inherent in individuals in their solitude (*in re*) but rather in individuals in solidarity or community (*inter res*). What things are, is known by virtue of the relations that hold between or among individuals or what relations might hold between or among individuals. In short, relational predicates come to have a primacy in describing the common world disclosed in experience which they lacked in most premodern and modern forms of science and philosophy.[8]

Although I have been speaking of the signification or representation of general terms and concepts, class terms, and relational predicates, Peirce's theory of symbols can be also extended to singular terms or names. That is, one can represent a unique individual in terms of a series of definite descriptions wherein one attempts to identify that unique individual in some unique respect or capacity. For example, I can represent my wife Amburn in the unique respect or capacity of being the daughter of Mildred and Jay Huskins, the natural mother of Jay and Joe Watson, the adoptive mother of Keith and Kevin Power, the youngest founder of the Athens Puppet Theater, and the wife of Will Power, who in turn is the husband of Amburn Power, and the only son of Ellis and Lauraine Power. To be sure, there are other definite descriptions which could be used to say who Amburn is and who I am. What is logically interesting, however, is that in each of the definite descriptions I have used, relational predicates play a decisive role. Thus, in saying who someone is, the user of language will invariably attempt to locate or point to that individual in some order generated by a relation of some sort. Contrary to Hume's maxim, whoever or whatever can be distinguished cannot be separated from its relationally ordered environment.

While many would disagree with his judgment, Peirce thought that epistemological realism is entailed by human inquiry and behavior. Peirce was a realist who believed that human beings lived in, interacted with, and were bonded to their human and nonhuman environments; and in terms of his semantics of linguistic and nonlinguistic signs, Peirce recognized that humans intend to accurately represent those extramental and extralinguistic environments. Our representations of extramental and extralinguistic reality, as well as our representations of mental and linguistic reality, are not perfect representations. On the other hand, to acknowledge that our representations are approximate and fallible, is not to fall into the extreme of denying that they represent at all. Our actual and possible environments are epistemically illusive, to be sure; yet, we know a good bit about the way things are and might be through our acritical common sense and our critical common sense or science, broadly

[8]In Aristolelian class logic only monadic predicates were used. The ontological import of this was that concrete individuals could exist apart from their relations to other concrete individuals. That is, relations could not be essential to the descriptions of metaphysics of empirical science. Relations were considered as accidental.

understood to embrace all domains of theoretical investigation or inquiry. Moreover, we can know a good bit more if we pursue inquiry long enough, all the while confessing the incomprehensibility of all that in principle can be known.

In regard to the representational or descriptive use of language, Peirce clearly distinguished between our linguistic worlds and our nonlinguistic environments.[9] By means of our linguistic worlds we represent our environments and discourse about them, but our linguistic worlds cannot, in Peirce's words "furnish acquaintance with or recognition of our nonlingulistic environments" (2.231). In short, knowledge by description is not identical with knowledge by acquaintance, even if the two are inseparably related.

In our common sense and in our critical common sense, we assume that there is an extramental and extralinguistic world; and in our everyday use of language and in our theoretical use of language, we assume that our discourse, at least in intent, corresponds to reality. Peirce accepted the correspondence theory of truth although modified it to take into account human fallibility and the unending task of formulating, explicating, and testing hypotheses by abductive, deductive, and inductive inferences (2.100-104, 5.189, 6.477, 522-28).[10] While viewing truth as the ideal end of inquiry and the search for truth as a communal endeavour, one can still accept a "rational reconstruction" of the correspondence theory of truth in terms of contemporary semantic theory. Indeed, the semantic theory of truth is the contemporary attempt to articulate in a more precise way the traditional correspondence theory. Thus, in the parlance of current semantics, a declarative sentence or statement is true if and only if the state of affairs asserted by that sentence or statement is the case. If one prefers to relate truth to belief rather to sentences and statements, then one can say that a belief is true or false depending on whether things are as believed. Thus, drawing on earlier examples one could say that the statement, "Human beings are the dominant sign-using, sign-interpreting, and sign-making animals" is true if and only if human beings are the dominant sign-using, sign-interpreting and sign-making beings. And the statement, "Amburn is the youngest founder of the Athens Puppet Theater" is true if and only if Amburn is the youngest founder of the Athens Puppet Theater. The task of determining whether these statements are true, however, is a practical or pragmatic one, wherein one attempts to justify a statement by means of inferential or noninferential procedures. As such, the semantic issue of

---

[9]Walker Percy, *Lost in the Cosmos* (New York: Farrar, Straus, and Giroux, 1983) 99. My use of "linguistic worlds" and "non-linguistic environments" draws on Percy's work on semiotics which is heavily indebted to Peirce.

[10]As generally understood, a deductive inference or argument is one such that if the premises are true then the conclusion *necessarily* follows; an inductive argument is one such that if the premises are true then the conclusion *probably* follows; an abductive argument is one such that if the premises are true then the conclusion *plausibly* follows. An abductive argument has the logical form of the deductive fallacy of affirming the consequent: Q, P $\supset$ Q/P.

truth and falsity is to be distinguished from the pragmatic issue of justification and refutation.

II

In Section I of this paper I have spoken of human beings, as *homo symbolicus* and *homo loquens* from the point of view of a Peircean logic or semiotics. Whether one views that logic or semiotics as a logic of common sense or instinct or as a logic of critical common sense—what Peirce called a *logica utens* and a *logica docens* (2.188)—I hope enough has been said to underline the realism of that point of view and the extent to which human beings use and interpret natural and artificial signs in order to represent and understand the environment in which they live and to which they are bonded by a multitude of relations. The question I now want to address is whether a Peircean or pragmatic semiotics is useful, *mutatis mutandis*, in understanding human beings as *homo religiosus*. An answer, I believe, is not hard to find.

The term "religion" is ambiguous and can be used in many ways. However, corresponding to its Greek cognates *threskeia* and *eusebeia* and its Latin cognates *cultus* and *religio*, it basically has two uses. It is used to signify or designate a community with its cultus, and it is used to designate a way of life which takes account of a or the divine reality by means of that cultus. In more traditional language, a religion is an objective cult and religion is piety. In the more recent language of Clifford Geertz, religion can be construed both as a cultural system and a style of life.[11] Geertz, interestingly enough, develops his interpretation of religion on the basis of a semiotic understanding of human culture which draws heavily upon the work of Susanne Langer.[12] Be that as it may, let me briefly sketch out my own interpretation of *homo religiosus* from a semiotic point of view, albeit more Peircean.

An objective cult or a cultural system is simply a community with its cultus. It is what we normally refer to as a religion. It is something finite, empirical, public, and observable. The community is an organized group of socially interdependent human beings, and its structure or polity, as well as its cultus, is designed to fulfill the aims of that group. Its form exists for the sake of its function. The community can be tribal, national, or international, and it is locatable in the spatiotemporal order. As such, an objective cult has an ongoing history and is subject to the usual conditions of historical continuity and change. These communities have different evolving life histories and different life spans. They come to be, endure for a time, and often perish.

---

[11]Glifford Geertz, *The Interpretation of Cultures: Selected Essays* (New York: Basic Books, 1973) 87-125, 126-41.

[12]Ibid., 91.

The cultus consists of an organic system of linguistic and nonlinguistic signs, encompassing such elements as stories, creeds, scriptures, doctrines, theologies confessions, prayers, chants, songs, artifacts, rites, rituals, sacraments, etc. Like any other cultural system, scheme, or network of signs, one can characterize a religious cultus as an intersubjective set of signs whose usage is determined by the implicit or explicit rules that govern the relations of signs to each other; the relations of the signs to the objects which the signs designate or denote, or stand for in some way; and the relations of the signs to the users or interpreters of these signs in some way. Thus, each religion has a syntactic, semantic, and pragmatic dimension; and each religion can and should be studied, if it is to be fully understood, in terms of its linguistic and nonlinguistic signs, the signification of its signs, and the significance of its signs for the way humans realistically can and should live.

Gathering together these various elements, one can describe an objective cult or a religion as a community which employs its oral and written languages and its nonlinguistic signs to proclaim, enact, and display a comprehensive worldview and to effect human ways of life on the basis of that representation. That is, the religious form of human culture functions to mediate an understanding and perception of sacred or divine things, human things, and natural things in their actual and possible interrelations so that human beings can live, lead a good life, and have a good life in their all encompassing environment. The way of life which is generated, formed, nurtured, and transformed by the objective cult is basically what we mean by piety or religious experience, and it encompasses the cognitive, conative, and affective dimensions of human existence in its solidarity and solitude. In short, a religion is a cultural system which functions to map the whole of reality, primarily ultimate reality and to acculturate in desirable ways or to civilize. At least this is the intent of most, if not all, religious cultural systems.

From this discussion, one can see that a religion exists for the sake of religion, and that religion is primarily a way of relating to sacred or divine reality by means of a religion. Of course, human relations to nondivine domains of our environing universe are not excluded. *Eusebeia*, *religio*, religion, piety, religious experience and the like is the taking account of that which is divine, sacred, or holy by means of *threskeia*, *cultus*, a religion, or a religious tradition. It is man and woman's recognition of and response to a or the divine reality, or as I prefer to say, a religious way of life. It is the *hodos* of Judaism, the *marga* of Hinduism and the *tao* of Taoism.

Those who are familiar with the recent literature on religious experience will no doubt find my exposition in harmony with much of what is written therein. There are two Peircean points, however, which I want to emphasize. The first is that there is no human experience without acculturation or the mediation of signs. As creators and creatures of culture, our apprehension of and response to reality is culturally conditioned from infancy onward. Even if we recognize that we live in a wider environment than our linguistic and cultural worlds, our taking account of that environment is a mediated recognition and response. As noted in Section I of this paper, this is the process of semiosis. In this process, a psychosomatic organism, agent, or interpreter takes account of the environment by means of signs. This "taking account of" manifests itself in a thought, an action, or a quality of feeling—Peirce's logical, energetic, and emotional interpretants. In short, there is no immediate experience. There is no culture free cognition, conation, and affection.

Just as scientific observation is theory laden, our experience of things divine is conditioned by some objective cult or aspect of a cultural system. That is, the interiorizing of a cultural system facilitates and predisposes humans to recognize and respond to that reality. Thus, our religious piety, to use an older and familiar expression, is not a two term relation, but a three term relation. One's piety or experience of that which is divine is a mediated awareness. Our relation to divine reality is a triadic relation, not a dyadic one. This is not to say that that which is "given" in experience, our extramental environments, do not influence us to alter our linguistic and nonlinguistic sign systems. We continually correct our mistaken beliefs about reality, as a cartographer corrects his or her maps of various topographies. We also continually construct new cultural forms to more adequately represent reality and to represent what is newly discovered and might be discovered. Acknowledging this fact, I still want to emphasize that our cultural and conceptual frameworks are inseparably related to our experience of the external world or extramental reality.

The second point I want to underline is that piety or religious experience cannot be reduced to some noncognitive or nonrational dimension of human existence. For example, religious experience cannot properly be defined or described exclusively as inward feeling affection, or emotion. The noetic dimension of experience is ever present. To be sure, such thought, intelligence, and rationality need not be critical and fully reflective. Indeed, one can argue that the thought, intelligence, and rationality of most religious believers, saints, prophets, and contemplatives is for the most part acritical. Only at the level of theorizing does cognition become critical. With various degrees of reflection, what is implicit is made explicit. Even then, such critical thought rests upon an acritical foundation. Be that as it may, the primacy of perception, insight, recognition, discernment, and the like in religious experience can hardly be denied, even though some have tended to interpret religious experience in noncognitive and nonrational terms.[13] Given my description of religion as a way of life, it is clear that the logos, ethos, and pathos of piety are inseparably bound together; and, in my judgment, logos is logically prior to ethos and pathos.

From my brief discussion of *homo religiosus*, one can see that there are three constitutive factors, aspects, or dimensions of religion. There is the cultural dimension, consisting of the oral and written linguistic and nonlinguistic signs of the

---

[13]One of the best discussions of this tendency is still that of John Baillie, *The Interpretation of Religion* (New York: Charles Scribner's Sons, 1928) 202-34.

community. Central in this cultural system is a religious community's worldview. Secondly, there is the reality and value dimension which is represented by the worldview. Lastly, there is the existential dimension which is effected by the cultural and ontological-axiological dimensions. That is, a person or community of persons takes account of divine things, human things, and natural things by means of a cultus. In this sense, the cultural and ontological-axiological dimensions function as necessary conditions for the specific forms of belief, praxis, and sensibility which constitute piety or religious experiences. Thus, religious ways of life can be viewed as receptive responses to the world of reality as mediated by the worldviews and other facets of the cultus of religious communities. At least this is how I interpret the notion of religion, and it is an interpretation which is harmonious with Peirce's thoughts on religion and the discourse of religious communities (6.429-50). If this interpretation is sound, then human discourse about God and human bonding with God will exhibit the semiotic structure I have been discussing. In short, semiotics can provide a framework for what Roposa calls a "theological semiotic."[14]

III

In terms of syntax, the term "God" is a singular term or name. As such, it can be taken as primitive in theistic discourse or it can be introduced definitionally by means of a definite description. Peirce understood the symbol "God" as "*the* definable proper name, signifying *ens necessarium* . . . [the] creator of all three Universes of Experience" (6.452). Peirce also affirmed that the name "God" is vague, indeed vaguer than most vernacular words (6.494). For the most part, he never attempted to explicate his conception of God, and basically left it vague. For that reason, Peirce scholars have found it difficult to identify his form of theism. There are elements of his theology which indicate that he primarily accepts classical theism, while there are other elements of his theology which indicate that he accepts a form of neoclassical theology.[15] Which ever is the case, however, Peirce thought that the term "God," for all its vagueness, served its purposes well as a *representamen* of God in the unique respect or capacity of being the necessary being and the creator of the universe or the common world disclosed in experience, namely, the world of possibility, actuality, and generality, and as an exemplar for the conduct of human life (6.494,452-85).

Peirce accepted "the doctrine of a personal God" and believed that human beings can have "a direct perception of that person and indeed be in personal communication with him" (6.162). As the Absolute Mind or perfect "disembodied spirit" (6.489) Peirce could designate God in respect of being omniscient, omnipo-

---

[14]Raposa, *Peirce's Philosophy of Religion*, 5.

[15]Ibid., 35-62. See also Charles Hartshorne, *Creativity in American Philosophy* (Albany: SUNY Press, 1984) 89-90.

tent, and omnibenevolent or unbounded agape. Indeed, the creative activity of God, which Peirce thought was necessary, although no particular created entity was necessary (6.218), is an expression of God's "cherishing-love" (6.287). The One Supreme Being is also represented as having "its being out of time," and is, therefore, immutable (6.490,4.67). God is also understood by Peirce to be free "from all experience" and "all desire;" and because God is incorporeal and without a brain, "God probably has no consciousness" (6.489). Thus God seems to be impassible. Because Peirce believed God cannot be acted upon or be affected, he refused to apply the category of secondness to God, and hence the notion of existence. For anything to exist, it must have the power of acting and being acted upon; therefore, God cannot be said to exists. This usage of the word "exist" in reference to God is somewhat different than that of Kant and Tillich, who restricted the use of the word to contingent beings.

If one views Peirce's thoughts and discourse about God as a vague presentation of divine perfection, then there is much to be desired. If one conceives of God as a personal being, then it hardly seems possible to eliminate the affective aspect of the divine psyche. Furthermore, if one takes seriously Peirce's logic of relations and his pragmatic maxim, then it would seem to be the case that God must have the capacity of acting as well as the capacity of being acted upon. Be that as it may, my main point in this brief sketch of Peirce's understanding of God is to indicate how semantically the word "God" functions as a symbol which represents its object in some respect or capacity for some interpreter. In short, the symbol "God" serves the semantic function of designating the theistic God in some unique respect or capacity along with the pragmatic function of effecting human thought, action, and feeling on the basis of that representation.

As long as the theistic conception or description of God remains vague and is arrived at by an acritical abductive inference manifest in musing on the common world disclosed in experience, as it is in Peirce's "humble argument" (6.486), then theology can be viewed as a method and product of common sense and an expression of acritical realism. However, if one can go on to explicate such a vague notion of God and critically justify that notion in the context of a speculative philosophy or what Peirce envisioned as a "scientific metaphysics," then theology can become a method and product of critical common sense and an expression of critical realism. Interestingly enough, just four years before his death, in his 1910 "Additament" to his 1908 "A Neglected Argument for the Reality of God" (6.452-85), he "hints" that such an endeavour is possible and necessary (6.490).

If Peirce is correct in his suggestion, and I believe that he is, then theological realism can be affirmed at two levels. At the first level, belief in the reality of God is available to all normal human beings at the tacit dimension of their experience. At this level of acritical thought, action, and feeling, the universe can be viewed as a "vast representamen" of God (6.459). The cosmos can be viewed as a system of interconnected signs which, if interpreted correctly, can signify the divine reality.

For Peirce, the universe is God's symbol, with indexical and iconic features (6.459). The general features of the cosmos as a vast developing environmental or ecological system can be taken as a symbol of God's purposes for the creatures; the emergence and movements of actual things and existents in the spatiotemporal order can be taken as indexical signs of the creative producer; and the objective and subjective qualities and relations manifest in experience can be taken as iconic signs of the divine nature and identity.

For Peirce, the cosmos is God's "great poem" (5.119) which signifies the divine artist and artistry. One can use other expressions to speak metaphorically of God's productive work, and I rather prefer to speak of the cosmos as God's "great story" or God's "great drama" in which each creature is called upon to live out their stories or participate as actors in the divine comedy. In any case, God's poem can evoke in us, according to Peirce, "a sort of sentiment, or obscure perception" of its author "the first and last, the Alpha and Omega," to whom we are inseparably related or intimately bonded (6.162). That is, musing on the common world disclosed in experience and abductively inferring God as its creator and consummator can awaken in us a latent awareness of God. This sense of the divine presence, Calvin's *sensus divinitatis*, is a kind of naive piety, religious experience, or instinctive discernment of God. Thus, at the first level of naivete, one affirms theological realism by abduction and by direct perception.

Theological realism can be affirmed at the second level of reflective thought and discourse to the extent that the idea of God can be made clear and theological statements can be justified in a theoretical framework or constructive theology and to the extent that piety or religious experience can be elucidated and the spirits assessed. In short, commonsense theology becomes critical commonsense theology when tested in "the cupelfurnace of measured criticism" (6.480), to use Peirce's apt expression. Thus theological inquiry begins in acritical musement and naive piety and ends in critical theory and refined piety. However, since inquiry is in reality a never ending task, like the reign of God, the fullness of theological truth lies in the future which is not yet. Such is the nature of a Peircean theosemiotic.

How Far Can Kaufman Go towards Naturalism? The Divine Plurality as a Test

Jerome A. Stone

In this essay I outline Gordon Kaufman's construction of the symbol/concept "God," showing that a hint of pluralism is overcome by a preference for personal/agential metaphors. After a brief sketch of discussions of divine plurality, I develop a similar construction with greater acknowledgement of the plurality of transcendent forces and ideals. Finally I argue for the merit of such a recognition on pragmatic grounds.

I

Kaufman's first main point is that our ideas of God are imaginative constructs. "All speech to and about God, and all 'experience of God,' is made possible by and is a function of the constructive powers of the imagination."[1]

Kaufman's second point is that God is the "ultimate point of reference to which all action, consciousness and reflection can lead." No regressive reflection, no devotion, no action toward the future can intend a reality "beyond" God. "God" is a limiting idea, "the idea of that beyond which we cannot go either in experience, thought or imagination."[2]

The image/concept of God includes the connotations of a "personal/agential" being. According to Kaufman there is a continuum from highly mythical and symbolic images of God (God as a personal being, for example) to abstract notions such as "the cosmic ground of our humanity." It is important to Kaufman that "the myth-

---

[1]Gordon D. Kaufman, *The Theological Imagination: Constructing the Concept of God* (Philadelphia: Westminster, 1981) 22. Sections of this essay are taken from Jerome A. Stone, *The Minimalist Vision of Transcendence* (Albany: SUNY Press, 1992).

[2]Gordon D. Kaufman, *An Essay on Theological Method*, rev. ed. (Missoula MT: Scholars Press, 1979) 11, 13.

ic and the metaphysical dimensions of the image/concept of God must be held together."[3] To this end images from the whole continuum must be used.

Very fascinating from the viewpoint of the older Chicago school, especially Shailer Mathews, is Kaufman's identification of God with the cosmic forces working toward humanization.

> "God" is a symbol that gathers up into itself and focuses for us all those cosmic forces working toward the fully humane existence for which we long. God symbolizes that in the ongoing evolutionary-historical process which grounds our being as distinctively human and which draws (or drives) us on toward authentic human fulfillment.[4]

Now the symbol of God is clearly a personifying symbol.

> Such a personification has a considerable advantage for some purposes over abstract concepts such as "cosmic forces" or "foundation for our humanity in the ultimate nature of things": the symbol "God" is concrete and definite, a sharply defined image, and as such it can readily become the central focus for devotion and service.[5]

We should note that he quickly glides from the plurality of "cosmic forces" in his metaphysical referent to the personified symbol of "god." Like Wieman, his concern for the religious power of the symbol of God is dominant.

II

This, I trust, is a brief but fair picture of Kaufman's reconstruction of the image/concept of God. It lacks reference to what Kaufman calls the other theological categories, humanity, the world, and Christ, but I think it will suffice for our present purposes. I would like to propose an alternative imaginative reconstruction which is rather similar to Kaufman's but is more explicitly pluralistic. But first I must examine my own historical roots. I could look at a number of modern thinkers who briefly explore theological pluralism: William James, Frederick R. Tennant, Edward Scribner Ames, John Dewey (especially in his exchange with Wieman), the early Meland, and recently the Jungian David Miller. However, I shall pass to the most relevant writer for our dialogue with Kaufman, Shailer Mathews.

As Mathews matured he developed a brief definition of God which I have found useful. I select the version from *Is God Emeritus?* The term *God*, according to Mathews, is

---

[3]*Theological Imagination*, 52

[4]Ibid., 50, 41.

[5]Ibid., 50.

> in reality an anthropomorphic concept of those personality-producing activities of the universe with which humanity is organically united.[6]

Note the parallel with Kaufman's discussion of God as the symbol for the cosmic humanizing forces.

III

Now I wish to propose a somewhat different experiment in theological imagination, a more pluralistic construction than Kaufman's. I have two motives for this proposal. First, this is a serious proposal which I put forward for public consideration. At other times I have called this my "minimal model of the transcendent" or a minimalist approach to the divine.[7] Second, I offer it as a dialogical approach to Professor Kaufman to see if he can accept or reject it. I suspect that he will reject it. However, I hope that my proposal will be a serious enough challenge that he will be moved to clarify further and justify his position. I trust that this is a useful and helpful thing to do.

I wish to begin with Kaufman's identification of God with forces working towards humanization. " 'God' is a symbol that gathers up into itself and focuses for us all those cosmic forces working toward the fully humane existence for which we long."[8] Note the explicit plurality in the phrase "all those cosmic forces" and also the move toward unification of this plurality in the phrase "'God' is a symbol that gathers up into itself and focuses for us all those cosmic forces." Shailer Mathews would be very interested in this, as am I.

Drawing upon Mathews, I would like to propose the following as a model for "God" or, as I prefer, "the divine" or "the transcendent." *"God" is a human symbol for a plurality of norms and creative powers which transcend the present situation as perceived.*

I believe that starting from either an empirical or a constructivist basis for religious inquiry the issue of plurality in the divine must be faced. I also believe that, using tentative and minimalist thinking, as I try to do, we cannot go on to affirm a significant unity to the divine, other than the bare minimum of the common generic properties of being situationally transcendent and also being a creative power or a compelling norm. In other words, God is a collection of situationally transcendent powers and norms. I wish to draw attention to four aspects of this model.

---

[6]Shailer Mathews, *Is God Emeritus?* (New York: Macmillan, 1940) 34. See Gordon D. Kaufman, *In Face of Mystery: A Constructive Theology* (Cambridge: Harvard University Press, 1993) 356.

[7]Jerome A. Stone, "A Minimal Model of Transcendence," *American Journal of Theology & Philosophy* 8/3 (September 1987): 121-35.

[8]*Theological Imagination*, 50.

1. The symbol is neither subjective nor objective. It certainly is not an illusion, although it is subject to illusion. It involves an interplay between objective factors in the world and a unifying, abstractive human response to these factors.

2. The symbols of "God" or the "divine" refer to both powers and norms. In terminology which I am trying to develop, the symbols refer to both real and ideal transcendence. As Kaufman phrases it, "God symbolizes that in the ongoing evolutionary-historical process which *grounds* our being as distinctively human *and* which *draws (or drives) us on toward authentic human fulfillment.*"[9] The temptation of some forms of naturalism is to ignore the real powers and treat God as a symbol for ideas or norms only.

3. These symbols refer not to just any powers and norms, but to those which are transcendent. In my minimalist language, these symbols refer to powers and norms which are transcendent to the present situation.

4. These symbols, "God" and "the divine," are singular but refer to a plurality of situationally transcendent powers and norms. It is not unusual to have a singular symbol referring to a plurality of factors. For example, the term "wood" is a singular term referring to a plurality of pieces and of items of wood. Again, employing minimalist thinking, we must acknowledge that there might be more unity to the divine than our pluralistic model suggests. However, I suggest that as a minimum, all that we can affirm with adequate warrant is that there are a plurality of situationally transcendent powers and norms which we can refer to with a single symbol.

The similarities between this view and that of Kaufman should be somewhat clear. The similarities are partly those of a sociological or historicist Kantianism, with a conceptual/pragmatic analysis of the concept of God owing much to Richard Niebuhr and Tillich. For both Kaufman and myself "God" is an imaginative construct, an image or symbol with reference to real forces at work and with powerful pragmatic import.

Kaufman's distinction between the relativizing and the humanizing functions of the image/concept of God is very similar to the distinction drawn by me between the ideal and the real aspects of transcendence. I think that Kaufman has seen something very similar to the two aspects of transcendence. There are some differences, however.

The first is that there is a unity to Kaufman's notion of a "Supreme Relativizer" which is lacking in the concept of ideal transcendence in my minimal model. The ontological reticence I am urging challenges this notion of a single Relativizer. This is related to the fact that I am suggesting a minimal model, not of God, but of a divine or sacred quality or dimension of experience.

The second difference is that his notion of a Supreme Humanizer also has a unity which differs from my notion of many experiences of real transcendence as

[9]Ibid., 41, emphasis added.

minimally understood. The experiences of real transcendent powers are all experiences of enhancement or nurturing of our humaneness, but again, Kaufman has introduced a unity to these experiences which may be closer to the traditional notion of God but which oversteps the bounds of legitimate metaphysical modesty.

Another difference is that in specifying the referent of the term "god" or "the divine" in my model, I do not make the cosmic-evolutionary sweep of the humanizing process the primary focus of attention. I recognize a deep kinship with Kaufman here. However, my attention is centered less on the evolutionary process than on the specific experiences of situationally transcendent qualities or forces. Recognition of a process is more of an intellectual construct, an inference from the data of science. On the other hand, the experiences of transcendence are concrete, real, and insistent. At this point I feel closer to Meland's comment that these experiences can at times be terribly real than I do to the cosmic vision of Smuts, Alexander or Mathews (however much I also feel a kinship with them). My model of the divine is not based on a *Weltanschauung* generalized from evolutionary theory. It does not reject such a worldview, but it is more closely tied to specific experiences of unexpected and unmanageable resource and healing.

Why speak of "God" or "the divine?" Why not use philosophical and empirical language for the plurality of powers and norms? Here I find myself in sympathy with Bernard Loomer. Having identified God as the "concrete, interconnected totality" of the world as a whole, Loomer raised the question "why deify this interconnected web of existence by calling it 'God'?" Loomer's identification of God with the web of the world as a whole is quite different from the pluralism proposed here which selects powers and norms from the world to deify. However, his justification for using the term "God" is worth listening to.

> In our traditions the term "God" is the symbol of ultimate values and meanings in all of their dimensions. It connotes an absolute claim on our loyalty. It bespeaks a primacy of trust, and a priority within the ordering of our commitments.[10]

My approach to a functional justification for using religious language for plurality of situationally transcendent powers and norms differs in detail from Loomer. I rely on a phenomenology of the transcendent, eliciting a triadic structure of transcendent blessing and judgment. But Loomer is fundamentally correct: "In our traditions the term 'God' is the symbol of ultimate values and meanings in all their dimensions."

Many people tend to think in traditional religious symbols. Further, those traditional symbols are helpful in eliciting appropriate attitudes of openness and dedica-

---

[10]Bernard Loomer, *The Size of God: The Theology of Bernard Loomer in Context*, ed. William Dean and Larry E. Axel (Macon GA: Mercer University Press, 1987) 42; cf. Kaufman, *Theological Imagination*, 41.

tion and also in thinking conceptually of the objects of these attitudes. The term "God" has power. It has power to support and challenge as probably no other word has in the Western languages. However, it also has the power to obfuscate and stifle and repel. To use it is a calculated risk.

I suspect that the situationally transcendent powers and claims may ultimately be in conflict. There may come a conflict between patriotism and love of humanity, between love of security and truth, between order and freedom. There may also be a conflict between the power of eros and the power of logos, between the powers of individuation and participation. I say that I suspect that these conflicts may be ultimate, but I don't know that. They may turn out to be the result of poor planning, lack of imagination or intelligence or good will. I urge that the unity of the transcendent powers and claims be held forth as a regulative ideal.

The pragmatic import of this regulative ideal is to attempt to hold these conflicts in a relative tension, to live out the hope that we will be able to resolve these conflicts in our living and not be torn apart by the warfare of powers and claims. Schelling's insight that the history of the gods is a preliminary stage in the history of mankind I transmute into the image that the gods are an underlying stage of the history of each self back into which we could fall. The hope by which we should orient our lives is that we shall be able to reconcile these conflicts creatively enough, that we shall achieve a significant degree of unity in our lives and in our world, that the living god is not a senseless symbol. We shall never exhaust this ideal, but its pursuit is not in vain.

My approach stresses the plurality of forces and values. Like Mathews and Kaufman I do find an imaginative or symbolic unity to these forces and values, but the forces of humanization or, to be less anthropocentric, the forces of creation have only a generic similarity, a family resemblance and the creative unity of our values is only a regulative idea, a living hope.

IV

Let me now argue briefly that this explicit recognition of plurality with symbolic or imaginative unity without Kaufman's personal-agential unity is a viable, indeed a preferable, position.

To begin, let us ask whether Kaufman has illegitimately trespassed the limits of proper ontological reticence. Why should we think of The Relativizer as a single limit? Why not a limiting idea of justice which is different from the limiting idea of truth? And why may the limiting idea of freedom not be different from the limiting idea of order? Justice, truth, freedom and order may turn out to be incompatible values when pursued in concrete decisions amidst the complexities of life. Why should the unifying idea of the ground of all experience turn out to be any one of these values? In other words, why not several limiting ideas, why one? Second, it is not clear that the idea of the absolute limit as explicated by Kaufman is only a regulative and not also a constitutive idea in the Kantian sense (even though Kaufman uses the term "regulative idea"). Despite Kaufman's disclaimers that this is a conceptual matter, his limiting idea does seem to be an ontological reality for him, supreme and unified; at least it seems to be pointing in that direction, which is why Kaufman is able to see this as the analysis of the idea of God.

The issue seems to lie in the nature of the divine unity. For Kaufman persons and agents provide a useful metaphor for God. I do not think that personal metaphors are that helpful. I think instead that there is an abstractive or generic unity to the divine. "The divine" is a common noun, just like "water." "Water" is what all the lakes, rivers, rain drops, muddy puddles, pollution pits, powerful floods, rivers, and oceans have in common. "Water" is a word which we use, not as a fiction, but because it is helpful to have a word to point to the common quality of all these experiences. Likewise "God" or, as I prefer, "the divine," is what is common to these sundry experiences in sanctuary and bedroom, in terror and joy, in sacrament and prayer, in guilt and in reconciliation, in forest and on sidewalks. What is common, as I analyze these experiences, is transcendent gift and transcendent call. In the technical language of my otologically cautious naturalism, I call them situationally transcendent gifts and continually challenging norms. They have a unity, but the unity is not analogous to that of a person, but to that of all the multifarious experiences of water.

This is a radical reconstruction of our traditional notions, to be sure, but Kaufman invites and encourages radical reconstruction and urges us to be responsible for our symbols.

Is this minimalist model of plurality with symbolic unity pragmatically useful? Especially, is it helpful in humanization, in building persons and communities? This is Kaufman's test. My answer is, yes, but the test must be used with reservations.

In a sense it is too early to tell if this model is pragmatically preferable. The tests of pragmatic usefulness cannot be done in a laboratory nor in a controlled field study. They require the long haul and in the long haul there are so many other variables, economic, social, genetic, nutritional, chemical, that we will never know, I suspect, the precise value of a symbol-system. In one sense you cannot make a pragmatic test, because the test is never over and if an image or symbol fails to build persons and communities we can always say that it was not tried and found wanting, but was wanted and not really tried.

Then, too, both Mathews and Kaufman point to the institutionalization of ecclesiastical embodiment of a symbol as both means and symptom of success.[11] However, without making some Kierkegaardan snipes at the dilution of prophecy in the reforms of Josiah, may I say that the success of experiments, including thought experiments, is not measured in either longevity or in popularity. Social and

---

[11]Shailer Mathews, "The Historical Study of Religion," *A Guide to the Study of the Christian Religion*, ed, E. D. Burton et al. (Chicago: University of Chicago Press, 1916) 69; Kaufman, *Theological Imagination*, 259.

temporal popularity are not to be despised, but neither are they to be overestimated. Plato's Socrates taught us that long ago. You do not have to be a gnostic to value technically wrought concepts in physics or philosophy even if they do not have popular appeal.

Nevertheless, a pragmatic test is possible in one sense, namely, it is imaginatively possible as a thought experiment. We can ask what would life be like if we tried this concept? While we will never know for certain, and while there will be personal judgment involved, we can make some reasonable guesses.

Comparing the probable pragmatic usefulness of the approaches of Kaufman and myself, what reasonable guesses can we make? Kaufman's model, I think, has three outstanding pragmatic strengths. First, it is a powerful conceptual instrument of criticism. Standing in the prophetic tradition, his notion of God is that of a supreme relativizer challenging the pretensions of all human values and programs.[12] Second, it is a source of hope and courage, partly because it points to real, presently operative cosmic and social forces. Third, concretely, it specifies a much-needed type of approach. When the category of Christ is added, the imperative of the model points to an enabling, responsive directive rather than to a hierarchical, controlling directive. Can my more pluralistic model match these strengths? Yes, but perhaps not as easily. It may require more imagination.

On the other hand, Kaufman has some potential weaknesses in his approach. In the first place, there is still a hierarchial potential at work, despite the nonhierarchical imperative. I think that exclusiveness is built into monotheism. It is difficult to fight idolatry without being imperialistic. It is difficult to fight idols without a hammer. The supreme principle, the supreme relativizer, easily falls into being a monoarche and it is a short step from a monoarche to a monarchy. I suggest rather that a more accurate picture of the human condition is that it is an untidy democracy where tough choices have to be made and where you cannot have your cake and eat it too, where you cannot have maximal freedom and maximal security, although you can bake two cakes if you put off the gardening and you can have a good mixed bag of freedom and security if you don't mind some compromise.

The second weakness in Kaufman's approach is that he moves beyond appropriate metaphysical modesty. We just do not know that all of the cosmic forces working toward humanization or creation can be appropriately denoted by a personal symbol. It would be nice, but I'm not sure it is possible.

I am suggesting that the pragmatic test can be an invitation to wishful thinking. If it is useful to believe in a personal-agential image of God, that does not mean it is proper to believe in it. We do not have a right to believe. There is something to be said for concern for error as well as openness to truth. Granted that we do need to believe in something, and granted that self-esteem can be based on a notion of

---

[12]*Theological Imagination*, chap. 3, "The Idea of Relativity and the Idea of God," 283n.10.

God's esteem of us, and granted that believing you can do it will help you jump the ditch, nevertheless, the workings of fantasy are in the neighborhood. For all of the naivete of his empiricism, Wieman's concern to route out fantasy is a needed voice in the chorus.

There is a time to realize that some ditches may not be jumped, that no white knight is coming soon. In short, I think that a renunciation of ultimates is needed. Just as maturity is needed to adjust to the loss of our parents, to the loss of our adolescent fantasies, so there is a need to adjust to the loss of our heavenly Parent.[13] Now such a renunciation of fantasy may not seem at first glance pragmatically useful. It can be hard and tearful, but surely grief work is part of humanization.

Further, one pragmatically important ground for human tenderness is the realization that we all hurt, that we are all vulnerable. Perhaps there is something pragmatically useful about growing up, about building community around the loss of God as a personal agent. We are sisters and brothers and need to protect each other because no God will do it for us. We are not our brother's keeper, but we are family. Can we have the sisterhood and brotherhood of mankind without the Fatherhood of God? Let us try it.

I grant that it is pragmatically useful to have with Kaufman, a way of speaking of an Archimedean point which relativizes our programs and projects and symbolizes a transcendent gift of healing. However, it is also pragmatically useful to be able to speak of this in a way that makes sense to the agnostic, naturalistic, secular strands of our cultures. Such a way of speaking may make sense only if it acknowledges the plurality of Archimedean points and transcendent gifts.

Two other points may be made about the pragmatic value of an approach which looks to resources that are situationally transcendent and values which are continually challenging, yet which are qualities within the world. First, this approach stresses the need for the nurture of sensitive discernment, or what Meland called appreciative awareness, in order to perceive the creativity of cosmic and social forces. I think that Kaufman would also encourage the nurture of appreciative awareness, although he does not make a generous empiricism as important methodologically as Meland and the later Loomer.

Further, my approach stresses the need for the relativization of all human programs. Kaufman's approach stresses this and I think that mine does equally as well.

As for the liberation of the oppressed, the discernment noted above is needed to see the dignity and worth of the victim. It is so easy to become isolated in our own tribes, our suburban or academic ghettos and treat the oppressed as faceless problems, as having no strengths, creativity, and resources. The shock of the white

---

[13]Jerome A. Stone, "What Religious Naturalism Can Learn from Langdon Gilkey: Uncovering the Dimension of Ultimacy," *God, Values and Empiricism: Issues in Philosophical Theology*, ed. by W. Creighton Peden and Larry E. Axel (Macon GA: Mercer University Press, 1989) 215-19.

liberal facing the shout of "Black Power" in the late American sixties is a paradigm of the helper who lacks sufficient discernment to see the power already in the supposedly helpless.

Further, liberation theologies are sometimes unnecessarily eschatological, overlooking the present workings of the creative process. The trouble with theologies of hope is that the eschaton delayed can lead to despair. Ken Cauthen has recently written of Shailer Mathews as providing a needed resource for all theologies of humanization, namely, involvement with the present workings of the processes building persons. I agree.

Also I suspect that liberation, Black and feminist theologies need to hear the work of relativization just as a white, male, middle-class oriented theology needs to hear it. We all need to. Both Kaufman's supreme relativizer and my notion of values as a continually challenging regulative idea provide this uncomfortable service. There must be a solidarity of relativization as well as a solidarity of suffering and of hope.

As to the care and nurture of our global home, the discernment of creative forces must extend beyond forces building persons and communities. Our environmental awareness needs to reach beyond the anthropocentrism of Mathews as Kaufman is moving. The nurture of sensitive discernment must learn to value and cherish other forms of life. And the principle of relativization needs to be directed against a self-enlarging, self-feeding, self-justifying production machine which needs to create consumer demand in order to feed itself. What new thought forms will be needed to be environmentally sensitive and yet responsive to the genuine needs of our ever-enlarging population with dwindling resources we can not yet tell. What I do suggest is that in the twenty-first century a minimalist naturalism recognizing a plurality of forces and values may have great pragmatic value.

Conclusion

I look to Gordon Kaufman as a fellow seeker after truth. I have drawn both encouragement and insight from his attempts at reconstructing our concepts and images. I urge him, in a fraternal way, to consider whether he has found too much unity to the cosmic and social forces making for humanization, whether the personal-agential metaphors for God are as pragmatically useful as he suggests. I don't wish to remove all God-talk. And I don't wish to supplant the language of devotion with technical language. But perhaps we need to have more renunciation of an ultimate point of reference and of the primacy of the personal metaphors. Along with this would go a greater recognition both of the plurality of the cosmic and social forces making for humanization and of the incompatible diversity of values among which we must choose. I think this would be both pragmatically useful and a defense against fantasy.

The Possibilities for Religious Language: A Dialogue between Gordon Kaufman and Ludwig Wittgenstein

Everett J. Tarbox, Jr.

"Is it meaningful or useful to speak or think of 'God' at all any more? or is talk about God simply a vestige of earlier stages of culture from which we must seek increasingly to free ourselves?"[1] With this question Gordon Kaufman forcefully stated the central problem for Western theologians in the late twentieth century. The first option is, for Kaufman, the only viable one. However, this option requires radical theological reconstruction if it is to be meaningful for our generation. For Kaufman, this necessity was a result of the crisis following the collapse of the neoorthodox theological consensus which had begun in the 1920s and had declined abruptly in the 1960s.

I agree with Kaufman's assessment. Not only have we witnessed an almost total collapse of revelation as a foundation for theological construction, but we have witnessed a loss of confidence in traditional metaphysical philosophy to provide such a base.[2] One major exponent of postmetaphysical philosophy is Ludwig Wittgenstein.

Ludwig Wittgenstein was chosen as the partner in philosophical dialogue with Gordon Kaufman for two major reasons. First, Wittgenstein has been recognized as one of the greatest and most innovative philosophers of the twentieth century. His *Philosophical Investigations* is considered to be the most important work of philosophy of our age. As one of the chief architects of the "linguistic turn" in philosophy, he has been instrumental in a reorientation of the magnitude of Kant's "Second Copernican Revolution."[3] As Kant sought to reorient the focus of philosophy from

---

[1]Gordon D. Kaufman, *An Essay on Theological Method* (Missoula MT: Scholars Press, 1979) ix.

[2]Cf. Langdon Gilkey, "New Modes of Empirical Theology," *The Future of Empirical Theology*, ed. Bernard Meland (Chicago: University of Chicago Press, 1969) 346.

[3]Immanuel Kant, *Critique of Pure Reason*, trans. Norman K. Smith (London: MacMillan, 1958) 22.

the external world to the internal structure or categories of the philosophers' minds, so Wittgenstein has proposed a "Third Copernican Revolution," reorienting the focus of philosophical analysis on language rather than on the categories of thought.[4]

Second, Kaufman has acknowledged that Wittgenstein's philosophy influenced his theology, especially in *An Essay on Theological Method* where he sets out his theological method.[5] I do not claim that Kaufman is a "Wittgensteinian." The influences of Kant and Hegel are all too evident. Rather I will argue that Kaufman did use Wittgenstein's later philosophy in significant ways in his theological reconstruction. Since my goal is to focus upon the possibilities for "God-language" in Kaufman's theology as a result of his use of Wittgenstein's philosophy, only those parts of each man's thought relevant to these possibilities will be examined. Further, primary attention will be given to their later thought.

It is necessary, however, to explore briefly the early stage of their thought. Wittgenstein, in the *Tractatus-Logico-Philosophicus*, asserted that the basic patterns of language, when uncovered by proper philosophical analysis, "mirrored" (or "showed") reality.[6] Kaufman, in his early stage, was moving out of his neoorthodox background. His theological education, as well as his early theological writings reflect his neoorthodox roots, especially in the thought of H. Richard Niebuhr, his teacher, and of Karl Barth.

Wittgenstein: Philosophy as Description

When Wittgenstein returned to philosophy in 1929 he began a process of radically revisioning the whole philosophical enterprise, especially as he came to see the errors of his earlier position. His new vision is most clearly seen in his masterpiece, *Philosophical Investigations*. He came to see that his earlier view of language in the *Tractatus* was in error. Instead of language "mirroring" the logical form of reality, the reverse was true: reality is a "shadow of language," a projection.[7] This projection is then internalized by later generations.[8]

Peter Hacker has documented this shift from Wittgenstein's early to later philosophy. He argues that one central insight of the later philosophy was Wittgenstein's recognition of the projective nature of language.[9] Rather than discovering the nature of the structure of reality, philosophers had discovered merely the "shadow cast by

---

[4]Cf. Nancy Frankenberry, *Religion and Radical Empiricism* (Albany: SUNY Press, 1987) 4ff.

[5]Kaufman, *Essay*, 1-20.

[6]Ludwig Wittgenstein, *Tractatus-Logico-Philosophicus*, trans. D. F. Pears and B. F. McGuinness (London: Routledge and Kegan Paul, 1961).

[7]P. M. S. Hacker, *Insight and Illusion* (Oxford: Clarendon Press, 1986) 179ff.

[8]David Pears, *The False Prison: A Study of the Development of Wittgenstein's Philosophy* (Oxford: Clarendon Press, 1988) 2:219.

[9]Hacker, *Insight and Illusion*, 179-85.

grammar." This dramatic change in Wittgenstein's thought led to the "re-allocation of the metaphysical from "the domain of ineffability" (in the *Tractatus*) to "the domain of philosophical illusion, a fit subject for the pathology of the intellect."[10]

Seen from this perspective Wittgenstein's descriptive philosophy functions at two levels. On the grammatical level, he seeks to describe the rules of usage as they are actually found in our language use. On the therapeutic level, he seeks to discover the "world-pictures" or "mythologies" which were originally projected by our linguistic usage and then internalized. Much attention has been focused upon Wittgenstein's grammatical investigations. He asserted that his goal was purely descriptive, seeking only to uncover the ideas and the logic of the ordinary language as it is actually used by persons in our culture. In *Philosophical Investigations*, he observed:

> We may not advance any kind of theory. There must not be anything hypothetical in our considerations. We must do away with all *explanation*, and description alone must take its place. And this description gets its light, that is to say its purpose—from the philosophical problems. These are, of course, not empirical problems; they are solved, rather, by looking into the workings of our language, and that in such a way as to make us recognize those workings: *in despite of* an urge to misunderstand them. The problems are solved, not by giving new information, but by arranging what we have always known. Philosophy is a battle against the bewitchment of our intelligence by means of language.[11]

Wittgenstein's vision of philosophy as a grammatical investigation, as will be shown, influenced Kaufman's theological method. However, equally important for Wittgenstein was the role of philosophical investigation as therapy. The goal of his philosophical therapy was to help us break loose from metaphysics, which he describes as "a bewitchment" by language and its forms.[12] One crucial element in our bewitchment is the projected world-picture of our Western culture which has been reified by philosophers, taking on an objective feel. A central theme in *On Certainty*[13] is the important role this world-picture plays in our language and our system of beliefs, especially when it is not recognized as a projection. Wittgenstein concluded that our world-picture is not acquired by rational choice. Rather we "swallow" it with the acquiring of our native language. The process of growing up as a member of the human race is in part a process of acquiring a language. Embedded in this language is a "mythology," or world-picture:

---

[10]Ibid., 179.

[11]Ludwig Wittgenstein, *Philosophical Investigations*, trans. G. E. M. Anscombe (New York: MacMillan, 1953) 1.109.

[12]Ibid.

[13]Ludwig Wittgenstein, *On Certainty*, ed. G. E. M. Anscombe and G. H. vonWright (New York: Harper, 1969) #95.

> I did not get my picture of the world by satisfying myself of its correctness; nor do I have it because I am satisfied of its correctness. No: it is the inherited background against which I distinguish between true and false.[14]

Therefore, Wittgenstein concluded that the "truth" of empirical propositions belongs to our frame of reference.[15] This insight led him to assert that at the foundation of well-founded beliefs lies belief that is not founded.[16] "The difficulty is to realize the groundlessness of believing."[17] It is within this context that Wittgenstein practiced his philosophical therapy.

In the *Philosophical Investigations* Wittgenstein began with a description of the "world-picture" of our Western intellectual culture: "the Augustinian picture of language."[18] Wittgenstein chose his target carefully, for in Augustine's writings he confronted a synthesis of the Greco-Roman and Judeo-Christian worldviews. Perhaps this picture could better be characterized as the "Platonian-Augustinian picture" since Wittgenstein saw it to be present from the early Greeks, especially Plato, through Frege, Russell, and his own early thought. Gordon Baker observed that the core of this picture is a pair of theses: "all words are names, and all sentences are combinations of names."[19]

> The importance of Augustine's picture for Wittgenstein is not that it represents one theory of language among others, but that it is a proto-theory or *Urbild* that shapes a vast range of philosophers' theorizing about language, like what Kuhn calls a scientific paradigm. . . . Hence, in confronting Augustine's picture of language, Wittgenstein did not see himself as tilting at a windmill. Rather he meant to engage the combined forces mustered by the most advanced philosophers of the modern era.[20]

Wittgenstein's careful descriptive analysis of this picture, or *Urbild*, uncovered the mythology upon which the correspondence theory of truth was founded. Every ostensive definition forged a "link between language and reality." He uncovered

---

[14]Ibid., #94.

[15]Cf. G. P. Baker and P. M. S. Hacker, *An Analytical Commentary on the Philosophical Investigations: Wittgenstein, Rules, Grammar, and Necessity* (Oxford: Blackwell, 1988) 2:229-38.

[16]Wittgenstein, *On Certainty*, #253.

[17]Ibid., #166.

[18]G. P. Baker and P. M. S. Hacker, *An Analytical Commentary on the Philosophical Investigations: Wittgenstein, Understanding and Meaning* (Chicago: University of Chicago Press, 1980) 1:33ff.

[19]Gordon Baker, "Following Wittgenstein: Some Signposts for *Philosophical Investigations* 143-242," in *Wittgenstein: To Follow a Rule*, ed. Steven H. Holtzman and Christopher M. Leich (London: Routledge and Kegan Paul, 1981) 37.

[20]Ibid.

three major "implicit" presuppositions: an "inner" and "outer" picture of the mind, a presumption of a prelinguistic self-consciousness, and a presumption of the intelligible self-knowledge of mental states. For Wittgenstein, exposure of this picture revealed its illusory character, its "bewitching power." Once described, its power to coerce is broken. Therefore, an examination and description of the way we actually use language is therapeutic. Wittgenstein stated his conclusion in a most graphic way:

> Where does our investigation get its importance from, since it seems only to destroy everything interesting, that is, all that is great and important? (As it were all the buildings, leaving behind only bits of stone and rubble.) What we are destroying is nothing but houses of cards and we are clearing up the ground of language on which they stand.[21]

Once the philosopher has escaped the "bewitchment" of our language and has come to recognize the entrenched "world-picture" as mythological, he is in a position to describe our actual language from a functional point of view: "How is language actually used?" Wittgenstein concluded that the solution to many, if not most, philosophical problems was to "dissolve the problem." As noted earlier, we have internalized the rules of language. Therefore, the philosopher elicits these rules from language by a careful description of what we do when we use language. In this sense Wittgenstein stood in the tradition of critical philosophy begun by Kant. Philosophy is a "conceptual investigation." It examines the language that we bring to the world, rather than the world on which we bring it to bear.

Later, I will explore Wittgenstein's understanding of the framework in which language functions, but it does not function as a part of Wittgenstein's philosophical investigations in a direct way. As Baker and Hacker, in their commentary, observed:

> Although it is philosophically important and illuminating to appreciate the *framework* within which our language-games are played, philosophical investigation—the examination of conceptual structures—moves *within* language-games. Our concern is with the rules we have and use, for it is their entanglement, our lack of a "Ubersicht" of them, which is the source of philosophical questions.[22]

Kaufman: Theology as Imaginative Construction

Kaufman, like Wittgenstein, experienced what has been called the "Third Copernican Revolution." As Kaufman came to understand theology as an imaginative construction, language and symbols came to play a central role in his thought. His writings in the 1960s and early 1970s reflect Kaufman's transition from neo-

---

[21]Wittgenstein, *Philosophical Investigations*, 1.118.

[22]Baker and Hacker, *An Analytical Commentary*, 2:238.

orthodoxy to his later views. These writings reflect his growing uneasiness with the heavy reliance upon revelation as foundational for theological construction. Like Wittgenstein, Kaufman had rejected natural theology and traditional metaphysics.[23] As long as he remained within the fold of neoorthodoxy, revelation provided a base. However, when Kaufman abandoned the concept of revelation, as set forth by neo-orthodox theologians, he did not have the options of turning to "reason" or "religious experience" as his predecessors had done a century earlier.

One of his early attempts to move toward theological reconstruction was to seek to redefine revelation. Starting with humanity, rather than with God, Kaufman sought to build a doctrine of revelation "from the ground up." Humans seek to mold their experience into a coherent whole that is seen to have meaning.[24] Certain events or experiences are selected, perhaps even unconsciously, from the totality of our experiences as being more "meaningful" or "significant." Then the rest of our experiences is organized into a meaningful whole. As a result, these central concepts are seen to be "revelatory."[25]

By the mid-1970s Kaufman broke completely with neoorthodoxy's view of revelation as foundational. He observed that the proclamation "God is dead!" made it clearly apparent that the "neoorthodox Emperor" had no clothes.[26] Therefore, it was at this stage that he began openly to address the questions of the grounds of belief and theology. No longer could he ignore the critical questions which had been ignored—or overlooked—during the neo-orthodox period. Most notable was the question of the problem of God, which had been the central concept on which the whole theological enterprise had rested. "What do we mean by 'God'? Can this notion be made intelligible at all to "modern man" or does it depend on outgrown mythological patterns of thought?"[27]

Theology as Description

The influence of Wittgenstein on Kaufman's theology is most apparent in Kaufman's formulation of his theological method in *An Essay on Theological Method.* Paralleling Wittgenstein's analysis of the Platonic-Augustinian world-picture by means of which Wittgenstein exposed its mythological and illusory character, Kaufman's analysis of our Judeo-Christian religious tradition led him to reject both revelation and religious experience as foundational for theological construction. He asserted that the claim about God's revelation should be a conclu-

---

[23]Gordon D. Kaufman, *God the Problem* (Cambridge: Harvard Univ. Press, 1972) 151.

[24]Gordon D. Kaufman, *Relativism, Knowledge, and Faith*, (Chicago: University of Chicago Press, 1960) 104ff.

[25]Ibid., 106. Kaufman acknowledges the influence of H. Richard Niebuhr at this point in n. 2.

[26]Kaufman, *God the Problem*, 226.

[27]Ibid., 4.

sion, not an opening premise. Religious experience was also rejected as foundational for theological construction. Kaufman's analysis led him to conclude that religious experience is never the "raw, preconceptual, prelinguistic experience" upon which theologies are built. Like all our experience, religious experience is a construction or composite.[28]

Wittgenstein's descriptive philosophy functioned at two levels, the grammatical and the therapeutic. Kaufman's theological construction, in its formal phase, has two similar levels. As formal analysis Kaufman's theological construction functions very similarly to Wittgenstein's descriptive philosophy. For Kaufman, our common language provides our principal foundation for theological analysis and construction. Therefore, Kaufman's analysis begins with our ordinary uses. For him, the language of the church and of the Scriptures are part of the common language of cultures in which they are found. In this common language of our Western society Kaufman finds the material for his analysis. He asserted:

> Theology is the disciplined effort to see what we are trying to do and say with these complexes of meaning so as to enable us to say and do them better—more accurately, more precisely, more effectively. In this sense, as Ludwig Wittgenstein has put it, "Theology [is] grammar."[29]

Kaufman observed that such a "grammatical analysis" involves both an attempt to determine how the language is actually used and an attempt to discover the rules governing its use so that one might distinguish clear and adequate uses from misleading and confusing uses.

> This prescriptive dimension of grammar—always founded upon and emergent out of descriptive studies of usage—enables it to help shape language into a vehicle which expresses our intentions with greater precision, thus facilitating a fuller and clearer consciousness of these intentions.[30]

Therefore, for Kaufman, the proper business of theology is the "analysis, criticism, and reconstruction" of the major symbols of the Christian faith, especially the symbol of "God."[31] His analysis reveals that God is not directly perceivable. "Nevertheless, the concept of God has usually been treated as though it referred to a structure or reality that was definitely *there* and *given* (as objects of experience are there and given)."[32]

---

[28]Kaufman, *Essay*, 4-8.

[29]Ibid., 9.

[30]Ibid.

[31]Gordon D. Kaufman, *Theology for a Nuclear Age* (Manchester: Manchester University Press, 1985) 22.

[32]Kaufman, *Essay*, 21.

Kaufman concluded that to regard God "as some kind of describable or knowable object over against us" is both a degradation of God and a serious category mistake. His formal theological reconstruction grows out of the dualities is evidenced in this understanding. Following Kant, Kaufman asserted that the concept of God is an imaginative construct. Therefore, there is no percept that corresponds directly to our concept of God. The implications of this insight, for Kaufman, are significant:

> It is essential for us to recognize that the peculiar logical status of the central concepts with which theology deals demands radical reconception of both the task of theology and the way in which the task is carried out. Theology can no longer conceive of itself as presenting straightforwardly a kind of picture or map of *how things are*—the old schema of God, humankind and the world in their structural relations with each other.[33]

Kaufman concluded that the concept or symbol "God," when used in the formal sense, functions primarily to provide orientation for persons living in our particular Western culture. "God," when used in this sense, indicates the last or "ultimate point of reference" to which all action, consciousness, and reflection leads.[34] "God," therefore, functions as a limiting concept, as an idea of that beyond which we cannot go in experience, thought, or imagination.[35]

Such attempts to construct a concept of God have been part of our theological heritage from its earliest times. However, they were not recognized as human imaginative constructions. Only recently have theologians understood this. "The fact that their work was thoroughly imaginative and constructive in character was simply not recognized."[36] However, once recognized, theological work can, and must, be carried on as a fully critical and self-conscious activity. Kaufman's formal analysis on this level has deep roots in our Western religious tradition. He observes:

> The important role of this formal element in the notion of God has long been recognized in the theological tradition. It finds expression in the Book of Job's powerful statement about humanity's littleness and ignorance before God, in the "negative way" of Pseudo-Dionysius, in Thomas' claim that all knowledge of God is at best only analogical. Sometimes this formal element has been concealed in formulas which appear to give a description of what God is, but in fact only state *rules* to guide our theological construction. Thus God has been spoken of as "that than which nothing greater can be conceived" (Anselm) or as "ultimate reality" (Tillich), and it may seem that

---

[33]Ibid., 28.
[34]Ibid., 11-12.
[35]Ibid., 13.
[36]Kaufman, *Theology for a Nuclear Age*, 27.

these phrases define or describe him. In fact, however, neither tells us anything about what or who God is; both are purely formal, expressing rules to guide our theological thinking.[37]

In Kaufman's formal analysis he has sought to establish two major arguments. First, theology's foundation is not to be found in either revelation or religious experience. Rather, it is to the common language of our culture that the theologian must turn for his data. Second, "God" is a construct of our human imagination, functioning as an ultimate point of reference. "When we realize . . . that all concepts of God are human constructions, we are protected against the destructive heteronomy of traditional images."[38]

Theology and World-Pictures

In his second phase, the material phase, of theological reconstruction Kaufman goes beyond Wittgenstein's descriptive philosophy. While agreeing with Wittgenstein concerning the "mythological" nature of our world-pictures, Kaufman also sees a positive role for world-pictures if they are seen to be imaginative constructions.

At least two possible readings of Kaufman's theological reconstruction present themselves. The first reading, which I find more acceptable, is that Kaufman is describing a major paradigm shift, a movement from one world-picture to another—a shift comparable to that implied in Wittgenstein's shift in the "riverbed" of language in *On Certainty*.[39] As observed earlier, for Kaufman one of the most important functions of the imagination is to provide us with imaginative pictures by means of which we may give meaning to our lives. Read this way, Kaufman's central thesis is that our old world-picture no longer works. On the one hand, it has been reified and, therefore, become "idolatrous." As such, it is dangerous to the planet and to humankind, threatening our survival. On the other hand, it is no longer viable for a large contingent of contemporary persons in our Western culture. He observes that many of the traditional concepts—including especially "God"—no longer seem related to our actual experience. "They seem to float free, as more or less empty forms with little contemporary meaning."[40]

Therefore, Kaufman proposes that a new world-picture has emerged. We must now conceive "God" in terms appropriate to this new understanding. He asserts: "God should today be conceived in terms of the complex of physical, biological and historicocultural conditions which have made human existence possible, which continue to sustain, and which may draw it out to a fuller humanity and humaneness."[41]

---

[37]Kaufman, *Essay*, 51.
[38]Ibid., 57.
[39]Wittgenstein, *On Certainty*, ##95-99.
[40]Kaufman, *Essay*, 7
[41]Kaufman, *Theology for a Nuclear Age*, 42.

Kaufman's proposed new "world-picture" is most clearly set forth in his later writings, especially *Theology for a Nuclear Age*. Central to this vision is a shift in the model used to picture our experiences of "relativization" and "humanization."

> We . . . experience our human existence as both relativized and humanized by forces and powers impinging from beyond us, from the context or matrix which has given birth to human life and which continues to sustain and transform it. It is through reflection on this contemporary experience and understanding of our relativisation and humanisation, and on that which unifies and holds these together in one, that we will begin to discern the outlines of a contemporary conception of God, of that ultimate point of reference to which we today can freely and wholeheartedly give ourselves in devotion and work.[42]

Kaufman, however, is not simply a naturalist theologian. He carefully develops a world-picture that interrelates the biological and sociocultural evolution of both our world and of humankind. He sets forth two stages of this evolution: a great web of life has gradually emerged and evolved on this planet earth. Human life is an expression of, and is continually sustained by, this web. As such, humankind is but one strand in this ancient and complex web, and could not exist apart from it. The second stage appears once an animal has evolved with a sufficiently complex nervous system to develop and sustain linguistic and other symbolic activity, thus making possible primitive consciousness, memory, and imagination. Therefore, for Kaufman, a long and complicated historical development was required before anything we would recognize as a truly human mode of existence could appear on earth. After spelling out in detail these two stages, Kaufman sets forth his "revisionist" view of God which is implied in this model.

> If we today are to speak of how we humans are created and sustained, it must be in terms of biological evolution and the ecosystem, on the one hand, and the long process of human history and the diverse sociocultural systems which it has produced, on the other. . . . It is in connection with them, and the metaphors and images that they make available to us, that we today must come to understand and speak of God—if we are to speak at all in ways connected with our contemporary experience and knowledge.[43]

As a descriptive analysis of a paradigm shift Kaufman's reconstruction is compatible with Wittgenstein's position. However, I suspect Wittgenstein wished to cure us of holding such mythologies.

The second reading of Kaufman's theological reconstruction reveals a "lingering Hegelianism," which tends toward a reification of the new world-picture. At times

---

[42]Ibid., 35.

[43]Ibid., 36-37.

Kaufman speaks of the symbol "God" as suggesting a reality, an ultimate tendency or power, which is working itself out in the evolutionary process. He speaks of "a *hidden creativity at work* in the historicocultural process."[44] Kaufman also speaks of humans as "the point farthest out" in the cosmic evolutionary-historical process. Again, in a move similar to Hegel, he connects our fate on earth with God's fate—God being understood as the ecological reality behind and in and working through all our history.

Conclusion

Kaufman is one of the few theologians which is addressing the problem of language about God in a genuinely postrevelatory and postmetaphysical way. I find my first reading of his material phase preferable. Read this way, Kaufman's understanding of theology as imaginative construction closely parallels Wittgenstein's view of theology as grammar. Also, Kaufman rejects, in strong terms, the correspondence theory of truth as applicable to God-language. In the "Epilogue" to *An Essay on Theological Method*, Kaufman states that the question of the relation of theological imaginative construction to "truth" was not directly addressed because the presupposition behind this question is that of the "perceptual model" of reality, where correspondence of our ideas with the reals "out there" is a proper issue.[45] This model of truth works when dealing with the way in which one item in our conceptual scheme relates to and represents one item in what we call experience of the world. But such a model is inadequate and misleading when applied to the "world-itself" or to God, because in both cases there is nothing outside our conception against which we can place the world or God to see whether they correspond![46] Therefore, for Kaufman, at this level of analysis, "only criteria of coherence and pragmatic usefulness to human life are relevant and applicable."[47]

It is at this point, however, that I find a major difficulty. How does Kaufman connect his formal analysis of God-language—an analysis rooted in "negative theology—with his material analysis? One attempt is to connect God as "relativizer" and "humanizer" with our experiences of mystery and awe, on the one hand, and with our experiences of humanization.[48] These experiences undergirded the traditional religious images of God as creator, sovereign lord of life and history, and images of God as a "humane" being, a 'father.' As noted above, Kaufman believes that we continue to have these experiences, but we must picture them in different terms. My problem with this approach is that it tends to reinforce the second reading of Kaufman as having retained a lingering strand of "Hegelian" liberalism.

---

[44]Ibid., 41.

[45]Kaufman, *Essay*, 75.

[46]Ibid.

[47]Ibid.

[48]Kaufman, *Theology for a Nuclear Age*, 33.

I propose that Kaufman continue to develop what I have called the first reading of his thought. Here I would like to return to Wittgenstein. Wittgenstein distinguished between the framework in which our language-games is played and the language-games. Central to this framework are, first, the relative stability of the world as a background condition for the application of our concepts,[49] and second, the common biological nature of humankind.[50] Wittgenstein, when read from this perspective, was developing an alternative to realism or to antirealism. Grammar, on the one hand, is autonomous and arbitrary, while, on the other hand, causally conditioned. As he observed in *Philosophical Investigations*:

> If anyone believes that certain concepts are absolutely the correct ones, and that having different ones would mean not realizing something that we realize—then let him imagine certain general facts of nature to be different from what we are used to, and the formation of concepts different from the usual ones will become intelligible to him.[51]

Kaufman's next step theologically is eagerly awaited. I wish him well in his exciting quest.

---

[49]Baker and Hacker, *An Analytical Commentary*, 2:229ff.
[50]Ibid., 234ff.
[51]Wittgenstein, *Philosophical Investigations*, 2:230.

About the Authors

Rebecca C. Axel is engaged in further graduate studies at Christian Theological Seminary. She is a graduate of the University of Indianapolis (B.S.) and Indiana University (M.A.). She is actively involved in the Lafayette Urban Ministry and is coauthor of *Indiana Poor Relief: The Myths and Facts About Township Assistance.*

J. Edward Barrett is Professor Emeritus of Religion at Muskingum College. He is a graduate of Susquehanna University (B.A.), Princeton Theological Seminary (B.D.), and the University of St. Andrews (Ph.D.). In addition to twenty articles, he is the author of *How Are You Programmed?* and *Faith in Focus.* He is Editor of *HIART News.*

Delwin Brown is the Harvey H. Potthoff Professor of Theology at Iliff School of Theology. He is a graduate of Anderson College (B.A.), Union Theological Seminar of New York (B.D.), and Claremont Graduate School (Ph.D.). He has published numerous articles in scholarly journals. Dr. Brown is Secretary of the American Academy of Religion.

David E. Conner is Senior Pastor of the University Park United Methodist Church in Denver, the youngest minister to hold that position in over thirty years. He holds degrees from Millsaps College (B.S.) and the Iliff School of Theology (M.Div., Th.D.), having also done Ph.D. work at the Claremont Graduate School where he was a C. G. S. Fellow and Elizabeth Iliff Warren Fellow. Dr. Conner is the author of four articles relating to empirical theology and process thought. He has recently been elected by the Rocky Mountain Conference as the first alternate delegate to the Western Jurisdictional Conference of the United Methodist Church.

Sheila G. Davaney is Associate Professor of Theology at the Iliff School of Theology. She is a graduate of Manhattanville College (B.A.) and Harvard University (M.T.S. and Th.D.). Dr. Davaney is noted for her scholarly contributions to process theology and to feminist theology. She is the author of *Divine Power: A Study of Karl Barth and Charles Hartshorne* and the editor of *Theology at the End of Modernity and Feminism and Feminism and Proces Thought.*

William Dean is Professor of Religion at Gustavus Adolphus College. He is a graduate of Carleton College (B.A.) and Union Theological Seminar in New York City (M.A. and Ph.D.) Dr. Dean is considered a leading voice in the empiricism renaissance in American religious thought. His two most recent books are considered major contributions to the empirical dialogue. The works are *American Religious Empiricism* and *History Making History: The New Historicism in American Religious Thought.*

Emanuel S. Goldsmith is Associate Professor of Yiddish Language and Literature at Queens College of the City University of New York. He is a graduate of City College of New York (B.A.), Jewish Theological Seminary (B.H.L., M.H.L., Rabbi, and D.D.), and Brandeis University (Ph.D.). Dr. Goldsmith is the author of nineteen books and monographs and numerous articles in scholarly journals.

Charley D. Hardwick is Professor of Religious Studies at the American University in Washington, D.C. In addition to degrees from Southern Methodist University and Drew University, he received his doctorate in philosophical theology from Yale University. As a student he received Danforth and Rockefeller theological fellowships. He has also been recipient of Guggenheim, American Council of Learned Societies, and the American University Sabbatical Support Fellowship. Dr. Hardwick is author of *Faith and Objectivity: Fritz Buri and the Hermeneutical Foundations of a Radical Theology* and also *Religious Truth in the Absence of God*, as well as numerous articles. He served as editor of the "Aids to the Study of Religion" and "Studies in Religion" monograph series sponsored by the American Academy of Religion.

Tyron L. Inbody is Professor of Theology at the United Theological Seminary in Dayton, Ohio. He is a graduate of the University of Indianapolis (B.A.), United Theological Seminar (M.Div.), and the University of Chicago (M.A., Ph.D.). He is the editor of *Changing Channels: The Church and the Television Revolution,* as well as author of numerous articles in scholarly journals. Dr. Inbody is the founding editor of the *United Theological Seminary Journal of Theology* and is also editor of the *American Journal of Theology & Philosophy.*

Jennifer G. Jesse is completing her doctorate at the University of Chicago in Religion and Literature. She is a graduate of Kent State University (B.A.), Butler University (M.A.), and Christian Theological Seminary (M.Div.). William Blake is a special interest of Ms. Jesse.

Gordon D. Kaufman is the Mallinckrodt Professor of Divinity at Harvard University. He is a graduate of Bethel College (B.A.), Northwestern University (M.A.), and Yale University (Ph.D.) Before joining the faculty at Harvard Divinity

School, he taught at Pomona College and Vanderbilt University. Kaufman has written eight books, including his latest *Theology for a Nuclear Age.*

James A. Kirk is Professor Emeritus of Religious Studies at the University of Denver. He is a graduate of Hillsdale College (B.A.) and the Iliff School of Theology (Th.M., Th.D.). After early teaching and writing in the philosophy of religion, his recent publications have been primarily in Asian religions: *Stories of the Hindus: An Introduction* and coauthor of *Religion and the Human Image.*

Randolph Crump Miller is the Horace Bushnell Emeritus Professor of Christian Nurture at Yale University and the emeritus editor of *Religious Education.* He is a graduate of Pomona College (B.A.) and Yale University (Ph.D.). Called the "Dean of American Christian Educators," Miller has earned the reputation for his outstanding scholarship and teaching in the field of Christian education. He has served as visiting professor and lecturer at more than twenty theological schools in the United States and around the world. Miller has also published twenty books, including *The American Spirit in Theology.*

Mason Olds is Professor and Chair of the Department of Religion and Philosophy at Springfield College. He is a graduate of Mercer University (B.A.), Colgate Rochester Divinity School (B.D.) and Brown University (Ph.D.). He is the author of *Story: The Language of Faith* and *Religious Humanism in America,* as well as numerous scholarly articles. Dr. Olds is editor of the journal *Religious Humanism.*

Karl E. Peters is Professor of Philosophy and Religion at Rollins College. He is a graduate of Carroll College (B.A.), McCormick Theological Seminary (M.Div.), and Columbia University (Ph.D.) He is co-editor of *Zygon: Journal of Religion and Science* and is the author of numerous scholarly articles.

William L. Power is Associate Professor of Religion at The University of Georgia. He is a graduate of the University of Mississippi (B.A.E.) and Emory University (B.D., Ph.D.) He is coauthor of *Perspective on Theology* and numerous scholarly articles.

Jerome A. Stone is Associate Professor of Philosophy at William Rainey Harper College. He a graduate of the University of Chicago (B.A., M.A., Ph.D.) and Andover Newton Theological School (M.Div.). He is Secretary of the Highlands Institute for American Religious Thought. In addition to numerous scholarly articles, Dr. Stone is author of *The Minimalist Vision of Transcendence: A Neo-naturalist Philosophy of Religion.*

Everett J. Tarbox, Jr. is Professor of Humanities at Indiana State University. He is a graduate of Texas Tech University (B.A.), Southwestern Baptist Theological Seminary (B.D., Th.D.), and the University of Chicago (M.A., Ph.D.). He is a Lilly Fellow, a Rockefeller Doctoral Fellow, and a National Endowment for the Humanities Summer Seminar Fellow. Tarbox is an active leader in the Indiana and the Midwest Region of the American Academy of Religion, having served as President of both groups. He is Treasurer of the Highlands Institute for American Religious Thought and serves as Director of the Institute's Public Lectures and Seminars. Tarbox is the author of numerous scholarly articles, many of which focus on the writings of Ludwig Wittgenstein, William James, and Donald Cupitt.